T0320032

Organizations, Markets and Imperial Formations

Organizations, Markets and Imperial Formations

Towards an Anthropology of Globalization

Edited by

Subhabrata Bobby Banerjee

Professor of Management and Associate Dean of Research, College of Business, University of Western Sydney, Australia

Vanessa C.M. Chio

Associate Professor, University of Washington Tacoma, USA

Raza Mir

Associate Professor, William Paterson University, USA

Edward Elgar
Cheltenham, UK • Northampton, MA, USA

© Subhabrata Bobby Banerjee, Vanessa C.M. Chio and Raza Mir 2009

All rights reserved. No part of this publication may be reproduced, stored in a retrieval system or transmitted in any form or by any means, electronic, mechanical or photocopying, recording, or otherwise without the prior permission of the publisher.

Published by
Edward Elgar Publishing Limited
The Lypiatts
15 Lansdown Road
Cheltenham
Glos GL50 2JA
UK

Edward Elgar Publishing, Inc.
William Pratt House
9 Dewey Court
Northampton
Massachusetts 01060
USA

A catalogue record for this book
is available from the British Library

Library of Congress Control Number: 2008943839

Mixed Sources
Product group from well-managed
forests and other controlled sources
www.fsc.org Cert no. SA-COC-1565
© 1996 Forest Stewardship Council
FSC

ISBN 978 1 84844 317 4

Printed and bound in Great Britain by MPG Books Ltd, Bodmin, Cornwall

Contents

v

Contributors

Abbas J. Ali, PhD, is Professor of Management and Director, School of International Management, Eberly College of Business, at Indiana University of Pennsylvania. He is the Executive Director of the American Society for Competitiveness. His current research interests include global business leadership, strategy, foreign policy, comparative management, competitiveness issues, organizational politics and international management. He has published more than 130 scholarly journal articles. His latest book, *Business and Management Environment in Saudi Arabia: Challenges and Opportunities for Multinational Corporations*, was recently published by Routledge. He serves as editor of the *International Journal of Commerce and Management, Advances in Competitiveness Research, Competitiveness Review* and *Competition Forum*.

Subhabrata Bobby Banerjee (PhD University of Massachusetts) is Professor of Management and Associate Dean of Research in the College of Business at University of Western Sydney. His research interests include sustainability, corporate social responsibility, indigenous ecology and postcolonialism. He has published widely in scholarly journals in a variety of disciplines and his work has appeared in *Journal of Marketing, Organization Studies, Journal of Management Studies, Organization, Management Learning, Journal of Advertising, Critical Perspectives on International Business* and *Human Relations*. His book *Corporate Social Responsibility: The Good, the Bad and the Ugly* was published by Edward Elgar in 2007.

Vanessa C.M. Chio (PhD University of Massachusetts) is currently an Associate Professor at the Milgard School of Business, University of Washington Tacoma. Her research focuses on globalization and knowledge transfers, sustainability and the UN Global Compact, and gender, diversity and pedagogy. She takes an interdisciplinary approach in her research, drawing on insights from critical sociology, cultural and social anthropology and postcolonial studies. Her book, *Malaysia and the Development Process: Globalization, Knowledge Transfers and Postcolonial Dilemmas*, was published by Routledge, NY in 2005.

Diya Das is Assistant Professor of Management at Bryant University. She received her PhD in Business Administration from Syracuse University.

Her current research interests include issues of identity under conditions of globalization, organizational cynicism and surveillance in organizations. Her research appears in *Human Resource Management Review* and Academy of Management Best Paper Proceedings. She is also a recipient of the Best International Paper Award from the Academy of Management's Organizational Behavior Division.

Ravi Dharwadkar is Professor of Management at the Whitman School of Management of Syracuse University. He received his PhD in Management from the University of Cincinnati. His current research explores the implications of ownership structures for organizational performance and multiple identifications at work. His research in corporate governance and organizational behavior appears in *Academy of Management Review, Academy of Management Journal, Strategic Management Journal, Organization Science, Journal of Marketing* and *Journal of International Business Studies*.

Suzette Dyer (PhD Waikato University, Hamilton, New Zealand) has been researching the impact of global changes on career for nearly a decade. Her particular interest is understanding the impact of the contemporary construction of career on individuals, communities, organizations and women.

Martin Fougère is Assistant Professor in Politics and Business at the Department of Management and Organization, Swedish School of Economics and Business Administration, Helsinki, Finland. Broadly positioned within Critical Management Studies (CMS), his work draws on Foucauldian and postcolonial perspectives to expose the dark sides of managerial discourses such as corporate responsibility, cross-cultural management and marketing.

Ali Mir (PhD University of Massachusetts) is Professor of Management in the School of Management at New York Institute of Technology, USA. He is currently working on issues related to migration/immigration and the international division of labor. He is on the board of directors of the Brecht Forum in New York City. He has published in several journals including *Journal of Management Education, Critical Perspectives on International Business, Cultural Dynamics* and *Organizational Research Methods*.

Raza Mir (PhD University of Massachusetts) is Associate Professor of Management at William Paterson University, USA. His research mainly concerns the transfer of knowledge across national boundaries in multinational corporations, and issues relating to power and resistance in organizations. He has published in journals from a variety of disciplines, including *Academy of Management Learning and Education, Critical*

Perspectives on International Business, Cultural Dynamics, Journal of Business Communication, Organizational Research Methods and *Strategic Management Journal.*

Agneta Moulettes is based at the School of Economics and Business Administration, Lund University in Sweden. She takes a critical stance towards traditional models in cross-cultural management and is particularly interested in postcolonial theory and its implications for international management research, the power of language in relation to globalization, and gender-related issues. In her research she takes an interest in investigating how national cultures have been constructed, diffused and reproduced through cross-cultural management discourses. She also has extensive teaching experiences in business administration, law and social science.

Martyna Sliwa is Senior Lecturer in International Management at Newcastle University, UK. Her research interests include post-socialist transition, migration and transnationalism, critical approaches to international business, and philosophy of management and organization.

Nikodemus Solitander is a doctoral candidate in Corporate Geography at the department of Marketing, Swedish School of Economics and Business Administration, Helsinki, Finland. His recent research focuses on the discourses of corporate responsibility and self-regulation, and critical appraisals of the rise of the creative economy.

Diana J. Wong-MingJi is an Associate Professor of Strategy and Organization Development at Eastern Michigan University. She received her PhD from the University of Massachusetts, Amherst. One of Diana's research streams focuses on leadership development in organizational change processes within the global economy. She teaches strategy, international management, organization development and entrepreneurship. Her recent project examines how cultural mythology shapes global leaders from different geographical locations.

PART I

Introduction

1. The imperial formations of globalization

Subhabrata Bobby Banerjee, Vanessa C.M. Chio and Raza Mir

> We need to anthropologize the West; show how exotic its constitution of reality
> has been; emphasize those domains most taken for granted as universal (this
> includes epistemology and economics); make them seem as historically peculiar
> as possible; show how their claims to truth are linked to social practices and
> have hence become effective forces in the social world.
>
> (Paul Rabinow, 1986: 241)

In this book, we explore the nexus between organization theory, globalization and imperialism. Rather than debate the convergence or divergence
produced by globalization between different spatial and temporal theat-
ers, we are trying instead to focus attention on what makes globalization
itself possible, as a form of economic or social organization. As a response
to Rabinow's call to 'anthropologize the West', we start by focusing our
attention on the 'facticity' of globalization as a phenomenon. It is an
approach whose purpose is to investigate and illuminate the myriad of
institutional and institutionalized practices, knowledge and relations (e.g.
between workers and organizations, headquarters and subsidiaries, the
West and the Rest) that intersect to make possible the very existence and
constitution of globalization. Such an approach helps us understand the
social, economic and procedural conditions giving rise to the production of
global relations, and the dynamics of power that are involved.

One very important unit of analysis in the process of globalization is
the firm, specifically the multinational corporation (MNC). This entity
has been implicated historically and currently in the coercive elements of
globalization. From recent events that link Halliburton to the Iraq War
(Tappan, 2004) to medieval activities practiced by the East India Company
in the 18th century (Guha, 1989), corporations have been linked with
allegations of malfeasance. These allegations involve actions that affect
customers, communities, countries and citizens in a variety of negative
ways, and bring the corporation as an institution into considerable dis-
repute, especially among poor citizens of the world. This phenomenon

occurs despite the fact that in this era of the hegemony of global capital, the governments of most poor nations are wooing MNCs to their shores with an increasingly competitive desperation.

One may choose to view these allegations against specific corporations as overblown cases of selective and even fraudulent reporting by interest groups inimical to corporate interests. Even if the role of individual MNCs in these acts of violence, fraud and environmental ravagement is acknowledged, they could also be explained away as acts of corruption by individual firms at a specific moment in history, relatively tangential to a social-science discussion of the theory of the corporation. However, we argue in this book that the sheer number of complaints by groups affected by corporations is too high to ignore, and that these data points suggest a trend. Similarly, the acts of resistance by world citizens against global corporations and their advocate institutions like the World Trade Organization (WTO) and the World Bank defy easy characterization as unlawful disturbances or resistance to change. The various chapters that constitute this book suggest that in today's environment of international governance, corporations (especially of the multinational kind) have internalized a culture of impunity, which has arisen out of the inability of national and global institutions to keep pace with their growing reach and power. To that end, organizations have become more *imperialist* in the era of neoliberal accumulation.

With the possible exception of comparative institutional theorists like Djelic (1998) and Guillén (2001), few scholars question the naturalness or implied superiority of Western economic development models and their links to globalization, focusing instead on the problems with knowledge that either limits researchers' ability to recognize divergence, or the inability of existing theories to explain or capture the divergent. While the primary focus of most of the organization and management literature is on economic globalization or on the degree and extent of its reach (whether convergent or divergent), few management scholars have questioned what globalization itself is constitutive of or constituted by, let alone explored the imperial formations of globalization. This book is an attempt at developing such a critique.

CORPORATE IMPERIALISM

In generic terms, imperialism can be seen as a special case of exploitation, where the appropriator of surplus value functions by shifting the locus of exploitation into specific geographical areas, for the gratification of other geographies. In other words, the heightened exploitation of one part of the world serves to ameliorate the effects of exploitation in another part (Brewer, 1980). The post-war welfare states in Europe and the USA have often been seen as a consequence of neo-imperialist and extractive practices of Western states (often through the medium of MNCs) in Asia, Africa and South America. Institutional, material and discursive power enable forms of organizational accumulation that result in dispossession (Banerjee, 2008), and the progressive marginalization of 'life, labor and language' in these societies (Chio, 2005; Escobar, 1995). Dependency theorists have referred to the phenomenon of *unequal development* (Amin, 1976), implying that much of the order that pervades the capitalist societies of Europe and North America is predicated on the suffering of poorer nations. MNCs have been implicated in these imperialist processes. Be it plantation corporations, mineral and oil producers, and increasingly, those that utilize poorer nations as sites of labor-intensive manufacture, MNCs have been implicated in the process of imperialistic exploitation.

The dynamics of imperialism have been transformed in the past several decades. Over three decades ago, Bill Warren presented empirical analysis to suggest that the emergence of regimes of national capitalism in the third world end up mitigating the effects of imperialism. This is not to say that exploitative regimes of accumulation are reduced, rather, Warren argued that exploitative systems

> originate not in current imperialist–Third World relationships, but almost entirely from the internal contradictions of the Third World itself; that the impe-rialist countries' policies and their overall impact on the Third World actually favour its industrialization; and that the ties of dependence binding the Third World to the imperialist countries have been, and are being, markedly loosened, with the consequence that the distribution of power within the capitalist world is becoming less uneven. (Warren, 1973: 3)

However, conditions in the past two decades (especially since the emergence of neoliberal regimes in many third world nations) have led to a resurgence of the older patterns of imperialism (Gatade, 1997). Corporations, through their promise of global investment (and periodic threats to withdraw it), have been able to influence nation states as well as local capitalists substantially, leading to the re-emergence of extractive regimes (the extraction refers here not only to materials such as minerals and crops, but also to surplus value through regimes of outsourcing and offshoring). They have been abetted by an entire secondary network of institutions that have aggressively pursued the goal of capital mobility, elimination of sovereign protection for local industries, currency convert-ibility, and immunity for corporations from local laws (Baker et al., 1998). Consider, for example, that much of debt provision to the poorer nations by the IMF and the World Bank has been linked to tariff reductions, corporate tax reductions, removal of barriers to MNC entry in specific industrial sectors, reduction of barriers to foreign exchange repatriation, currency convertibility, reduction of administrative tasks by foreign investors, and in specific cases, immunity from local laws relating to labor and environmental protection.

Many theories of globalization are problematic because they construct a false opposition between globalization and the territorial State resulting in a neglect of the role of the State to the extent that in some discourses of globalization the State scale vanishes almost entirely. In their haste to escape from the territorial trap, therefore, many globalization researchers veer toward an equally problematic inversion of State-centric approaches. Theorists such as Henri Lefebvre (1991) point to more complex readings of late capitalism where the globalization of capital/labor and the structure of territorial states are not posed as oppositional. Instead, the global economy is premised precisely on a system of states. Globalization in such a reading is characterized not by the vanishing nation state but on the contrary, by the central implication of the territorial state in the production of a globalized world. It is the structured permanence that provides the organization of space, and the control of its networks. For Lefebvre, the State controls the flows and stocks, assuring their coordination and serves as a social architecture that is constantly engaged in the production of matrices of global social relations. The past two centuries have culminated in the rationalization of the State mode of production where the state as a unit is central to a whole array of global networks and flows and practices of managing space. What we have in place today then is an 'inter-state system', through which the political space of the planet has been 'subdivided, parcelled, and territorialized' (Brenner, 1997: 150). In this reading, globalization is the marker for the final hegemonic triumph of the State mode of production. The nation state then is a fundamental building block of globalization, in the working of multinational corporations, in the setting-up of a global financial system, in the institution of policies that determine the mobility of labor, and in the creation of the multi-state institutions such as the UN, IMF, World Bank, NAFTA and WTO (Banerjee and Linstead, 2001).

Thus, while the interest of this book coincides partially with emerging critiques of knowledge forwarded by scholars investigating institutions and divergence, our interest also differs from theirs. Our focus is primarily on those institutions – academic, development, multinational, managerial, state – that are centrally engaged in the active production of this global and globalizing reality, that organize the particular form and shape it takes including the institution of knowledge and knowledge production.

The contributions in this book examine the location of knowledge and the centrality of practices, whether of knowledge construction, of administration and management, strategy and development planning, and the institutional and discursive production and regulation of a variety of social and economic spaces, places and people making up the web of globalization.

THE COLONIAL ROOTS OF DEVELOPMENT

While our analysis is located primarily in the present age, we contend that actions by states and political actors on behalf of international capital are not new; in fact they present a continuum from earlier actions, which we have now come to recognize as being inherently imperialistic in character. For example, in the 18th century, the physical and military security of the East India Company was underwritten by the British Army. Headrick (1988: 379) points to the fact that 'trade did not follow the flag as come wrapped in it'. Likewise, the rule of Central American colonies by the Spanish from 1520 to 1820 was administered by private enterprise, and once it moved to the United States (vide the Monroe Doctrine of 1823), US troops were sent 36 times to this region between 1822 and 1964 to support the interests of US corporations (Faber, 1993). Imperialist adventures form the basis of many actions that are now accepted MNC practices. The first joint stock company was formed by Genoan merchants to run plantations (Verlinden, 1970). The first instance of a joint venture between a government and a private entrepreneur was between Queen Elizabeth I and a slave trader (Rodney, 1974: 83). The East India Company, which was active in a number of nations in the 18th century, was organized into national subsidiaries reminiscent of a geographically specialized MNC. Essentially, many organizational forms as we know them were experimented on in the regimes of colonialism (Mir et al., 2003).

It has often been the case that development and globalization are used interchangeably. Generally understood to be a post-World War II phenomenon, globalization as we know it is associated in this instance with the emergence of the development apparatus (Escobar, 1995), and its stated aims to effect the systemic transition of nations and societies towards a 'developed' end-state; albeit effected here via the planning activities of development officials, and progressive transformation of the social and economic spheres of target nations and sectors (Chio, 2005). Contemporary discourses of globalization inform a particular form of development: namely, neoliberalism, and its implicit and explicit focus on and privileging of markets as both the generator and organizer of activities and practices. Within this context and historicized conjuncture, modern development studies are the result of an agglomeration and 'merging' of capital (or market-oriented ways of organizing) and the equally modernist beliefs in science, reason and progress, and their application to the context of economic transformation and development (Chio, 2005; Escobar, 1995).

Both development and globalization have their roots in colonial histories. Colonialism entailed both conquest and theft of land and reformation of the natives' minds (particularly in terms of knowledge systems and culture). Consequently, multiple local economic histories became incorporated into a Western narrative of progress and development (Mudimbe, 1988). The emergence of postcolonial scholarship in the 1950s and 1960s reflected radical critiques of colonialism, imperialism and neocolonialism. Inspired and informed by political activists, freedom fighters, and anti-colonial activists from Africa, India, South America and other regions, postcolonial perspectives called for nations emerging from colonialism to 'decolonize their minds' (Ngugi wa Thiong'O, 1981) and to contest the unquestioned sovereignty of Western epistemological, economic, political and cultural categories (Prasad, 2003). In a broad sense, the postcolonial approach seeks to understand contemporary problems in developing countries through a 'retrospective reflection on colonialism' (Said, 1986: 45). As Prasad (2003) points out, a postcolonial perspective can be intellectually productive in the sense that it can reveal the neocolonial assumptions that underlie management disciplines, especially international management and cross-cultural management. Neocolonialism can be understood as a continuation of direct Western colonialism without the traditional mechanism of expanding frontiers and territorial control, but with elements of political, economic and cultural control.

However, in addition to emphasizing the ongoing significance of colonialism in today's world, the postcolonial perspective also brings something new and different in the way it undertakes the study of colonialism. Specifically, in contrast to certain earlier Western scholarly approaches that, by and large, adopted Eurocentric perspectives in the course of mostly examining political and/or economic aspects of Western colonialism and neocolonialism, postcolonial theory stakes a position firmly committed to critiquing Eurocentrism, and gives significant attention not only to political and economic issues, but also to the cultural, psychological, philosophical, epistemological and similar other aspects of (neo)colonialism. In a nutshell, therefore, postcolonialism may be viewed as a much more comprehensive critique and deconstruction of the constitutive practices and discourses of (neo)colonialism.

Postcolonial insights can enable us to understand the discursive formations of development and globalization, the politics of representation, the accompanying forms of knowledge and systems of power that organize

their practice, and the subjectivities they foster (Chio, 2005). When recon-
ceived in terms of this discursive production and regulation of subjects,
and resituated in reference to the series of material practices and relations
organizing this production and regulation, it becomes possible not only to
understand development and globalization as singularly historicized phenomena, but also how it is that they have become the effective mechanisms
or regimes of transformation and rule at the center of most postcolonial
and development scholars' critiques of 'the economic, material, and cultural conditions that determine the global system in which the postcolonial
nation is required to operate' (Young, 2001: 57). Implicit in discourses
of the globalization of capital is that capital became globalized *after* its
European invention and influence and that development and globalization would produce 'local versions of the same narrative' (Chakrabarty,
2000: 7). Cultural ethnocentricism and Western ideologies of development
continue to inform postcolonial modes of development as well as Western
notions of environmental conservation and sustainable development
(Banerjee, 2003).

CONTENT OF THE BOOK

While the contributions in the volume are informed by a variety of
theoretical and research frameworks, they implicitly or explicitly seek to
bring attention to the socially constructed nature of globalization and its
non-natural and non-neutral character. Through a variety of topics (e.g.
careers, intellectual property, social responsibility, sustainability, knowledge management, human resource training practices), the authors draw
attention to components of the management and organizational discursive
formation contributing to the construction of this global and globalizing
world:

- Forms and procedures of knowledge (professional, managerial,
  scientific/academic; visibilities attached, functional or ahistorical
  orientation of concepts/theories, their economized nature)
- Modes of power (visibilities produced and reproduced, practices of
  construction and organization, political economy, history and relations between West and the Rest)
- Subjects/subjectivities (constructions of Other, constitution of environment, of workers, reconstitution of subjects/subjectivities)

The chapters in this book reflect the intersection of factors that make
imperial formations of globalization possible – histories of development,

(post)colonialism, practices of knowledge construction and conceptual entry-points, structural adjustment policies of multilateral institutions, and the political economy. Chapters include theoretical and empirical contributions that critique ethnocentric assumptions that inform popular notions of culture in international management textbooks, examine Western economic and corporate interests that inform discourses of 'global' sustainability, discuss the political economy of knowledge and analyze the discursive production of subjects in emerging economies.

Martin Fougère and Agneta Moulettes (Chapter 2) interrogate the treatment of 'culture' in international management textbooks. Employing a postcolonial perspective the authors argue that most international management textbooks reproduce stereotypical images of the 'Other' that are grounded in colonial and neocolonial discourses. They show how discourses of culture become subsumed to managerialist discourse, resulting in reductive, simplistic notions of 'international cultures' where cultural sensitivity is framed as a business opportunity that enables corporations to sell their products in international markets. Western forms of knowledge facilitate the production of subjects by essentializing 'national cultures' while shifting the focus from the Western self to the generalized Other, thus producing and sustaining a 'guilt-free Western subjectivity'. The authors show how discourses of culture create subjectivities of both the 'international manager' and the 'local' where the former is given simplistic tools to 'manage' cultural diversity while the latter enacts the cultural subject position that is presented as 'knowledge'.

Martin Fougère and Nikodemus Solitander (Chapter 3) critique contemporary discourses of sustainable development and corporate social responsibility. Analyzing two influential texts on sustainable development the authors show how discourses of sustainability result in the capitalization of nature. The appropriation and reconstitution of nature by corporate interests reflect a dominant managerialist discourse that constructs environmental problems and articulates solutions that focus more on enhancing the profitability of corporations than on the protection of the environment. Such a capture is enabled by discourses of corporate social responsibility, which the authors argue present sustainability issues as 'win–win' (make profits by saving the world). Sustainability is thus accepted as a goal only if it is profitable for corporations.

Diana Wong-MingJi (Chapter 4) examines the relationship between globalization and boundaries with particular reference to the contested terrains of nation states, intellectual capital and e-commerce. Specifically, Wong focuses attention on understanding boundaries as contested terrains with both spatial and temporal properties and as outcomes of power relations between actors such as nation states, transnational corporations, non-governmental organizations and citizens. In Wong-MinJi's conceptualization, boundaries are not static but are part of a more dynamic process involving conflicts, negotiations, compromises and ambiguous sovereignties. Wong-MinJi shows how conventional static notions of boundaries such as the boundaries that determine a sovereign nation state are constantly transgressed and shifted by transnational corporate activity and state and civil society actors. Boundary spanning in the context of nation states and transnational capital enables the control of economic exchanges in the global market through the creation of intellectual capital boundaries that privilege global capital flows. The dynamic nature of boundaries implies that old boundaries are dissolved and new ones created, reflecting the 'positional powers of competing actors in a contested space'.

Raza Mir, Subhabrata Bobby Banerjee and Ali Mir (Chapter 5) problematize the notion of organizational knowledge, particularly in the historical experiences of power differences and economic imbalances that underlie 'knowledge transfer' between multinational corporations and their subsidiaries. They describe the results of an ethnographic study of knowledge transfer between a US multinational and its Indian subsidiary and argue that much of the interaction reflected older relationships in the era of colonialism. Their analysis points to a colonial understanding of knowledge that highlights disjunctures between theoretical descriptions of knowledge transfer and the empirical realities of MNC–subsidiary relations.

Abbas Ali in his chapter on 'Evangelical capitalism' (Chapter 6) argues that the global neoliberal hegemony promotes a universal form of capitalism and economic organization that is foisted on non-Western states irrespective of their cultural and economic conditions. The evangelical zeal with which these policies are pursued on a global scale reflects the colonial project in its focus on appropriating resources of other countries. Departing from conventional theories of the firm, Ali takes an evolutionary perspective to help understand the connections between business firms and the political economy. Rather than conceptualize a firm as a separate entity or 'nexus of contracts' Ali shows how a variety of factors in the political economy determine organizational goals and the influence of national economic policy in shaping firm strategy.

Suzette Dyer (Chapter 7) interrogates discourses of flexible careers in the political economy of neoliberal globalization. Structural changes in the political economy have fundamentally changed the conditions of employment and notions of what it means to have a 'career'. 'Career management' strategies create particular subjectivities that reflect less the needs of the individual but more the neoliberal requirement of 'flexibility' in employment, which requires the construction of a subjectivity that 'takes responsibility for the self'. However, the political economy of 'flexible careers' does not provide all individuals with the same freedom, choice, or opportunity to enhance their wellbeing. Rather discourses of career management tend to manufacture consent in a political economy that reproduces particular forms of power and domination within contemporary society.

Diya Das and Ravi Dharwadkar (Chapter 8) examine the practice of offshoring of service work, in particular the emergence of call centers in the context of corporate globalization. Adopting a postcolonial perspective the authors argue that globalization of work produces new forms of postcolonial hybrid subjectivities. Contemporary theories of organizational identity, they argue, do not explain the complexities, contradictions, tensions, forms of power and control and resistance that arise from call centers in former colonies like India. The findings from their empirical study of call center employees in India indicate that new postcolonial identities are being produced as a result of globalization and that subjects are 'trained into new identity orientations' through a process of mimicry and Anglicization. The often hostile reception faced by call center employees from their customers seems to reinforce postcolonial concepts of ambivalence and mimicry – to quote Bhabha (1994: 86), 'the subjects were Anglicized and not English – thereby maintaining a difference and therefore a subject of a difference that is almost the same, but not quite'.

Martyna Sliwa (Chapter 9) analyzes the discursive production of subjects in 'transition economies' such as Poland and its experience with market-based forms of economic and social organization. She problematizes the taken-for-granted positive outcomes of economies in transition as 'having arrived'. Sliwa describes the experiences of some residents of Krakow in south eastern Poland and the social reconstitutions to daily life, language and labor that accompanied the transition to market economies. The transition experience in Polish society was characterized by a decreased role of government, changed employment conditions, increased inequalities, and spatial segregation between the 'haves and have-nots'. The exercise of power in transition economies like Poland resulted in significant shifts in subjectivities and perceptions of self and others arising from the introduction of market and managerialist-infused notions of what constitutes 'value' in the market economy.

The chapters in this book thus produce an interesting patchwork quilt of approaches to globalization. Their collective effect, however, is to provide an innovative critique of globalization, implying a confluence of newer forms of power relations with older patterns of imperialist exploitation. However, there are some resonances between our conclusions and those of preceding theorists. For instance, as Chakrabarty (2000) has pointed out, one of the problems of capitalist modernity in an era of globalization is not just the transition of non-Western countries but the translation of forms of organization, practices and knowledge into universal categories, despite their European origin. The contributions in this volume present some examples of the problems associated with transition and translation as well as demonstrating the need for more research on the politics of translation. What is needed for a richer and more politically informed approach to globalization is not just abstract analytical histories that describe the transition to global capitalism, but also *affective histories* (Chakrabarty, 2000) that describe human narratives about interrupting and deferring the universalizing and totalizing discourses of globalization in an attempt to reclaim historical difference.

REFERENCES

Amin, S. (1976). *Imperialism and Unequal Development*. New York: Monthly Review Press.

Baker, D., G. Epstein and R. Pollin (1998). *Globalization and Progressive Economic Policy*. Cambridge: Cambridge University Press.

Banerjee, S.B. (2003). 'Who sustains whose development? Sustainable development and the reinvention of nature', *Organization Studies*, **24** (1): 143–80

Banerjee, S.B. (2008). 'Necrocapitalism', *Organization Studies*, **29** (12): 1541–63.

Banerjee, S.B. and S. Linstead (2001). 'Globalization, multiculturalism and other fictions: colonialism for the new millennium?', *Organization*, **8** (4): 711–50.

Bhabha, Homi K. (1994). *The Location of Culture*. London & New York: Routledge.

Brenner, N. (1997). 'Global, fragmented, hierarchical: Henri Lefebvre's geographies of globalization', *Public Culture*, **10** (1): 135–67.

Brewer, J. (1980). *Marxist Theories of Imperialism*. London: Routledge.

Chakrabarty, D. (2000). *Provincializing Europe: Postcolonial Thought and Historical Difference*. Princeton, NJ: Princeton University Press.

Chio, V. (2005). *Malaysia and the Development Process: Globalization, Knowledge Transfers and Postcolonial Dilemmas*. New York: Routledge.

Djelic, M. (1998). *Exporting the American Model*. Oxford: Oxford University Press.

Escobar, A. (1995). *Encountering Development: The Making and Unmaking of the Third World, 1945–1992*. Princeton, NJ: Princeton University Press.

Faber, D. (1993). *Environment Under Fire: Imperialism and the Ecological Crisis in Central America*. New York: Monthly Review Press Books.

Gatade, S. (1997). *Globalisation of Capital: An Outline of Recent Changes in the Modus Operandi of Imperialism*. New Delhi: Lok Dasta Press.

Guha, R. (1989). 'Dominance without hegemony and its historiography', in R. Guha (ed.), *Subaltern Studies VI*. New Delhi: Oxford University Press, pp. 210–309.

Guillén, M.F. (2001). *The Limits of Convergence*. Princeton, NJ: Princeton University Press.

Headrick, D. (1988). *The Tentacles of Progress: Technology Transfer in the Age of Imperialism.* New York: Oxford University Press.

Lefebvre, H. (1991). *The Production of Space.* Oxford: Blackwell.

Mir, R., A. Mir and P. Upadhyay (2003). 'Toward a postcolonial reading of organizational control', in Anshuman Prasad (ed.), *The Gaze of the Other: Postcolonial Theory and Organizational Analysis.* New York: Palgrave, pp. 47–75.

Mudimbe, V.Y. (1988). *The Invention of Africa.* Bloomington: Indiana University Press.

Ngugi wa Thiong'O (1981). *Decolonizing the Mind.* London: James Curry.

Prasad, A. (ed.) (2003). *Postcolonial Theory and Organizational Analysis: A Critical Engagement.* New York: Palgrave Macmillan/St Martin's Press.

Rabinow, P. (1986). 'Representations are social facts: modernity and postmodernity in anthropology', in J. Clifford and G. Marcus (eds), *Writing Culture: The Poetics and Politics of Ethnography.* Berkeley: University of California Press, pp. 234–61.

Rodney, W. (1974). *How Europe Underdeveloped Africa.* Washington, DC: Howard University Press.

Said, E. (1986). 'Intellectuals in the postcolonial world', *Salmagundi*, **70/71**: 44–64.

Tappan, S. (2004). *Shock and Awe in Fort Worth: How the U.S. Army Rigged the Free and Open Competition to Replace Halliburton's Sole-source Oil Field Contract in Iraq.* New York: Pourquoi Press.

Verlinden, Charles (1970). *The Beginnings of Modern Colonisation* (Trans. Yvonne Freccero). Ithaca, NY: Cornell University Press.

Warren, W. (1973). 'Imperialism and capitalist industrialization', *New Left Review*, **I** (81): 1–20.

Young, R.J.C. (2001). *Postcolonialism: An Historical Introduction.* Oxford: Blackwell.

PART II

The construction of culture and the reinvention of nature

2. On 'cultural' knowledge in international management textbooks: a postcolonial reading

Martin Fougère and Agneta Moulettes

INTRODUCTION

Training a managerial elite able to conduct business efficiently on the global market is unanimously presented as of utmost importance for success in today's globalized economy. Underlining the too widespread underestimation of cultural differences by managers, international management literature problematizes culture as a critical factor for global competitiveness. It especially stresses the need for global managers to be 'culturally sensitive', and it has become an important endeavour for various educational institutions to provide courses that may address this issue. Presumably because of this increasingly pressing need, many a textbook on international management claims to be taking the cross-cultural challenge seriously, directly or indirectly referring to culture in their title – or on their front page.

Evidence from previous research (Fougère and Moulettes 2007; Kwek 2003; Westwood 2001, 2006) has shown that the main works within the cross-cultural management field (especially Hofstede 1980) can be seen as characterized by a (neo)colonial, orientalist worldview. Since these main cross-cultural management works are heavily used in the broader field of international management, it may be interesting to look at how 'culture' is discussed in some of the most known international management textbooks. We see postcolonial theory as potentially providing an insightful lens for examining power relations concealed in this literature largely constructed from a central (Western) position that views the rest of the world as peripheral. The aim of our chapter is to analyse, with a broadly postcolonial sensibility (inspired by authors such as Prasad 2003; Said [1978] 1995; and Young 2001), the discourses on culture found in some of these well-known books that: (1) especially claim to emphasize the cultural factor, and (2) present themselves as 'international', supposedly appropriate for reading in all parts of the globe. We more specifically aim to emphasize how the future international managers who acquire cross-cultural 'knowledge' through these books are meant to see the world as a result.

In the following two sections we introduce some theoretical discussion on how a postcolonial perspective can be relevant for the study of international management textbooks and on how education has been central in colonial and neocolonial processes. We then proceed to a brief presentation of the selection of our five textbooks and our methodology. Our analysis follows, divided in four parts dealing respectively with how the books promote the essentializing of national cultures and cultural differences; the generalization of basic cultural differences to larger cultural groups; the 'tolerance' for all cultural practices as long as there are business opportunities; and the Western 'universalist' perception of today's global world and its history. In a final section we discuss the particular hybrid subjectification processes of Western-educated non-Western managers-to-be, provide some suggestions for further research and offer some concluding thoughts.

EXPLORING INTERNATIONAL MANAGEMENT TEXTBOOKS THROUGH A POSTCOLONIAL LENS

Before proceeding with our exploration of management textbooks, some words on postcolonialism and closely related terms, such as imperialism, colonialism and neocolonialism, are in order. To begin with, imperialism does in its most general sense refer to the formation of an empire through the extension of a nation's territorial borders. In this general definition of imperialism, focus is on a metropolitan centre's domination and control over other territories. A somewhat extended definition of imperialism is offered by Said, who claims that 'imperialism' refers to 'the practice, the theory and the attitudes of a dominating metropolitan centre ruling a distant territory; "colonialism", which is almost always a consequence of imperialism, is the implanting of settlements on distant territory' (Said [1993] 1994, p. 8). Said further points out that 'in our time, direct colonialism has largely ended; imperialism . . . lingers where it has always been, in a kind of general cultural sphere as in specific political, ideological, economic, and social practices' (Said [1993] 1994, p. 8). Neocolonialism, which is a term that came into use after the period of decolonialization during the middle of the 20th century, refers to a continuation of Western colonialism by nontraditional means (Prasad 2003, p. 6). It has usually been associated with the economic and political power that former colonizers continued to exercise in these newly independent nations. However, neocolonialism has in more recent years developed into a modified version now including

Western control also over the cultural dimension. The diffusion of Western ideas through international management textbooks is one example of this cultural dimension of Western neocolonialism.

Postcolonial theory, from which we find the inspiration for our discussion on international management textbooks, is used here in Said's broader sense as a continuity of Western colonialism. In a nutshell postcolonial studies attempt to investigate the effects of the colonial and neocolonial encounters between the West (European former colonial powers and North America) and the non-West and their current influences on the economic, political, ideological and cultural spheres (see Ashcroft et al. 2004; Mills 1997; Prasad 2003; Young 2001). This perspective was originally developed to enhance our understanding of the historical process of colonization and its consequences for the Occident's constitution of the Orient (Said [1978] 1995). It not only examines colonial history and the Western endeavours to gain control of non-Western territories, but also problematizes the power relationships between centre and periphery (Aizenberg 1999; Mishra and Hodge 1991) and, for instance, the current representation of cultural differences along imperialist lines. It is our contention that such neocolonial power relationships between centre and periphery appear clearly in the representations found in those Western-produced international management textbooks that are aimed at a global audience. That is why we see postcolonialism as a useful lens for examining the power relations concealed in 'global' international management textbooks.

Moreover, as highlighted by scholars like Banerjee (2003), Bhabha (1994), Prasad (2003) and Said ([1978] 1995), colonialism was one of the most profound and significant experiences that shaped Western people's perception not only of non-Western people but also, and perhaps mainly, of themselves – as well as the non-Western people's perceptions of themselves. Even though Western travellers spent a lot of time producing knowledge about the Orient, they rarely learned much about or from the local inhabitants. Instead they documented their observations of the Middle East on commonly held assumptions about the Orient (Said [1978] 1995, as referred to by McLeod 2000). The resulting orientalism discourse (Said [1978] 1995), which largely served as justification for colonization, has been characterized by a 'starkly dichotomous view of "the Orient" and "the Occident"' and 'essentialist statements about the former' (Prasad 2003, p. 10). Similar claims may be raised towards international management textbooks, which reproduce assumptions about national culture constructed by cross-cultural management scholars like Hall and Hall (1990), Hofstede (1980), Lewis (1996), and Trompenaars (1993). A colonial mindset is discernible in the binary opposition and hierarchical ordering of nations constructed by these scholars. Models of national cultures broadly divide the world in two (Fougère and Moulettes 2007): on the one hand a modern, developed West, and on the other hand the non-West and its primitive, mystical and passive people of colour.

POSTCOLONIALISM AND EDUCATION

Education has certainly been one of the most important (however insidious) vehicles of colonialist appropriation (see Altbach 2004; and as shown in Macaulay [1835] 2004) and in the wake of globalization it is now being transformed into new shapes. During the colonial era it was part of a planned policy for the survival of the colonial order to educate the colonial subjects. Although the consequences may have differed between countries, education was, as pointed out by Altbach (2004), a direct political means designed to gain power and control over the colonies. Thus, instead of an educational system that could have furthered the internal development in the colonies, what was developed was a system oriented towards the training of an administrative elite that permitted the colonizer to stay in power. For example, the educational scheme generally stressed language training that made a selective group of natives fluent in the metropolitan language; that is, French, English, Spanish or Portuguese, and put special emphasis on the training of civil servants and lawyers according to the metropolitan administration and law systems. At the same time as the natives received the training needed for entering civil services and legal professions, thereby forming a local elite, they were disciplined according to the underlying metropolitan values that guided their educational cursus.

While the domination relationships of clearly exploitative forms of neocolonialism raise critical voices all over the world – which sadly does not mean they are getting more uncommon – the question of a 'softer' neocolonialism that characterizes today's world – connected to the practice of development and development aid in particular – is a heated issue of debate where contradictory views concerning victors and victims of the global venture are articulated. While these 'softer' aspects are considered a much-needed philanthropic mission by their ardent advocates, who feel a responsibility to distribute both goods and knowledge to those 'less fortunate', their critics rather think of them as a continuation of the colonial oppression under the same 'civilizing' guise. As argued by Altbach (2004) the reliance on educational systems dictated by the former colonial powers has remained almost total in ex-colonies, but influences of Western educational systems are discernible also in countries that had not been under colonial domination, such as Thailand, Liberia and Ethiopia. The motivation of gaining direct political control may no longer be as obvious as before – although that is debatable – but the Western world's sense of 'mission' to dominate non-Western societies on behalf of their development still is (Escobar 1995). We argue that the conquest of territory endures and that past practices and planned policies of the Western world maintain their grip on their non-Western world – only now this primarily takes place between actors on the global market.

Now that cultural models delineating differences between countries have seemingly been well established among management scholars and managers, the latter are mostly concerned with how to disseminate this knowledge and use it as a factor potentially providing a competitive advantage. In the educational system this fashion is visible in the increasing amount of managerialistic courses offered by universities, university colleges and various kinds of business schools. Educational institutions with some standing have thus included international (and cross-cultural) management courses in their curriculum. A brief survey on the Internet clearly shows that courses focusing on globalization, international management and cross-cultural relations attract students and businesspeople all over the globe. Besides International Management, Intercultural Understanding, Cross-cultural Communication, Cross-cultural Project Management, Cross-cultural Training, or Global Diversity Consulting are some of the themes that are now being marketed all over the world wide web. The objectives and contents of these courses are very similar even though they are supposed to belong to various disciplines. Participants are drawn to these courses in order to obtain a deeper understanding of intercultural phenomena, to enhance their knowledge about cultural identities, to learn about cultural differences, to learn how to manage in cross-cultural situations and how to interact with the natives. The courses generally claim to provide the participants with methods for enhancing their own cross-cultural awareness, cross-cultural competencies, and what is most often referred to as 'cultural sensitivity'. Irrespective of where these courses take place the source of information is usually based on Anglo-American international management textbooks.

Based on a strongly held belief that the world can be made a familiar place to organizations and thereby rationally managed, these textbooks, which are usually targeted to MBA students, have become a significant means for the training – or, with more of a Foucauldian lens, the disciplining – of the managerial corps. What can be noticed is that these textbooks share some common characteristics. In order to live up to the growing demand for normative models dealing with cross-cultural issues, the authors of the textbooks have uncritically taken advantage of the largely self-proclaimed success that models of national cultures – especially Hofstede's – have received.

SELECTION OF TEXTBOOKS AND METHODOLOGY

The selection of the five international textbooks that we have analysed was guided by three criteria. First, we chose to analyse popular textbooks that are available in Sweden and Finland (where we respectively live) and that can be found in university libraries – having lectured in courses connected to international management, we even received some of these books as inspection copies. Second, we selected textbooks that explicitly state that they are written for a worldwide audience and intended for use by both undergraduate and MBA students who are undertaking studies that have an interdisciplinary and international context. Third, we chose textbooks that contain an extensive discussion of culture.

Among the five chosen textbooks, three very explicitly mention culture as of focal importance to international management in their title: *International Management: A Cultural Approach* (Rodrigues 2001, 2nd edition), *International Management: Culture, Strategy and Behavior* (Hodgetts and Luthans 2005, 6th edition), and *International Management: Managing Across Borders and Cultures* (Deresky 2006, 5th edition). The other two books we will examine are *International Business: An Introduction* (Woods 2001), which shows its specific interest in culture by advertising the 'Foreword by Geert Hofstede' on its front page, and *International Management* (Holt and Wiggington 2002, 2nd edition), less explicitly 'cultural' than the others at first sight.

From a first reading of the textbooks three main topics emerged, namely (1) the call for 'cultural sensitivity', (2) the role of culture as strictly subjugated to international management needs and (3) a general tendency to essentialize national cultures. After further reading, the second topic was broadened: it became clear that the reductionism characterizing the discussion of 'the role' of culture in all the books is strongly connected to the underlying managerialism of international management discourse. The topics were further reordered several times in order to make the analysis clearer: the first and third topics were switched in that process. One section that had initially been treated separately, discussing both the claimed global audiences of the books and the view of history present in them, was also included as an integral part of the analysis.

Drawing on insights from postcolonial theory and the Foucauldian notion of power/knowledge, we take an interest in the international management discourse that has acquired a dominant position thanks to the 'textual attitude' (see Said [1978] 1995) that has arisen from such formatted textbooks. We attempt to show how international management textbooks reproduce stereotypical images of culture that are grounded in colonial and neocolonial discourses reminiscent of orientalism. We adopt

Foucault's (1971) concept of discourse referring to 'a strongly bounded area of social knowledge, a system of statements within which the world can be known' (Ashcroft et al. 1998, p. 70) and argue that cross-cultural management models have paved the way for the cohesive and stereotypical image of 'others' now being replicated in international management textbooks. In our analysis we are particularly interested in exploring how Western-educated managers (MBA style) are supposed to see the world through these textbooks. We are inspired by Foucault's articulation of disciplinary power, which conceptualizes power as constituting human beings as objects of knowledge while at the same time making them subject to knowledge (Foucault 2000).

In our analysis we try to represent how those who are subject to this 'knowledge' are meant to see the world and develop an appropriate subjectivity for their future managerial careers. In the textbooks that we analyse, both the 'international managers' and the 'locals' are objects of knowledge, and they are made subjects/subjected in different ways. The former – as students who will presumably become managers – are given simple tools to manage cultural diversity, while the latter are merely expected to enact the stereotypical 'cultural' subject positions that are presented as 'knowledge' about them as passive objects (see also Westwood 2006). Particularly interesting subjects are those international management students who also see themselves as 'locals', Western-educated (at least through the use of these textbooks) yet non-Western at the same time. While in most of the chapter we focus on future international managers' worldviews without distinction – assuming that the manager is a Westerner since the books systematically take Western businesspeople going abroad as examples – we more specifically discuss the case of the subjectification of international-managers-to-be who are not of Western origin at the beginning of our discussion.

ANALYSIS

Although the emphasis on culture varies in the textbooks there is no doubt that it is central in all five of them. Ironically the most explicitly 'cultural' of them, Rodrigues (2001), also has the most naïve and unproblematic approach to cultural issues, while Holt and Wiggington (2002) are perhaps the ones who develop the potential critique the most despite their less explicit interest in culture at first sight. On the whole, culture is defined in similar ways across all five books. To start with, there is a taken-for-granted assumption among all the authors that all nations have their own specific cultures that distinguish them from one another. Relying on an essentialistic understanding, the authors see culture as characterized by 'the shared values, understandings, assumptions, and goals that are learned from earlier generations' (Deresky 2006, p. 83), or by shared solutions to universal problems with a core consisting of traditional (i.e. historically derived and selected) ideas and their attached values (Woods 2001). They present culture as 'an anthropological concept that relates to a *shared system* [emphasis in original] of beliefs, attitudes, possessions, attributes, customs and values that define group behaviour' (Holt and Wiggington 2002, p. 284), or as an 'acquired knowledge that people use to interpret, experience and generate social behaviour' (Hodgetts and Luthans 2005, p. 108). Considering that all of the authors dedicate much attention to culture they all seem to share an assumption that knowledge about these cultural differences is a critical need for the international manager, and that this need arises precisely because of the international dimension of her/his work. Woods (2001) further emphasizes that, since patterns of behaviour and social values vary between countries, management styles are also likely to differ from country to country.

After reading the five books we find that very similar discursive patterns characterize the conceptualizations of culture found in them. Broadly speaking, these texts are all meant to address the growing demand for normative models dealing with cross-cultural management issues – a demand that stems from an increasingly globalized business environment and a strongly held corporate belief, originating in the West, that the world can be rationally managed. When we look at the texts with a postcolonial or Foucauldian lens, we see in them a disciplinary power, an institutionalized way of looking at the world that is supposed to shape the readers' subjectivities as future international managers. We explore how the textbooks that we have chosen for our analysis are meant to develop subjectivities that make it possible to: (1) essentialize national cultures and cultural differences in an acceptable way, with appropriate disclaimers, (2) generalize basic cultural differences to larger cultural groups in a way that merely confirms existing preconceptions, (3) tolerate all 'different cultural practices' – even intolerable ones – as long as there are business opportunities, and (4) perceive the global business field and history with Western 'universalist' eyes.

Essentializing in an 'Acceptable' Way: First Disclaimers, Then Dichotomies

A large number of courses and textbooks are devoted solely to the study of comparative management practices in different cultures, and trying to cover the topic in a single chapter is clearly going to result in a relatively brief summary of key theories. Nonetheless it is included here because the author believes that students need to understand the importance of cultural empathy to business success. (Woods 2001, p. 10)

From this citation, it is clear that the author establishes a strong link between the need for 'cultural empathy' and a number of 'key theories'. From that statement one would be led to imagine that these 'theories' would have more to do with how to develop cultural sensitivity – see (3) – than with simple, 'ready-to-use' knowledge about different (national) cultures. Strangely enough, they (whether one refers to Hall and Hall 1990; Hofstede 1980; Javidan and House 2001; Lewis 1996; or Trompenaars 1993) turn out to be almost exclusively dealing with the latter.

To their credit, all the authors are quite cautious when introducing these models. In every book – with perhaps the notable exception of Rodrigues (2001) – there are disclaimers regarding the limitations to the relevance of such research on national culture. On the other hand, however, if there are so many disclaimers before the description of these models classifying national cultures it is also because they are the main (if not the only) general 'theories' that the authors refer to about culture. In a sense it seems that whatever is written in initial disclaimers should be read as meaning their very opposite: the authors are telling us, for instance, that cultures are 'not monolithic', that it is hard to separate culture from economic and political issues, that defining the degree of cultural difference is always subjective, and that the significance of national cultures is diluted in the global movements that characterize today's world (see Woods 2001, p. 72) before presenting models (especially Hofstede 1980, which is presented at length in every book) that directly contradict all of these points. Similarly, Deresky (2006, p. 89), after pointing out that 'good managers . . . consciously avoid any form of *stereotyping* [emphasis in original]', immediately follows up with the claim that 'however, a cultural profile is a good starting point to help managers develop some tentative expectations'. We are thus led to believe that even though stereotyping should be avoided, stereotyping should be pursued.

In addition to the initial disclaimers, there are also at times deeper criticisms of the models, but in most cases these criticisms are only there to be eventually ruled out. Holt and Wiggington's (2002) surprisingly thorough discussion exemplifies this theme best. The authors acknowledge that Hofstede's work 'is somewhat controversial because it attempts to classify patterns of behavior for individual countries without taking into account subcultural differences or ideological orientations' before stating that 'nevertheless, the model has significantly changed the prevailing view of behavior in various cultures and, in particular, how to understand work-related values among many of the world's nations' (Holt and Wiggington 2002, p. 294), and proceeding with a ten-page description of Hofstede's model. To their credit, they do point to quite a few limitations regarding this model, but they introduce these limitations with the sentence:

'Hofstede has been criticized on a number of issues, and although the criticisms are valid, they do not outweigh the importance of his work (Triandis 1982)' (Holt and Wiggington 2002, p. 299). And then of the three main limitations they underline, two are ruled out: the fact that Hofstede's initial study was limited to the managers of one company is not such a shortcoming since there have been many 'successful' replications, and the critique that the original research was heavily Western in context is mitigated by the claim that Hofstede 'chose to view these issues as opportunities for further research, and his early endeavors have subsequently become the building blocks for a significant number of studies in eastern culture [sic!]' (Holt and Wiggington 2002, p. 301). Eventually, the only limitation that remains relatively problematic to the authors after their discussion lies in the fact that national identities are described without regard for subcultural differences within a country, but the rationale brought forward is not very convincing to say the least: 'these shortcomings become obvious in places like the former Yugoslavia, now splintered through ethnic strife, or the former Soviet Union, which was an amalgamation of more than 160 ethnic societies' (Holt and Wiggington 2002, pp. 301–2). From this strange formulation it seems that if these countries had remained united, then the problem wouldn't have arisen – this assertion is misleading at best, and lies on a denial of colonialism. The authors seem to be unaware of the fact that if so many different ethnic societies have been amalgamated into huge, culturally meaningless countries, it is to a large extent a result of colonization.

Despite all the disclaimers and limitations, then, there is a general tendency to essentialize national cultures, presenting them as static and homogeneous. This is largely because of an overwhelming reliance on simplistic models that classify national cultures according to a few general dimensions, such as Hofstede's framework. For instance, Hodgetts and Luthans (2005, p. 31) maintain that Hofstede's (1980) and Trompenaars's (1993) works are useful points of departure not just for recognizing cultural differences, but also for providing guidelines for doing business effectively around the world. The importance given to national differences is evident in the fact that they return to Hofstede, Trompenaars as well as Hampden-Turner and Trompenaars (1997) throughout the entire book. But the importance given to cultural differences is shown also by a considerable number of illustrations from various countries that follow at the end of each chapter. In a section they call 'In the international spotlight' they include examples from India, Vietnam, France, Saudi Arabia, Taiwan, Mexico, Japan, Gulf States, Poland, Peru, Australia, Spain, Singapore, Germany, Russia, Argentina, and Denmark. The same tendency to focus on the national level in almost all 'cultural' examples is to be noticed in all the other books, to the extent that sometimes whatever varies from one country to another is deemed 'cultural': national and cultural are more or less equated in those cases. For instance, when Woods (2001, p. 84) discusses the 'impact of culture' on 'Operations Management' and 'Finance', most of the discussion focuses on national differences in technology, institutions or political systems. While there may indeed be underlying cultural differences helping to explain how there have come to be such differences, they are merely alluded to at best. To the author, pointing out, for example, institutional differences between countries seems to be exactly the same as discussing cultural differences. Despite so many disclaimers stating that national cultures are not homogeneous, general descriptions of cultural traits within big, extremely diverse countries abound: for instance, Chinese culture is presented as having easily identifiable 'main characteristics' (Deresky 2006, p. 214) in all five books, usually with much of a focus on the cultural trait called *guanxi*, which is always presented as 'a purely Chinese phenomenon' (Woods 2001, p. 90; but also Deresky 2006, pp. 208–15; Rodrigues 2001, pp. 357–60). If the authors were content with writing up general descriptions of 'national cultures' their texts could probably be useful – the same way that a tourist guide can be. However, in order to be grounded in a pseudo-scientific legitimacy (without which the discourse would be deprived of much of its power) they also need to demonstrate the relevance of the universal models they have presented and thereby are led to make very speculative assertions that even Hofstede would not dare formulate: for example, Woods (2001, p. 83) establishes a systematic connection between the country score on the power distance index (PDI) and the differences in pay levels between employees that the master himself would not corroborate, insofar as we understand what he claims PDI to represent.

No matter how neutral the models dealing with national cultures are claimed to be, they tend to favour one-dimensional oppositions that easily become loaded with a judgement of value. The picture that is painted soon becomes one of a world divided between a modern West and a backward rest (Fougère and Moulettes 2007). For example, to reproduce the image of Asia as a mysterious part of the world, Holt and Wiggington (2003, p. 289) have included a story about a solar eclipse.

The solar eclipse of October 1995 was seen most prominently in Thailand, where superstitions gained as many headlines as the eclipse itself. Four native language newspapers, including Thailand's largest mass-circulated newspaper, *The Rhath*, ran front-page stories and features full of astrological predictions for nearly a month before the occasion. Most warnings spelled doom and gloom for the country. Supported by astrological calculations, soothsayers predicted famine, inflation, flooding, and other national calamities, including a military coup by the end of the year.

Giving weight to people's superstition they mention a number of events of the year that prompted many people to take precautions. For example, Thailand's queen mother and the former prime minister both died unexpectedly, Bangkok experienced unusual floods, monsoon storms were predicted, political infighting led to military intervention to prevent a coup, the royal princess changed her plans for the week and substituted a secret itinerary, many merchants announced that they would close their doors and one third of the population was expected to shut themselves indoors. The reason for all these strange actions, we learn, has to do with the fact that, according to Hindu mythology, eclipses are the result of an act of a misfit god, Rahu, who drank Wishnu's sacred water to achieve immortality. And of course the Asian cultures' devotion to mysticism and Hindu mythology lives on today. The authors go on to emphasize the importance of the number 8 in many Asian cultures (a lucky number for some, it can also be associated with death), and then describe all kinds of rituals meant for Rahu involving that number. The exoticism – and cultural backwardness – of such behaviour, of course, is implied throughout.

Ironically, it should be pointed out that similar behaviour could be found in the West. For example, in connection with the turn of the century, many stories about Armageddon circulated in the press and among certain religious groups. Moreover, if many Asian people have a superstitious relation to the number 8, many Westerners have a similar superstitious relation to the number 13. However, nobody would even think of describing Western cultures on bases of mysticism and superstition. No textbook would include anecdotes about managers going to fortune-tellers asking for advice before making a difficult decision or about a HR department using horoscopes in order to hire the 'right' employee. On the contrary, the examples used in text books would rather depict Westerners and Western cultures in terms of how developed, modern, active and rational they are. Consider Hodgetts and Luthans's (2005) example of Jim, an American acquisition editor who goes to Colombia to visit an old school friend, and, more importantly, to establish some business contacts. In short the story tells us how Jim arrives at the first meeting at the university where he is to have a discussion with three of the professors. The excerpt that follows gives an account of the small talk taking place between Jim and the professors in the conference room. It also reveals Jim's thoughts after having had lunch at the local restaurant: 'It's been an hour and a half, and we haven't discussed anything.' At the end of the meeting a decision is made to visit Monserate, the mountain overlooking Bogotá and 'the myth and traditions that surround it'. The story ends with describing how Jim, once back at his friend's house, sits in the living room thinking: 'I just don't get it. The Colombians couldn't have been happier with the way the meeting turned out, but we didn't do anything. We didn't even talk about one book. I just don't understand what went wrong.' Luckily, his Colombian friend is there to explain: 'Here in Colombia, Jim, we do business differently. Right now, you're building friendship. You're building their trust in you' (Hodgetts and Luthans 2003, p. 567).

In this anecdote, it is obvious that the authors' aim is to emphasize that you do not carry out business in Colombia as you do in the USA. The Americans are presented as focusing on business, they are used to moving quickly and do not want to waste their time in any small talk that has nothing to do with business. The Colombians, on the other hand, need to build friendship and trust so that they know who they are dealing with before getting down to business. This is a good example of the type of binary oppositions that are recurring all the time in the books and tend to depict 'the others', from the Western viewpoint, as not so modern and rational. But in a sense the example could also be reconstructed as portraying the Colombians as culturally sensitive and the Americans as rather backward when it comes to cultural sensitivity, especially if we consider Beeth's (1997, p. 17, as quoted in Rodrigues 2001, p. 31) claim that 'you cannot motivate anyone, especially someone of another culture, until you have been accepted by that person'. But there is no such explicit ambition in that passage. The ultimate point seems to be that Jim, because he is American, likes to be efficient and get down to business quickly, while the Others like to develop relationships. The dichotomy is not questioned, it is the point as such. Instead of developing subjects who would understand that intercultural interactions are all about *relating* to the Other, the books reproduce essentialist binary oppositions while using disclaimers to make this focus on oppositions acceptable. So Jim can safely continue to see himself as more rational and modern than his South American counterparts.

Generalizing Further and Further: Infinite Reductionism

> In fact, the differences can be narrowed down by the creation of clusters of countries which demonstrate similar characteristics, and reference to such clusters can be helpful to the businessperson who when dealing with a country for the first time can simply look at the salient features of the culture of the relevant group, with which he may find he is in fact familiar . . . [The figure] demonstrates that there is a level of cultural affinity between groups of nations, and so a general understanding of management practice is made easier if one realises that it is only necessary to grasp the key characteristics of the seven groups. (Woods 2001, pp. 79–80)

We have pointed out above that the authors make an awkward connection between the need to be culturally sensitive and the use of simplistic models that tend to essentialize national cultures and classify them according to a few supposedly universal dimensions. But, as shown in the citation above, they go even further than that, suggesting that being aware of 'clusters of countries' that share 'cultural affinities' may be enough, in the sense that 'it is only necessary to grasp the key characteristics of the seven groups'. And so the authors move back and forth between a call for 'true' cultural sensitivity and the contradictory emphasis on broad, stereotypical cultural features that are supposed to apply to national and even supranational groups. This confirms that the disclaimers are only there to anticipate potential critiques (by making them their own in a superficial way) and thereby make it in turn possible for the authors to introduce extremely reductionistic approaches to the study of cultural differences. This reductionism, of course, is not surprising in such textbooks. It has to do with the managerialism that characterizes them: a need to provide simple tools that supposedly can help to solve concrete problems encountered by managers, while at the same time rooting these simple tools in (pseudo-) academic, prescriptive research in order to have a legitimate claim to knowledge. As we will see in the fourth subsection, his managerialism is 'tailor-made' for the 'global audience' to which the books are addressed.

The division of the world into national cultures is refined through 'cultural mappings' and regroupments into clusters that single out those nations for which it is worth being 'culturally sensitive' (e.g. China) while further excluding those national cultures (or should we say markets) that are too backward to offer a good potential for business in the near future. All books present some clusters putting a number of national cultures together: examples include Gupta et al. (2002, as quoted in Deresky 2006) who divide the world in ten cultural clusters, 'South Asia, Anglo, Arab, Germanic Europe, Latin Europe, Eastern Europe, Confucian Asia, Latin America, Sub-Saharan Africa, and Nordic Europe' (Deresky 2006, pp. 93–94); Ronen and Shenkar (1985, as quoted in Holt and Wiggington 2002) who include the originality to add four 'independent' national cultures (Brazil, Japan, India and Israel) to their eight clusters ('Arab', 'Near Eastern', 'Nordic', 'Germanic', 'Anglo', 'Latin European', 'Latin American' and 'Far Eastern'), which conspicuously exclude Africa; and, in the most extreme case, Hickson and Pugh (1995, as quoted in Woods 2001) who propose the seven clusters of 'East-Central Europe', 'Northern Europe + Israel', 'Arab Nations', 'Asians', 'Developing Nations', 'Latins' and 'Anglos' (Woods 2001, p. 80). In a convenient arrangement, the latter classification pushes all the backward 'developing nations' into the same cluster, presumably because there is not much interest for international-managers-to-be there anyway; and Israel, of course, had to be distinguished from its neighbours and brought back together with the modern and developed West – no, there is nothing far-fetched about associating it with Northern European cultures.

The almost systematic absence of Africa should not be very surprising. In one of the very rare attempts to discuss issues connected to the idiosyncracies of African cultures, Rodrigues (2001, p. 21) introduces 'the African thought system (*Ubuntu*)' (Mangaliso et al. 1998) in the following way:

> Just as there is no totally homogeneous thought in other regions of the world, such as Europe and South America, there is no totally homogeneous thought in Africa. There is in fact a diverse sociocultural, linguistic, and historical composition among the African nations. However, as is the case in the other regions throughout the globe, there is an underlying pan-African character that results from a unique geographical, historical, cultural, and political experience. Therefore, Africans can be identified by certain characteristics in their daily lives. Just as there is an Asian thought system (*Confucianism*), for example, there is an African thought system – *Ubuntu*.

We can notice here the usual pattern of a disclaimer followed by its negation with the adverb 'however' in between. It is difficult to imagine a more reductionistic cultural generalization than the one outlined in this short discussion. Just like in the case of *guanxi* for China, the use of the 'local-looking' word-concept *Ubuntu* is supposed to act as a legitimation for the presentation of a cultural idiosyncracy. The citation above takes up approximately half of the half page of text (only one paragraph) that is devoted to *Ubuntu* in the book, which means that there is not much room for a substantial description of what *Ubuntu* stands for. The main insight we get about it is expressed in the sentence 'similar to *Confucianism*, the individual is strongly connected to the group' and in the conclusion of the paragraph: 'this means that, in many organizational situations in Africa, a reward system emphasizing group achievement is often more effective than a reward system emphasizing individual achievement' (Rodrigues 2001, p. 21). Good to 'know', because our international manager subject (let's call him John this time), if he ever has any business interaction with 'Africans', will probably be mostly concerned, as a manager, about how he should reward them for their labour. If anything, what is surprising after this shallow description is that no author has used this 'evidence' to unite African '*Ubuntu*' cultures and Asian Confucian cultures into one big cluster.

The reductionism that characterizes the textbooks is also particularly visible in the subjugated 'role' that culture is given. Literally, authors write entire chapters titled 'the role of culture in international business' (Woods 2001, pp. 70–90) or 'understanding the role of culture' (Deresky 2006, pp. 79–115). It thus seems that culture only comes to play a role in connection with the main subject at hand – international management. The authors chiefly problematize culture in terms of its 'effects on organizations' (Deresky 2006, pp. 83–7), or 'impacts' on various management functions (Rodrigues 2001, pp. 9–12; Woods 2001, pp. 79–85) such as planning, staffing, coordinating or controlling. Culture is thus not seen as all-encompassing; it is only studied to the extent that it affects other things, and as such it is a factor to take into account when managing, not so much a factor to manage – the emphasis on organizational culture is very light in these textbooks – although such an understanding is alluded to at times. In the type of research referred to, such as Hofstede's (1980), culture (decomposed in dimensions) is usually the independent variable, and the idea that cultures may be changing over time is downplayed. Another way of reducing culture to a simple notion that managers-to-be can readily understand can be found in a metaphor of culture as 'rules of the game' used by Hofstede himself in his preface to Woods's (2001, p. 7) book: 'a multicultural perspective implies restraint in passing judgment: the ability to recognize that in different environments, different rules of the game of business apply'.

In addition, as a result of the need to keep the discussion simple, definitions of central concepts relating to culture often lack rigour and are complemented – or sometimes even altogether replaced – by illustrations that are not always appropriate. For example, Woods (2001, p. 71) is quite misleading in her description of 'beliefs':

> People's beliefs are most obviously expressed in religion, but the importance of religion and the specific beliefs vary across countries. For example, in Middle Eastern countries, Islam is a very important influence within societies, but in Western societies which are predominantly Christian, the social significance of religion is declining rapidly.

The above statements may be valid to some extent, but are we to believe that people in Western societies have no beliefs? This formulation is typical of the lack of rigour that characterizes the textbooks: there is no word about what people's beliefs may consist of besides their 'most obvious expression', and the discussion is not focused on beliefs per se but rather on an opposition between Middle Eastern and Western societies regarding the importance of religion. 'Values' and 'behaviour' are also only addressed by Woods (2001, pp. 71–2) in an illustrative manner that presents only one example in lieu of definition. Similarly, Holt and Wiggington (2002, p. 293), while they try to define the concepts with more rigour and describe them in more detail, mostly resort to examples that are not necessarily illustrative of the concept itself: for example, they mention Islamic law and the obligation for women to be covered from head to toe in the United Arab Emirates within their discussion of 'values'. Generally speaking, there is a notable tendency to use Arabic/Muslim examples, with a kind of post-Huntingtonesque orientalism, when dealing with the general aspects of culture, in order to have sharp contrasts with Western customs to present and thus make the points particularly salient to an audience that seems to be neither expected nor encouraged to be very culturally sensitive – to say the least. Seemingly the underlying logic is that because our subject John does not know so much about different cultures, it is better if his preconceptions are confirmed so at least he is more confident that he knows something.

Tolerating the Intolerable, Relativizing without Relating: Fake Cultural Sensitivity

> Successful international managers take great care to avoid misunderstandings by trying to understand cultural differences, which is a conscious effort to be *culturally sensitive*. *Cultural sensitivity* [emphasis in the original] means to have the empathy to accept cultural differences without allowing one's own values to surface in unproductive or confrontational ways (Mead 1994). It implies that an individual has become sufficiently aware of differences to function effectively without becoming openly judgmental. Expatriate managers do not have to abandon their values to be empathetic, but they must avoid imposing their cultural beliefs on others. Even when 'their way' seems to be right, and other ways seem to be wrong, managers must accommodate cultural differences to be effective. It is not a matter of right or wrong, or win or lose, but of avoiding *ethnocentric* or *parochial* behavior (Ferraro 1994). (Holt and Wiggington 2002, p. 291)

In all five books there is a unanimous call for 'cultural sensitivity', which is presented as a skill – one of the 'being skills' referred to by Woods (2001, p. 268) – that should be found in international managers. This call is nearly always one of the first issues addressed within the discussion of culture. Other terms alternatively used for cultural sensitivity are 'cultural empathy' (Deresky 2006; Woods 2001) or 'cultural savvy', which Deresky (2006, p. 82) presents as 'a critical skill for managing people and processes in other countries . . . that is, a working knowledge of the cultural variables affecting management decisions'. The view put forward is thus quite utilitarian: the value of cultural sensitivity is to be understood in terms of the benefits it can bring for management decisions.

Even when cultural sensitivity is not immediately emphasized as one of the prime aspects of the discussion on culture, as in Rodrigues (2001), it is nonetheless presented as a central skill for the managers of today and tomorrow to have, and the utilitarian angle remains quite clear. Examples include classifying cultural sensitivity as a 'core skill' for the '21st-Century

Expatriate Manager' (Howard 1992, p. 96), defined as 'quick and easy adaptibility into the foreign culture' and as characterizing 'an individual with as much cultural mix, diversity, and experience as possible' (Rodrigues 2001, p. 32); or introducing the 'Multicultural Manager' (Beeth 1997, p. 17) as follows (Rodrigues 2001, p. 31):

> You cannot motivate anyone, especially someone of another culture, until you have been accepted by that person. A multilingual salesperson can explain the advantages of a product in other languages, but a *multicultural* [our emphasis] salesperson can motivate foreigners to buy it. That's a critical difference.

Being a 'multicultural' salesperson has value to the extent that it allows someone to sell more. In most of the instances in these books, there is no other reason for cultural sensitivity than a matter of the business bottom line.

But there is worse. While any reader could be sympathetic to the willingness to develop cultural sensitivity insofar as it is clearly a pressing need in our globalized world, the way this need is instrumentalized here has insidious implications. Especially, cultural sensitivity often seems to be equivalent to a willingness to accept anything as long as there are business opportunities, as in the following quoted example (Deresky 2006, pp. 79–82):

> 'Foreign companies have had mixed success in Saudi Arabia, due in large part to how well they understood and adapted imaginatively to Saudi customs . . . Saudi Arabian sanctions seem harsh to many outsiders. Religious patrols may hit women if they show any hair in public. The government carries out beheadings and hand-severances in public and expects passers-by to observe the punishments, some of which are for crimes that would not be offences in other countries. For example, the government publicly beheaded three men in early 2002 for being homosexuals . . . In spite of contrasts and paradoxes, foreign companies find ways to be highly successful in Saudi Arabia' (Daniels et al. 2004).

This section's opening profile describes how an understanding of the local culture and business environment can give managers an advantage in competitive industries. Foreign companies – no matter how big – can ignore those aspects at their peril. Such differences in culture and the way of life in other countries require that managers develop international expertise to manage on a contingency basis according to the host-country environment. According to numerous accounts, many blunders made in international operations can be attributed to a lack of cultural sensitivity. *Cultural sensitivity*, or *cultural empathy*, is an awareness and an honest caring about another individual's culture. Such sensitivity requires the ability to understand the perspective of those living in other (and very different) societies and the willingness to put oneself in another's shoes.

Judging from the use and commentary of this 'opening profile', it seems as though the idea of 'cultural sensitivity' can be used to mean not only that the 'locals' should be understood in their own terms, according to their own cultural values, but also that when some local practices strongly contradict with what has been established within one's own society as basic human rights, it may be better, for the sake of business, to choose to ignore these issues altogether in order to avoid 'blunders'. The notion of cultural sensitivity thus can become convenient in order to justify largely unethical business practices in certain foreign contexts. Anything is acceptable on behalf of cultural sensitivity and the pseudo-tolerance it entails towards other cultures, as long as it is in the name of business – money, after all, has no smell. Global (Western-educated) managers are obviously not meant to feel any guilt for the colonial and neocolonial facts, but in addition their 'missions' in the 'backward rest' (Fougère and Moulettes 2007) do not need to make them feel guilty of being unethical missionaries, since their handy cultural sensitivity allows them to ignore the horrors committed in the countries in which they do business. As outsiders, they might find the beheading of homosexuals to be slightly harsh as a sanction, but they want to do business with these people, and because they are culturally sensitive, they are not going to take stands: it's all about cultural traditions, who are they to judge them?

Now, this is particularly interesting from a postcolonial perspective because the relativism that makes it possible for international managers to selectively tolerate the intolerable resonates – at least to some – with the cultural relativism that often characterizes postcolonialism. While we do of course call for more relativism in terms of how different cultures should be portrayed in international management textbooks, is it possible to strongly criticize these same textbooks for their occasional, selective relativism? We contend that not only is it possible, it is also desirable and even crucial. First, because the fact that certain authors strategically appropriate a postcolonial worldview or a similar language here and there can in fact be an efficient way to neutralize the subversive potential of the postcolonial critique. Gikandi (2000, as referred to by Westwood 2006) for instance has shown that postcolonialism has been appropriated by neo-liberal globalization proponents such as Robertson (1992) or Huntington (1996). Second, because if we accepted relativism as the founding princi-ple of all claims, then we might as well not say anything anymore. Any attempt at emancipation or powerful critique has to go beyond relativism: it has to speak from somewhere, and be 'judgemental' in some way. Third, and most importantly, because extreme postmodern relativism and the associated emergence of 'a self-critical Eurocentrism' only '[abandon] the Other altogether in the name of non-interference' (Radhakrishnan 1994, p. 309). The expression of an interculturally ethical behaviour cannot just be based on the commitment not to interfere at all with the Other. Similarly to the idea that the postcolonial critique of the West 'cannot be a project of cultural relativism' (Chakrabarty 2000, p. 43), the Western redemption cannot come from a superficial 'relativist' acceptance of differences – valid only as long as these differences do not directly threaten Western values – combined with an avoidance of meaningful cultural interaction. The idea of 'tolerance' within the currently fashionable discourse of multiculturalism (which is 'used and abused of' according to Radhakrishnan 2003) is often merely a way to retain a safe distance from the Other, 'an attempt to conceal a deeper horror of the Other' (Žižek and Daly 2004, p. 117). As Žižek puts it, 'this logic of respect for the Other cannot be the ultimate horizon of our ethical engagement' (Žižek and Daly 2004, p. 124). Relativism of the 'cultural sensitivity' kind as described in international management textbooks is merely a way to not engage, to not *relate* with the Other, while still trying to take advantage of the opportunities business exchanges provide.

Perceiving Geography and History with Western Eyes: Globalism and Universalism

As we have pointed out above, all five textbooks see themselves as being addressed to a global audience of business students. For example, Deresky (2006, p. xiv) claims that her text 'places the student in the role of a manager of any nationality, encouraging the student to take a truly global perspective in dealing with dynamic management issues in both foreign and diverse host environments'; Woods (2001, p. 9) explains that '[her] book is intended for use by both undergraduate and MBA students who are undertaking university courses that have an interdisciplinary and international content', adding that 'a key feature of the text is its broad geographic scope which includes examples and cases studies from around the globe'. But in both these examples, it seems that 'around the globe' could in most cases be replaced by 'across the triad' (Woods 2001, p. 261) made up by North America, Europe and East Asia. Indeed, both writers make some specifications in their respective prefaces: Deresky (2006, p. xiv) points out that 'cross-cultural management and competitive strategy are evaluated in the context of global changes – the expanding European Union (EU), the North-American Free Trade Agreement (NAFTA), and the rapidly growing economies in Asia – that require new management applications'; and Woods (2001, p. 10) states that 'students from Western Europe, South

East Asia and North America will all find scenarios and examples which discuss familiar products and concepts'. So the 'global scope' of the books seemingly only refers to the three parts of the world that are most developed economically, and where standardized MBA programmes are more and more becoming the norm of business education. And although this 'special international edition' of Deresky's (2006) book is prohibited from being sold in the United States and Canada, it seems to be mostly written from the viewpoint of Americans: for example, after 'various research results about cultural variables' have been studied, there is a specific section (titled 'Cultural Operational Value Differences') devoted to identifying 'some specific culturally based variables that cause frequent problems for Americans in international management' (Deresky 2006, p. 98).

Ironically, this awareness of a worldwide readership, instead of allowing the books to present diverse, potentially alternative approaches, results in more formatted and simplistic communication (which, not unlike today's global mainstream Hollywood movies, seems to cater for 6-year-olds) in order to reach everyone at a uniformly superficial level, which neutralizes any possibility of critical thinking. The way of communicating 'knowledge' is too often simplistic – 'user friendly', as Rodrigues (2001, p. xxi) puts it – thereby spreading the superficial views on how culture should matter to international managers. The books' reliance on pseudo-scientific models provides legitimacy to their prescriptive managerialism, and there is no doubt that this in turn contributes to a uniformization of the stereotypical perceptions of cultural differences among future managers around the economically successful world.

In our view, the claimed 'global' book audiences are constructed on the legacy of colonial thinking in the sense that the knowledge is meant to be propagated through a one-way communication from the Western, mostly Anglo-Saxon, world (through standardized MBA education) to a rest of the world that is considered as economically and culturally peripheral. The same books, with their overwhelmingly 'naïve-American' approach to intercultural interactions, are read by students from all parts of the world – or all those that have enough economic development potential to have been deemed worth having MBA programmes. This constructs a global subject who has very minimal requirements indeed in terms of her/his necessary understanding of cultural dynamics.

In addition, the books are characterized by a strange relationship to 'history'. Rarely is there any explicit discussion of history in these kinds of books – colonial history, in that context, is better silenced, and international managers should live in the present and think about the future not the past. However, Woods (2001) does assign a 'role' to history – in a similar way that she does to culture. While she points out that 'the distribution of wealth across the world today is a consequence of several thousand years of economic change' and that 'the countries which are economically powerful and rich in technology, versus those which are relatively poor, can look to history for an explanation of their current position' (Woods 2001, p. 17), she does not even allude to the impact that colonialism has had in terms of worldwide economic and political inequalities – although she briefly mentions, in a surprisingly inspired piece of prose that suggests admiration on her part, 'the merchant venturers of the past, who raided the treasures of the Spice islands and helped to found empires' (Woods 2001, p. 18). It sounds from her formulation that the poor countries can blame their fate on something called 'history' that they would be responsible for. Moreover, Woods seems to assume that the world order has been the same for a thousand years and that the West has always been holding the dominant position in economic and political terms. Such an assumption reveals very limited knowledge about the history of globalization and an overconfidence in technology as the one explanatory factor for economic take-off. It is clear that this view of history is connected to the Western 'historicism' that has been much critiqued from a postcolonial perspective, particularly 'the idea of development and the assumption that a certain amount of time elapses in the very process of development' (Chakrabarty 2000, p. 23), which are critical to the understanding of the term 'historicism'. This Western-centred perspective on history is problematic because, while 'produced in relative, and sometimes absolute, ignorance of the majority of humankind', it claims to 'embrace the entirety of humanity' (Chakrabarty 2000, p. 29). At the core of the Western social scientists' views of their approaches as the only ones that can claim universal applicability, there is the belief, expressed for instance by Husserl at a lecture in Vienna in 1935, that European thought can produce 'absolute theoretical insights' because of its status as '*theoria* (universal science)' as opposed to the oriental '"practical-universal" and hence "mythical-religious" character' (as cited by Chakrabarty 2000, p. 29). This type of universalism has always been an instrument for the West to express its superiority over the rest, and it clearly permeates the textbooks in both their vision of a global audience and their unproblematic – and sometimes even nonexistent – discussion of global history.

DISCUSSION, SUGGESTIONS AND CONCLUSIONS

In our analysis the subjectification we have focused on has been that of a Western international management student, largely because of the way that the books seem to be written by Westerners for Westerners, and perhaps also because of our own identity as Western academics. But the subjectification of the 'other' business student, coming from and studying outside of the West, is also of interest. When subjected to the knowledge provided by these international management textbooks, the non-Western student can both define her/himself as a 'local' and a future manager of an international workforce. When assuming the latter subject position, he or she becomes a modern, rational Westerner, and likely rejects her/his local identity, which is presented as passive and 'there to be managed'. This type of process typically leads to the production of a hybrid subjectivity. The concept of 'mimicry' (Bhabha 1994; see also Das and Dharwadkar, Chapter 8, this volume), originally referring to English-educated Indians mimicking British people's behaviours during the colonial time, can provide insight into these processes of hybridization and in-between identity construction. Through these processes, Western-educated international managers from the non-West can become, as professionals, 'almost the same [as Westerners] but not quite', to quote Bhabha's (1994, p. 89) well-known formulation. According to Bhabha (1994), this cultural mimicry should provide a space of resistance that can destabilize authority. But in this case, while the non-Western managers may construct hybrid identities from which resistance – or at least mockery, parody or irony – is possible, what may also happen is that, having succeeded according to the legitimate criteria of the dominant system (that is, by graduating from a very Westernized institution), they become 'more Western than the Westerners' and thereby a most efficient instrument for the hegemonic domination of those locals whose subjectivities are fixed by the stereotypical accounts found in international management textbooks.

This leads us to two suggestions for further research – that is, research we intend to go further with. First, we see it as important to empirically study the reception of these or similar textbooks in international management courses taking place in non-Western universities and business schools. Processes of subjectification – as Western managers, passive locals, or both and neither – in these contexts should be studied, although this does potentially pose a number of methodological problems. Second, we aim to more specifically deconstruct these discussions of culture, looking at conspicuous absences and deafening silences; to propose alternative, mirror readings of certain passages in order to expose some of the underlying assumptions about culture – by providing an account of an 'Eastern' view of a 'Western culture' posited as culturally homogeneous in its extreme individualism, for instance; to suggest reconstructions and the development of alternative types of textbook material that could offer the possibility for people from different cultures to be on an equal footing so that they could communicate, learn from their interaction, and be truly 'culturally sensitive'.

As a conclusion, we would argue that in a way similar to the colonial educational systems, which trained the natives according to the requirements needed for entering civil service and legal professions, a dissemination of Western values is implicitly implemented in today's education of business managers all over the world. This way of using ready-made models that describe all the world's cultures resembles the colonial idea of writing the history of the colonized people before taking their territory into possession (see Bhabha 1994; Fabian 1986). To us, these textbooks mainly serve as a reproduction device for the domination of Western 'knowledge' and as an efficient means to maintain cultural binaries between the West and the non-West. We contend that books like these, greatly undermining the burdens of history and especially the colonial and neocolonial facts, contribute to producing a guilt-free Western subjectivity – even more so since managers are invited to selectively close their eyes on behalf of 'cultural sensitivity'; hybrid identities of non-Western managers mimicking Western ways of managing – and thereby furthering Western hegemony albeit in an ambivalent way; and a collective cultural responsibility on the part of the people from so-called 'developing countries' – since their underdevelopment can be blamed on what Hofstede calls their 'programming of the mind' alone.

REFERENCES

Aizenberg, E. (1999), 'I walked with a zombie: the pleasures and perils of postcolonial hybridity', *World Literature Today*, **73** (3), 461–6.

Altbach, P.G. (2004), 'Education and neo-colonialism', in B. Ashcroft, G. Griffiths and H. Tiffin (eds), *The Post-colonial Studies Reader*, London: Routledge.

Ashcroft, B., G. Griffiths and T. Tiffin (eds) (1998), *Key Concepts in Post-colonial Studies*, London: Routledge.

Ashcroft, B., G. Griffiths and H. Tiffin (2004), *The Post-colonial Studies Reader*, London: Routledge.

Banerjee, S.B. (2003), 'Who sustains whose development? Sustainable development and the reinvention of nature', *Organization Studies*, **24** (1), 143–80.

Beeth, G. (1997), 'Multicultural managers wanted', *Management Review* (**May**), 17.

Bhabha, H.K. (1994), *The Location of Culture*, London: Routledge.

Chakrabarty, D. (2000), *Provincializing Europe*, Princeton, NJ: Princeton University Press.

Daniels, J.D., L.H. Radebaugh and D.P. Sullivan (2004), *International Business: Environment and Operations*, 10th edn, Upper Saddle River, NJ: Pearson Prentice Hall.

Deresky, H. (2006), *International Management: Managing Across Borders and Cultures*, 5th edn, Upper Saddle River, NJ: Pearson Prentice Hall.

Escobar, A. (1995), *Encountering Development: The Making and Unmaking of the Third World*, Princeton, NJ: Princeton University Press.

Fabian, J. (1986), *Language and Colonial Power*, Berkeley and Los Angeles, CA: University of California Press.

Ferraro, G.P. (1994), *The Cultural Dimension of International Business*, Englewood Cliffs, NJ: Prentice Hall.

Foucault, M. (1971), 'Order of discourse: inaugural lecture delivered at the Collège de France', *Social Science Information*, **10** (2), 7–30.

Foucault, M. (2000), 'The subject and power', in J.D. Faubion (ed.), *Power: The Essential Works of Foucault: Volume 3*, New York: The Free Press, pp. 326–48.

Fougère, M. and A. Moulettes (2007), 'The construction of the modern West and the backward rest: studying the discourse of Hofstede's *Culture's Consequences*', *Journal of Multicultural Discourses*, **2** (1), 1–19.

Gikandi, S. (2000), 'Globalization and the claims of postcoloniality', *South Atlantic Quarterly*, **100** (3), 627–58.

Gupta, V., P.J. Hanges and P. Dorfman (2002), 'Cultural clusters: methodology and findings', *Journal of World Business*, **37** (1), 11–15.

Hall, E.T. and M.R. Hall (1990), *Understanding Cultural Differences*, Yarmouth, ME: Intercultural Press.

Hampden-Turner, C. and F. Trompenaars (1997), 'Response to Geert Hofstede', *International Journal of Intercultural Relations*, **21** (1), 149–59.

Hickson, D. and D.S. Pugh (1995), *Management Worldwide*, London: Penguin.

Hodgetts, R.M. and F. Luthans (2005), *International Management: Culture, Strategy and Behavior*, 6th edn, New York: McGraw-Hill.

Hofstede, G. (1980), *Culture's Consequences: International Differences in Work-related Values*, Beverly Hills, CA: Sage.

Holt, D.H. and K.W. Wiggington (2002), *International Management*, 2nd edn, Fort Worth, TX: Harcourt.

Howard, C.G. (1992), 'Profile of the 21st-century expatriate manager', *HR Manager* (**June**), 96.

Huntington, S. (1996), *The Clash of Civilizations and the Remaking of World Order*, New York: Simon & Schuster.

Javidan, M. and R.J. House (2001), 'Cultural acumen for the global manager: lessons from Project GLOBE', *Organizational Dynamics*, (**Spring**), 289–305.

Kwek, D. (2003), 'Decolonizing and *re*-presenting culture's consequences: a postcolonial critique of cross-cultural studies in management', in A. Prasad (ed.), *Postcolonial Theory and Organizational Analysis – A Critical Engagement*, New York: Palgrave Macmillan.

Lewis, R. (1996), *When Cultures Collide: Managing Successfully Across Cultures*, London: Nicholas Brealey.

Macaulay T. ([1835] 2004), 'Minute on Indian education', in B. Ashcroft, G. Griffiths and H. Tiffin (eds), *The Post-colonial Studies Reader*, London: Routledge.

Mangaliso, M.P., M.A. Mangaliso and J.M. Bruton (1998), 'Management in Africa, or Africa in management? The African philosophical thought in organizational discourse', paper presented at the International Management Division, Academy of Management Annual Meeting, San Diego, CA, August 1998.

McLeod, J. (2000), *Beginning Postcolonialism*, Manchester: Manchester University Press.

Mead, R. (1994), *International Management: Cross-cultural Dimensions*, Oxford: Blackwell.

Mills, S. (1997), *Discourse*, London: Routledge.

Mishra, V. and B. Hodge (1991), 'What is post(-)colonialism', *Textual Practice*, **5**, 399–414.

Prasad, A. (ed.) (2003), *Postcolonial Theory and Organizational Analysis – A Critical Engagement*, New York: Palgrave Macmillan.

Radhakrishnan, R. (1994), 'Postmodernism and the rest of the world', *Organization*, **1** (2), 305–40.

Radhakrishnan, R. (2003), *Theory in an Uneven World*, Malden, MA: Blackwell.

Robertson, R. (1992), *Globalization: Social Theory and Global Culture*, London: Sage.

Rodrigues, C. (2001), *International Management: A Cultural Approach*, 2nd edn, Cincinnati, OH: South-Western College Publishing.

Ronen, S. and O. Shenkar (1985), 'Clustering countries on attitudinal dimensions: a review and synthesis', *Academy of Management Review*, **10** (3), 435–54.

Said, E. ([1993] 1994), *Culture and Imperialism* (first published by Chatto & Windus Ltd, 1993), London: Vintage.

Said E. ([1978] 1995), *Orientalism: Western Conceptions of the Orient* (first published by Routledge & Kegan Paul, 1978), London: Penguin Books.

Triandis, H.C. (1982), 'Review of *Culture's Consequences: International Differences in Work-related Values*', *Human Organization*, **41**, 86–90.

Trompenaars, F. (1993), *Riding the Waves of Culture*, London: Economist Books.

Westwood, R.I. (2001), 'Appropriating the Other in the discourses of comparative management', in R.I. Westwood and S. Linstead (eds), *The Language of Organization*, London: Sage.

Westwood R.I. (2006), 'International business and management studies as an orientalist discourse: a postcolonial critique', *Critical Perspectives on International Business*, **2** (2), 91–113.

Woods, M. (2001), *International Business: An Introduction*, New York: Palgrave.

Young, R.J.C. (2001), *Postcolonialism: An Historical Introduction*, Oxford: Blackwell.

Žižek, S. and G. Daly (2004), *Conversations with Žižek*, Cambridge: Polity.

3. Sustainable development in the age of natural capitalism: making the world while saving profits

Martin Fougère and Nikodemus Solitander

INTRODUCTION: THE BUSINESS CASE FOR SUSTAINABLE DEVELOPMENT

> Some business leaders were drawn to the concept [of sustainable development] as they realized not only was it not anti-growth but also it called for serious economic growth to meet the needs of the current population. (Holliday et al. 2002: 15)

After years of trials, tribulations and tripartite schizophrenia, the discourse of sustainable development (SD) seems to have found a corporate articulation that accommodates concerns for economic, social and ecological developments. Since the introduction of the concept in *Our Common Future* (WCED 1987) in 1987, SD has become a global priority that has greatly affected practice and policy at different socio-spatial scales (Bryant and Wilson 1998). As a dominant discourse SD forms and reforms our conception of 'nature', what is 'natural' and 'sustainable', and how we are to stabilize the biophysical foundations of earth that are threatened by economic growth. *Our Common Future* marked a turning point in representing nature as capital instead of, as in the modernist vision, a passive and free natural resource. It served as a core document during the United Nations Conference on Environment and Development ('Earth Summit') in Rio in 1992, where some elements of SD were further refined. Central to this was the unprecedented corporate involvement in the task of finding out who destroys the irreplaceable natural resources, who produces the pollution, and how this is to be halted. Both the release of the report and the conference constituted the genesis of 'corporate social responsibility' (CSR): a rebuttal of the historical antagonism (see Friedman 1970; Levitt 1958; Velasquez 1992) between the corporation's traditional legal obligations to its shareholders and its newly alleged environmental and social responsibilities. During the last ten years the efforts to further dilute this antagonism have gathered momentum.

In parallel with this naturalization of the notion of SD and its mobilization by powerful institutional actors, SD discourse has been contested from many perspectives and on many grounds. The emerging dominant SD discourse has been criticized for creating arenas that amplify the neoliberal voices that in the name of community empowerment call for a dismantling of the welfare system (Haque 1999; Raco 2005). SD has also been considered a paradigm for the privileged (Saha 2002), which shifts blame onto the poor countries for their social and environmental problems while keeping them out of the market with unfair commodity prices and subsidies (Banerjee 2003).

In this chapter we focus on the issue of how the dominant discourse has been affected by the critique it has faced. In doing so we contend that there is a need for a careful examination of the *corporate actors* who posit themselves as sympathetic to the SD cause, and who, when faced with controversy over the compatibility between SD and corporate capitalism, have reshaped the discourse.

It is clear to us that SD, in all its articulations, remains largely a monocultural and Westerncentric concept. Our aim is not to discuss its definition, or the lack thereof, in its emergent dominant form (see Adams 2001; Banerjee 2003; Haque 2000; Robinson 2004). We approach SD and its significance by asking 'who puts substance into it and for what purpose?' (Harvey 1973; Saha 2002). We specifically focus on the representation of the relationship between (transnational) corporations and nature, and reflect on the social dimension where relevant – in particular in those cases where a focus on the social is used to distract from environmental concerns, or conversely. Because of our specific focus on certain recent articulations of SD discourse, we do not thoroughly engage with the political economy of sustainable development.

We have chosen to examine the discursive substance that is provided by proponents of 'natural capitalism', whom we argue have appropriated a large part of the current SD discourse. We approach this issue by analyzing two influential texts on SD, *Natural Capitalism: The Next Industrial Revolution* (Hawken et al. 2000) and *Walking the Talk: The Business Case for Sustainable Development* (Holliday et al. 2002). While we do not wish to argue that these two texts represent an epitome of the modern SD discourse, they are still considered most influential by business practitioners and environmental experts alike (see GlobeScan 2005[1]). We do not mean to pick unfairly on the authors of these two books; rather we analyze the texts in order to situate them in the emergent discourse of natural capitalism, which, we argue, shapes the understanding of SD today. We are especially interested in examining how the two books under scrutiny address and appropriate some of the harshest critiques (see Escobar 1995, 1996) that have been directed at the way the SD discourse has been deployed within the capitalist frame. To us, this appropriation is chiefly an attempt at neutralizing these critiques by adopting its language and thereby shifting boundaries between antagonistic discourses.

The chapter is structured as follows. In the following section we briefly present some of the critical voices and themes that have affected geographic and political ecology research on the SD discourse, with a particular focus on Escobar's (1995, 1996) critique. We then analyze the corporate reconstruction of SD through the two texts: *Natural Capitalism* and *Walking the Talk*. After having critically described the deployment of the discourse, we proceed to the discussion where we focus specifically on how the critiques are appropriated in an attempt to neutralize them.

SUSTAINABLE DEVELOPMENT AND ITS DISCONTENT(S)

While there is no one clear hegemonic articulation of SD, there is a form of SD that is more dominant than others (Adams 2001). The dominant discourse, exemplified by organizations such as the UN or the World Bank (Castro 2004), is based on a modernist ideology, commonly referred to as developmentalism (Adams 2001; Escobar 1995), where it is inherent not to challenge the capitalist model of industrialization. The discourse constructs a seemingly manageable global environment, where issues such as global warming and biodiversity depletion are at the forefront (Adams 2001; Escobar 1995), and marginalizes issues such as poverty and the North–South division (Sadler 2004; Saha 2002). This bias has given birth to a number of countercurrents.

Considering the vague definition of SD, the border between radical voices of opposition and a dominant mainstream is not always clear. The concept of SD has faced critique from many quarters, ranging from Marxist perspectives to corporate interests. These voices juxtapose their critique with an imaginary mainstream SD. The 'critical' voices have increased to such an extent that arguably most of the present approaches would locate outside a mainstream. A typical example of the positioning of CSR is provided in *Walking the Talk* (2002: 104–5):

> [David] Henderson concludes that CSR 'has caught on'. This we find surprising, as we [World Business Council for Sustainable Development] see only a minority of companies even mentioning it, much less trying to practice it.

In the citation above it is suggested that CSR has to be something that is not mainstream, only practiced by a few pioneering transnational corporations (TNCs). But the authors fall short of specifying who has not 'caught on'. A review of the top 500 corporations of Fortune Global 500 for the year 2006 reveals that 229 corporations have published a CSR report following or in accordance with the Global Reporting Initiative's[2] guidelines; of the top 100 corporations 38 participate in the UN Global Compact;[3] further, 30 of the top 100 and 93 of the Global 500 are members of the World Business Council for Sustainable Development (WBCSD). It should be clear that if there is a mainstream, it is represented by this organization, despite its claims to the contrary. CSR does not, of course, deliver sustainable practices, but CSR is heralded as the corporate commitment to SD (Holliday et al. 2002), and, with the emphasis on economic-led development, as the main vehicle to achieve SD. In the following section we briefly present some of the strong voices of opposition.

Ecomarxist, Ecofeminist and Postcolonial Critiques

The dominant radical voices that we consider most influential historically for political ecology are ecomarxism, ecofeminism and postcolonialism. From a historical perspective it is not an understatement that Marxist theories have overlooked nature and the negative effects that human action has had on it (Adams 2001; Smith 1996), even though issues of resource depletion have a longstanding history in Marxist writing (Bryant and Wilson 1998). For Marx and certainly for Engels, the social struggle with nature was deemed inevitable and man's mastery of nature is part of Marxist utopianism (Smith 1996). Since the 1980s Marxist writing has increasingly addressed the environmental impact of capitalism, and a theoretical framework of a Marxist theory of nature has developed (Adams 2001). Geographers such as Harvey (1996), Smith (1984, 1996), Swyngedouw (1999; Swyngedouw and Heynen 2003; Swyngedouw and Kaika 2000), or Peet and Watts (1993, 1996) have played significant roles in this development. Marxism has offered a powerful influence on the rethinking of both development studies and political ecology throughout the 1990s (Peet and Watts 1993). For example, research on third-world political ecologies often resorts to Marxist analysis (see Blaikie 1985; Watts 1983). In Marxist writings non-human nature is defined in relation to the specific societies that utilize it (Harvey 1996). The analyses and critiques have, among other things, evolved around the commodification of nature within the capitalist system (O'Connor 1994). Ecomarxism does not, however, represent an ecocentric view of nature, as social concerns – mostly in the form of wealth distribution – are in focus, while nature is mainly acknowledged as something that affects these social concerns (Adams 2001).

The stream of thought labeled 'ecofeminism' is characterized by different perspectives positing that the process of exploitation of nature stems from the same patriarchal hegemony that causes the subjugation of women (Shiva 1988, 1997). This view focuses on the difference between men and women, and on women's alleged closeness to nature. However, this perspective has been challenged by a number of feminists (Nesmith and Radcliffe 1993), and its essentialism has even been claimed to be part of the problem, facilitating the oppression of both women and nature (Jackson 1994).

Ecofeminists, whether essentialists or not, are related to postcolonial theorists through a shared concern with exploitation at the hands of technocratic, imperialistic Western (male) capitalists. Following the Rio conference in 1992 there were several voices that criticized SD as a 'paradigm for the privileged' (Saha 2002: 20), which fails to address the limits to growth in the industrialized countries and instead shifts blame onto developing countries for their environmental degradation (Banerjee 2003). Many accounts of environmental degradation provide a stereotypical image of the failure of Western actors to restrain the developing countries from destroying the environment, exemplified in debates over illegal logging in the Amazon region, and the release of methane gas into the atmosphere by large cattle stocks in developing regions (Saha, 2002). It has been argued that we live in a third phase of colonialization characterized by 'the white man's burden to protect the environment' (Mies and Shiva 1993, as cited in Banerjee 2003: 143). The postcolonial critique argues that the salvation of nature cannot be achieved through an old colonial order based on the white man's burden as the two are ethically, economically and epistemologically conflicting (ibid.). This position is shared by Escobar (1995, 1996), as we will see below.

The Symbolic Appropriation of Nature as Exposed by Escobar

In his critique of the development discourse, Escobar highlights four particular aspects of SD (Escobar 1995: 194–6). First, he underlines that this relatively new discourse problematizes sustainability in terms of 'global survival' (ibid.: 194), thereby effecting a globalization of the environmental problem. Second, he exposes how the discourse blames the poor as responsible for the environmental problems because of their alleged irrationality and their lack of awareness of the need to protect nature, 'thus shifting visibility and blame away from the large industrial polluters' (ibid.: 195). Third, he shows how SD is used to reproduce the main aspects of 'economism and developmentalism': it is economic growth rather than the environment that is to be sustained. Growth is to help eliminate poverty, and somehow this process will subsequently protect the environment. Fourth, Escobar argues that the reconciliation between managerialism and nature is facilitated by 'the transformation of "nature" into "environment"' (ibid.: 196): nature is not anymore an entity with its own agency, because the world is now seen as a resource to be exploited and managed.

Escobar introduces what he calls the 'symbolic conquest of nature' (Escobar 1996: 56), drawing on O'Connor's (1994) critique of the capitalization of nature. By capitalization of nature, O'Connor denotes that 'nature' enters the realm of capitalism through 'designating as valuable stocks erstwhile "uncapitalized" aspects of the physical environment (nature) and of civil society (infrastructure, households, and human nature)' (O'Connor 1994: 128). Nature and human nature are thus 'codified as *capital incarnate*' (ibid.: 131). O'Connor shows how 'local communities and social movements . . . may be enticed to cooperate, through representing them as the *stewards of the social and natural "capitals"* whose sustainable management is, henceforth, both their responsibility and the business of the world economy' (ibid.: 128). It is thus not only nature that is 'made to participate' (Baudrillard 1981: 201), thereby extending the influence of the system of capital, but also the local communities and the social movements. There is thus 'a coopting of Non-Occidental societies into the world economy' (O'Connor 1994: 130) in the same way as there is a coopting of the workers when they are 'liberated' as consumers in order to better serve the extension of the domain of capital (Baudrillard 1975).

When Escobar discusses the symbolic conquest of nature, he refers to 'the postmodern form of ecological capital' (1996: 56), as opposed to 'the modern form of capital' (ibid.: 54). Through this postmodern form of ecological capital capitalism symbolically appropriates nature by claiming that the capitalist frame is best suited for sustaining, if not saving, nature. Thus we can encounter such oxymoronic constructions as, for instance, 'the environmentally friendly and culturally sensitive uranium mine'[4] (Banerjee 2000: 16). According to Escobar, this second form of capital does not only refer to the symbolic conquest of nature and local communities, but also requires 'the semiotic conquest of local knowledges'. These knowledges that help sustain nature are to be valued as 'useful complements to modern biology' (Escobar 1996: 56–7). It is thus not only nature and people that are to become internalized production conditions within natural capitalism, but also local knowledge.

ANALYSIS OF *NATURAL CAPITALISM* AND *WALKING THE TALK*

Natural Capitalism describes a great deal of original and successful initiatives intended to tackle the growing concern for sustainability. We do not mean here to criticize everything, for we are sympathetic to many of the actions described and prescribed in this book. However, we are looking at the perverse effects of this discourse, which, if appropriated by corporate capitalism – as is most likely given the way the book is conceived – could become very detrimental to the sustainability of local communities. We seek to show how the way the book is designed can contribute to a legitimatization of further appropriation of global space and the local places by corporate capitalism.

We consider *Walking the Talk* as a continuation of the perimeters set up by *Our Common Future* and a pro-corporate implementation of the ideas of *Natural Capitalism*. It is easier to be less sympathetic to this account on the mere basis that it is produced within the confines of TNCs that support a largely unregulated free market. However, the book is also a testimony to the different shades of corporate views on the relation between humans and nature. It is especially important to consider this a *transnational corporate environmentalist account*, since it tends to identify certain actors, who can be considered extremely sympathetic to the capitalist framework, as adversaries.

NATURAL CAPITALISM: FROM DOMINATION TO APPROPRIATION OF NATURE[5]

Natural Capitalism is the result of collaboration between bestselling environmentalist Paul Hawken and the co-founders of Rocky Mountain Institute, physicist Amory Lovins and sociologist/political scientist Hunter Lovins. While the initial idea was to mainly discuss an emerging resource productivity revolution, the project went on to make much larger claims, ending up seeing itself as a 'revolutionary paradigm for the industrial economy' (cover page) that allegedly manages to reconcile ecological with economic goals through the interdependence and the mutual reinforcement of four principles: 'radical resource productivity', 'biomimicry', 'service and flow economy' and 'investing in natural capital' (pp. 10–11).

It's About and For Business

As the acknowledgements (pp. xv–xvi) suggest, the book is about (and for) business: many TNCs are thanked for having 'generously aided this research with data and insights' (p. xvi). The authors are grateful 'for the help of [these companies'] pioneering managers and practitioners' (ibid.). It is true that the authors do also underline, early on (pp. 20–1), that 'many of the techniques and methods described here can be used by individuals and small businesses', while 'other approaches are more suitable for corporations, even whole industrial sectors' and 'still others better suit local or central governments'. The 'radical change' that *Natural Capitalism* promises thus concerns everyone, a testimony to the all-encompassing ambition, as well as ubiquitous positioning, of the book. Yet it is business that is presented as the driving force in processes that should involve everyone. In their founding statement the authors point out that the economy now has to shift from an emphasis on human productivity to an increase in resource productivity. As an explanation for the decision to write this book, it is contended that 'a shared framework was needed that could harness the talent of business to solve the world's deepest environmental and social problems' (p. ix). Business is thus depicted as if on a mission to save the world.

The forces that may prevent 'business' from fulfilling its salutary mission are criticized and opposed. Especially, 'dogmatic' economists are presented as an opposing force throughout the book (e.g. pp. 56, 113, 261): the 'talent of business' and engineering – *contra* economists – allows corporations to appropriate local places as a response to the problems caused by (the economists') global views of the economy. In a way, critiques directed to economists (such as those from Escobar 1995, 1996, or O'Connor 1994) are thereby also appropriated and incorporated within the frame of corporate capitalism. For instance, 'economic dogma' (p. 113) is opposed to 'actual engineering practice' (p. 114): note the 'dogma' opposed to 'practice', 'economic' to 'engineering', and the 'actual', which is used several times by the authors as self-legitimating evidence that things are 'actually' like that, and not the way dogmatic economists would have it. It is not only engineers who are opposed to the guardians of economic dogma, but also certain kinds of 'more environmental' economists, such as Robert Ayres or Herman Daly, whose texts are drawn on to explain how, when the environment becomes the limiting factor, 'economic logic remains the same, but the pattern of scarcity in the world changes, with the result that behavior must change if it is to remain economic' (Daly 1994, as cited p. 159) – this suggests that the economic logic driving natural capitalism is at once different from and the same as what drives 'conventional capitalism'.

Governments and their public policies are also presented as troublemakers more often than not. For example, when discussing issues connected to protecting the climate, the authors claim that 'the genius of private enterprise and advanced technologies reduced sulfur and CFC emissions billions of dollars more cheaply than by using government regulation' (p. 258). Throughout the book, when 'subsidies' are mentioned, they are associated with 'diverted taxpayers' money' (p. 13) or 'deliberate distortions in the marketplace' (p. 15), directed to 'environmentally damaging industries' (p. 58), or are more generally deemed 'perverse' (pp. 160–2) or 'irrational' (p. 163), and thus are presented as responsible for the extreme 'imperfection of markets' (p. 264: 'worldwide subsidies exceed \$1.5 trillion annually', a global figure that is presented as such as a great problem). The only occurrence where subsidies are presented with a positive connotation is when the authors present 'the services provided by natural capital' as providing 'in effect annual "subsidies" [note the quotation marks] to production worth tens of billions of dollars' (p. 156). It is clear that the description does not refer to real subsidies, but to how natural capitalism provides a more viable alternative.

The authors do not, however, reject the need for a strong working tax system, quite the opposite. They propose a 'tax shift', which is 'not intended to redefine *who* pays the taxes but only *what* is taxed' (p. 164). As Ayres (1998, cited on p. 165) has explained, if the use of resources is taxed more heavily and if labor is taxed less, the economy can be expected 'to substitute the cheaper factor (labor) for the more expensive one (resources)' and thus an increase of 'the tax burden on activities that damage the social or natural environment' should 'discourage such activities and reduce the resulting damage'. However, this way of expressing the problem from the angle of *what* is taxed tends to divert the reader's attention away from *what the tax money is to be used for*, which should remain a central issue: for instance, if more money is to be spent on environmental protection, what will the implications be for social security systems? Nothing is written on that issue, which could be an open door to interpretations of the tax shift as shifting budgetary resources away from state-funded social protection.

Nature Is Capital, Capitalism Is Natural

A striking aspect of *Natural Capitalism* is that contrary to the original SD rhetoric, the book does not portray 'the environment' as something that one can manage (see especially how this trend is underlined in Escobar 1995), rather it deals with 'nature'. In this sense, the book goes much further than the usual sustainability discourse in appropriating nature into the realm of capitalism – an appropriation that is operated in the very title of the book. The concepts of environment and nature at times seem to be reversed: the environment is 'an envelope containing, provisioning and sustaining the entire economy', while nature is *enveloped* by capitalism through its incorporation as 'natural capital' (these are the first two 'fundamental assumptions' of natural capitalism, on p. 9). The way that this notion of 'natural capital' is introduced in the book is interesting: it is presented as an absolute given in a sentence, and then defined as including 'all the familiar resources used by mankind: water, minerals, oil, trees, fish, soil, air, et cetera' (p. 2). Nature is thus immediately framed within the hinted all-encompassing system of capitalism: no alternative is possible, it is implicitly meant. '*Actually* [italics added], an economy needs four types of capital to function properly' (p. 4), these are 'human capital', 'financial capital', 'manufactured capital' and 'natural capital'. There is no argumentation explaining why such an understanding of the economy is articulated, instead it is hinted that this is how things *naturally* are.

The reader is intended to believe that 'the conventional wisdom is mistaken in seeing priorities in economic, environmental and social policy as competing', since a 'design integration' can achieve 'all of them together' (p. xi). The world is thus claimed to be more *naturally* harmonious than it is understood to be by 'the conventional wisdom'. In order to revert to how things should *naturally* be, there should be a 'general direction of a journey that requires overturning long-held assumptions, even questioning what we *value* [italics added] and how we live' (p. xi). 'Value' is used with a double meaning: a matter of the cultural values that guide our ethical choices, but also a matter of what we grant (monetary) value to.

An example of this conceptualization of value in an ambivalent cultural-and-capitalist sense can be found in the authors' claim that the goods that used to be/are thought of as 'free' should be given monetary value, because 'as long as it is assumed that there are "free goods" in the world – pure water, clean air, hydrocarbon combustion, virgin forests, veins of minerals – large-scale, energy- and materials-intensive manufacturing methods will dominate, and labor will be increasingly marginalized' (p. 15). The problem is turned on its head in order to convince that the commodification of all natural resources is in the interest of the poor, the weaker, and the marginalized.

Turning problems on their head is a recurrent theme in the book. One of the missions of corporate capitalism is to 'make the world' (title of the section starting on p. 62), using elements of the managerial discourse to that end (see p. 64 on e.g. 'corporate culture'). For that purpose, corporations use tools such as (sustainable and 'naturally harmonious') architecture: corporate office buildings that make the company a great place to spend time in, or even to live one's life in, with a stress on 'less absenteeism' and on, for example, 'a bank whose workers don't want to go home' (p. 82). This is a good example of allegedly softer 'social policies', which extend the domain of corporate capitalism and colonize people's lives further.

Despite the seemingly harsh criticisms directed at economists who believe that markets can 'replace ethics or politics' (p. 261), natural capitalism is a framework that is meant to be implemented in market-based societies. As the authors put it, markets make 'a good servant but a bad master and a worse religion', yet they also stress that 'worldwide experience confirms an abundance of market-based tools whose outcomes can be environmentally, economically, and ethically superior' (ibid.). One of the fundamental assumptions of natural capitalism is that 'future economic progress can best take place in democratic, market-based systems of production and distribution' (p. 9). This depiction of 'democratic, market-based systems' seems to suggest that democracies and markets *naturally* fit together, regardless of the fact that a true democracy should allow its people to decide whether they want to organize their economy chiefly based on the dynamics of the market(s) or not. The expression 'natural capitalism' suggests that capitalism is the *natural* way to go, and that if given the choice people will always opt for it.

Ubiquitous Theory and Place-based Practice: Allowing for Blissful Optimism

The book is claimed to be containing both 'theory and practice' (p. x). The 'theory' covers many different aspects that are lumped together without too many attempts at designing a coherent whole, and the 'practice', on the other hand, is either extremely technocentric about particular problems to be addressed or very anecdotal, dealing with specific, if not unique cases/places. The definition of 'capitalism as if living systems mattered' (p. 9) is claimed to be based on a mindset radically different from 'conventional capitalism' (p. 6). What is striking is the inner contradictions contained in the fundamental assumptions made. These contradictions are a result of the aspiration to be radically different while remaining within the realm of capitalism. An awkward position, which only an enhanced – schizophrenic ubiquity – not only being everywhere at once, but also being every*thing* at once – can achieve. One of the central contradictions lies in seeing the environment as 'an envelope' containing all the economy, while presenting natural capital as merely 'the limiting factor to future economic development' (p. 9). Another contradiction is the imposition of 'market-based systems of production' to optimize 'future economic progress' (ibid.), while calling for 'true democratic systems of governance that are based on the needs of people rather than business' (p. 10). This dialectical exercise between softer issues regarding nature, mankind and the need for 'true democracy', and economic demands such as the primacy of the market and the capitalization of all these softer areas of life, allows the authors to have natural capitalism frame everything, including social and environmental concerns, in order to make the world better: this is what makes their blissful optimism possible.

Regarding 'practice', as opposed to theory, there is an exclusive focus on successful, 'feel-good' cases. Texts are built around numerous 'examples and references, included to show that the move toward radical resource productivity and natural capitalism is beginning to feel inevitable rather than merely possible' (p. xiii). Echoing Smith's (1996) claim that environmentalism is as much about making its advocates feel good about themselves and their world as it is about nature, the text focuses on showing that things are being done and that we should be optimistic. This enthusiasm tends to divert the reader from many of the most significant problems, since these are rarely addressed in detail; this is especially visible in the lack of discussion on who is to be held accountable.

This optimistic tone, extremely obvious in the very first words of the first chapter (p. 1) where a 'possible' future world is depicted, is a significant shift away from the much more pessimistic founding reports that have acted as initial inspirations for the notion of SD: most notably, The Club of Rome's *The Limits to Growth* (1972) and the Brundtland Report *Our Common Future* (WCED 1987). These two global reports had to cover all the relevant problems in the most comprehensive fashion possible, and thus ended up as rather depressing accounts of the state of the world. The authors of *Natural Capitalism* display no obligation to focus on problems; they deliberately choose to concentrate on the positive aspects found in some of the most constructive (mostly local) initiatives that are meant to address, at their own level, the global problems. They act on a 'mode of seduction', which allows for the diversion mentioned above; as Baudrillard (1990a) has explained, seducing means 'making things disappear'. Their enumeration of successful examples of local sustainable action gives an impression of an imminent solution to the problems by creative action designed by engineering and implemented by business.

Few examples are given from developing countries, and virtually all those that are given are presented as successful feel-good cases (such as the Curitiba 'success story' in Brazil, discussed over more than 20 pages with only six lines to cover the city's remaining problems, pp. 288–308). When writing about problems related to the supply of water (pp. 213–33) there are very few illustrations from the poorer areas of the world. Again, all of this contributes to the diversion from some of the most pressing environmental problems that the world is facing. The reasons for these problems are often veiled by mystery, especially when they are problems that could be blamed on the activities of certain easily identifiable companies – some of which are acknowledged at the beginning of the book (p. xv). For example, even though agriculture is one of the central topics addressed and there is a full chapter on 'food', there is no word about genetically modified organisms (GMOs), despite the fact that Monsanto is mentioned – in the acknowledgements section that is.

WALKING THE TALK: GOING PLACES WHILE APPROPRIATING SPACE[6]

Walking the Talk has been produced within the confines of a corporate non-governmental organization, the World Business Council for Sustainable Development (WBCSD). The Swiss-based WBCSD is described as a 'coalition of 160 international companies . . . united by a shared commitment to sustainable development via the three pillars of economic growth, ecological balance, and social progress' (www.wbcsd.ch). Indeed, the idea of 'sustainable – albeit limitless – growth' is fundamental to the discourse of natural capitalism: 'sustainability requires new products and services that are less greedy on natural resources, create less pollution and waste, and are more affordable to poor people' (p. 23). SD is equated with 'sustainable progress' (p. 25) and 'sustainable growth' (p. 15).

Since the propulsion of *Our Common Future* into *the* document of reference for the sustainable development, TNCs have become much more active in the domains of 'ecological balance' and 'social progress'. The implicit rationale is almost impeccable: (1) transnational business is paramount in economic development and economic globalization; (2) SD is a tripartite project involving the construction of three dimensions: the economic, the ecological and the social; (3) these dimensions are inseparable; as a result of 1, 2 and 3, TNCs are paramount in the reconstruction of the two remaining domains, the social and the ecological. At the same time the authors assure that small and medium sized enterprises (SMEs) in developing countries have a burden to carry themselves as they produce 'a disproportionately high amount of pollution because they are under-regulated and lack high visibility of bigger companies' (p. 93). It is clear, however, that small and medium sized enterprises do not qualify for WBSCD membership. The council is represented as an 'elite margin'. In this perspective TNCs form a vanguard of SD, as they are presented as a *minority* taking environmental matters seriously. To an extent WBCSD is echoing Ali and Camp's (2003; see also Ali, Chapter 6, this volume) notion of 'evangelical capitalism', in that the WBCSD is a powerful elite establishment that leads and thinks for more unsophisticated and less powerful actors, in their quest to generate universally valid principles for their version of the free market economy. And in natural capitalism discourse this is done by exaggerating best practice and good news while overlooking or ignoring win–lose situations.

The council and its publications can be considered a fair representation of the SD discourse that developed after the Earth Summit in 1992. As the authors put it: 'It is not surprising that business therefore decided to take a keen interest in what was to transpire at Rio and to make sure it was business-friendly' (p. 15). Albeit a recent representation, this form of

environmentalism is a 'natural progression' of the spaces and meanings of
sustainability as staked out by *Our Common Future*. This advent has seen
the infusion of a number of new concepts inherent to the corporate cause:
corporate citizenship, CSR, voluntary action, and eco-efficiency to name
a few. In the following section we review how the authors portray the
progression of SD into CSR since the publication of *Our Common Future*
in 1987.

The Corporate Mission of Sustainable Development

The end of the 1980s is portrayed as a time of upheaval and a reformation of the holistic grasp of business leaders and managers. There is the
emergence of a 'new paradigm' (p. 25) for business and an 'environmental
revolution' (p. 25). There is a not so subtle hint to reluctant business leaders
that the green wheels of change are already in motion, thus the corporate
response should not be about resistance but about changing the course of
the 'revolution':

> [Y]ou [skeptical business leaders] may as well join us in fighting for those
> changes so they benefit your company . . . The smart CEOs not only are going to
> orient their companies toward sustainability, but also are going to try to orient
> society toward sustainability. (p. 19)

Accordingly, effort has been put into reshaping the discourse of SD. The
'revolution' does not indicate an alternative to constructing the corporation as anything but a machine for maximizing profit. But as the concept of
'maximizing shareholder value' has been criticized as a vehicle for making
the top 1 percent of the population wealthier, more vague concepts of
'stakeholder value' and 'partnerships' are created and infused into the
discourse (Gaines 2003).

The pervading view in the discourse is that the market should be 'largely
free of entangling rules that could diminish its usefulness as a tool for
human development' (p. 41). In a similar manner nature is depicted as
a tool for human development. It is a tool that has to be sharpened and
taken care of, but a mere tool for human development nonetheless and
the market is portrayed as the best way to foster it. It reveals the modernist promise that nature is manageable, similar to the environment of a
company. So as to reinforce the managerial attitude towards nature, the
latter is reformed into 'the environment' (Escobar 1996). Escobar (1996)
posits that this construct positions the human agent and her creations as
the active principle, whereas nature is limited to a passive role in the flow
of resources. It is a representation of the mobilization of scientific expertise
and corporate technological skills embedded with a rational process of

political-economic decision-making (Harvey 1996) and where the possibility of 'global management' is inherently present. There is a strong reliance on 'science' in the reinvention of nature within the realms of economics. According to Pedynowsky (2003) environmental decay can be undone if there is no science-based mean that can position it in material representations of reality. Nature, the environment, and environmental decay become social constructions (Proctor 1998). The concept of eco-efficiency has developed into the foremost vehicle for CSR, not least because it is a concept that is dependent on scientific Western knowledge and technology, and because it in no way binds a company to ecological preservation. It is in this context that *Walking the Talk* should be considered as a medium for corporate environmentalism that has market-based capitalism as its core and TNCs as its engine. What is new in the corporate discourse is the *representation* of the 'ecological balance' and 'social development'. Business is portrayed as being 'part of civil society and inseparable from it' (p. 18), it is claimed that 'with increasing market globalization during the 1990s it became clear that business has a broader social responsibility . . . [it] also marked a radical rethink of the respective roles of the state and business in society' (p. 106). Through increasing privatization governments delegate to business a leading role in the spreading of SD, especially in developing countries:

> In parts of the developing world where media coverage is weak and/or government-controlled, companies do not feel as compelled to adopt CSR strategies . . . It is the subsidiaries of multinational companies . . . that are most likely to lead CSR in developing countries. (p. 107)

Natural Crisis Management

Apart from the actual development of corporate environmentalism, the critique aimed at neoclassical economic visions of nature has arguably been beneficial in the legitimization of a 'business case' for SD. The critique of modernism (Escobar 1995, 1996; O'Connor 1994; Shiva 1997) has helped to retouch the capitalistic framework into embracing the notion of natural capitalism (Hawken et al. 2000), where the critique is appropriated and turned into strength.

The authors of *Walking the Talk* adopt a refined version of the objective path set by *Our Common Future* (WCED 1987). The social dimension of SD was at the time of the report's release virgin territory for the corporate discourse. The report acknowledged the need to alleviate poverty in order to reach SD, implicitly the environmental agenda was not to become another hindrance to trade that would beset developing nations. Yet the stronger infusion of social concerns into the agenda required a reworking of the moral geographies (Sadler 2004). For business, the green agenda had been easier to capitalize on, as it was anchored in the rationale of science and concepts of efficiency. The construction of the corporate relation to poverty is not to be based on philanthropy as becomes evident in *Walking the Talk*. A turning point for the successful appropriation of all dimensions of SD has come through a crisis of legitimization. Amid critique and allegations of child labor, disempowerment of local interests, and union persecutions (see Barchiesi 2001; Escobar 1995; Frankental 2001; Klein 2000), the corporate discourse has turned its interest towards the local level. This has partially been a response to the critique that the poor and the local conditions were neglected. This appropriation of the critique has proven successful as the following account of Shell's former vice president of SD testifies: '[The mid-1990s problems at Shell were] the best things that ever happened to us' (p. 21). These crises did amount to a representation of what Sadler (2004) labels the moral geographies, and a representation of both the role of the TNC and the local community.

Think Locally, Act Globally

Walking the Talk is rich in peculiar details and anecdotes of corporate engagement on the local level, inspirational and upbeat, win–win examples only, similar to those of *Natural Capitalism*. A large part of the anecdotes represent developing locales. These local narratives strengthen the images of the marginalized poor trapped in unsustainable locales. In addition, the texts display the conceptual transformation of 'aid' towards 'development' and 'village' towards 'community'. The notorious Nigerian oil crisis is used as a case in *Walking the Talk*. Shell's retrospective view on an unsustainable locale is formulated in the following way:

> [Shell Petroleum Development Company of Nigeria Limited] has had a long history of assisting the communities in which it operates. However, discussions with NGOs, resulting in part from contacts made during the Ogoni crisis – a crisis that led to the execution of Ken Saro Wiwa – convinced the company that it needed to change its approach from community assistance to community development. SPCD will continue its drive to improve the lives of its host communities and increase its business in the region. (p. 35)

Similar to the crisis that somehow 'led to the execution of Ken Saro Wiwa', the discourse portrays communities as being constantly threatened by the [self-] destruction of nature, as in the following examples: 'Western Australia's worst environmental problem: salinity and land degradation' (p. 120); 'Fresh water is becoming scarce in many regions; globally 1.2

billion people lack access to clean drinking water' (p. 164); 'In response to public concern about the destruction of the world's forests' (p. 191). There is little or no discussion of what actually causes the destruction of the environment, although we are given some clues to the perpetrators: 'Industrialization can be hard on the environment, but not as hard as large populations forced to seek survival by mining topsoil and water systems to produce cheap commodities or to cut down into forests to clear farmland' (p. 52). There is little explanation on what forces the large populations to self-destruct, but the remedy is clear: freer access to global markets and an increased presence of TNCs. The negative impacts of globalization on poverty and environmental destruction are, however, recognized, without shifting the blame on the poor (thereby addressing common critiques from e.g. Escobar 1995 or Banerjee 2003).

Integrating the Poor into the Corporate Value Chain

'The ultimate business opportunity. Nearly two thirds of the planet's people are poor' (WBCSD 2004). The market is portrayed as the warden of nature, and with the lack of a market economy, nature will more often than not be [self-] destroyed: 'To survive, much less to thrive, they [the poor] need more. If they cannot get more, or even the basic necessities, through market access, they will be forced to destroy natural capital to support themselves' (p. 41). Economic growth is made paramount. This doctrine of growth was already visible in *Our Common Future*, and the subsequent development of natural capitalism is marred by a similar lack of discussion on the paradox of raising the consumption levels in developing regions without similarly reducing them in the developed regions. There are shades of Prometheanism visible in the response to these concerns:

> How then can poorer nations and people raise their standards of living while industrial nations maintain their standards of living and both respect environmental thresholds? The answer . . . is to mobilize markets in favor of sustainability, leveraging the power of innovation and global markets for the benefit of everyone, not just those in the developed world . . . As we have argued before, the poor need a liberal, open, global market. (p. 243)

In the passage above, there are strong shades of what Harvey (1996: 149) is criticizing in the capitalist appropriation of SD:

> There is, in short, nothing more ideologically powerful for capitalist interests to have at hand than unconstrained technological optimism and doctrines of progress ineluctably coupled to a doom-saying Malthusianism that can conveniently be blamed when, as they invariably do, things go wrong.

Walking the Talk does, however, address the critique that has been directed at Western-based business-minded analysis of developing countries, by identifying subsidies in industrialized countries and unfair commodity pricing as among the major obstacles for SD in developing countries.

> These markets are not free in the sense that they are rigged by more powerful nations . . . Ironically, industrial nations are the ones constantly urging developing nations to rid themselves of 'market distorting' policies. (p. 54)

While the poor are not blamed for environmental degradation, they are still left in the margins of the discourse. The culprits are depicted as the same as the adversaries of environmental entrepreneurism: overzealous governing bodies in the North, corrupt governing bodies in the South, dogmatic economists in the North, and anti-globalization activists in the North. By singling out 'economists' as part of the problem the authors of *Walking the Talk* are fast in drawing up a dividing line between managerial CSR and environmental economists. In fact the only critique in the text with a stated and named address is aimed at countering the claims of two 'academic economists', David Henderson and Milton Friedman. Their criticism towards SD is described as mirroring 'the views of those corporate bosses who have thought little about their company's wider responsibilities to society' (p. 104). The 'we' in the book is rather an image of an evangelist CEO of a TNC (based in the North or South), rather than a larger group of Northern-based free market defenders.

The Implementation of Full-cost Pricing

In the book the authors repeatedly show support for 'full-cost pricing', and the idea that ecological balance can be achieved once natural resources are given a price tag:

> We do not protect what we do not value. Many of nature's resources and services are currently not monetized. Establishing such prices – in ways which do not cut the poor off from crucial resources – could reduce resource waste and pollution. (p. 219)

As in *Natural Capitalism*, the double meaning of *value* is here drawn on: the claim that we can only value what we give monetary value to. It is claimed that full-cost pricing would enable a market that is not skewed because of 'government "tinkering"' (p. 17). The failure of science and economists is the inability to provide the market with implements and gauges for measuring all costs: financial, environmental and social.

Indeed, the marketplace is pretty good at reflecting short-term economic realities . . . However, it is not so good at reflecting environmental realities and longer-term economic realities . . . the *lack of ownership* [emphasis added] of certain crucial resources . . . can send exactly the wrong signals. They can signal abundance of environmental goods and services when in fact supply is dwindling dangerously. (p. 17)

The pricing of natural 'goods' would enable the complete ownership of nature. And with this we come to the least revolutionary aspect of natural capitalism, the commodification of nature.

In the text the authors refer to and defend perhaps the most contested of commodities: water. It is argued, falling back on testimonies of 'expert economists', that equitable water pricing is one of the most important mechanisms of SD. 'When water is free (from well, river, or pipe), consumers do not place value on its efficient use or conservation. Eliminating subsidies, and pricing water to cover infrastructure investment, treatment, and delivery costs will go a long way to getting the prices right' (p. 231). The authors acknowledge 'an adequate protection of the poor' (p. 232) as a necessity in these ventures of commodification and full-cost pricing, but fall short of specifying what is adequate. In order to achieve profit, corporations tend to get involved in privatization projects that target the middle classes, industry and drinking water supplies. Once the marginalized are within the geographic perimeters of the project it becomes problematic, as in the case of French TNC and WBCSD member, Suez in La Paz – El Alto, presented as a success while very different pictures have been painted about the case in the independent press and academia (see Chávez 2005; Olivera and Lewis 2005; Shiva 2002). The rights of 'the poor' and how profit-seeking corporations should drive the alleviation of poverty are issues that remain unclear, even to the authors. We are brought back to the difficulty of transnational CSR to deal with social issues. As Gaines (2003) notes, the corporate paradox lies in the fact that if the motive is profit, it will not equal making the system work for everybody.

DISCUSSION: OPTIMISM, UBIQUITY AND SCHIZOPHRENIA

The analysis in the previous section raises the issue of transnational CSR, which has been able to gather momentum as a discourse of resistance through its critique of a postulated industrial 'unsustainability' rooted in the economists' inability to put a monetary value on natural resources. As repeatedly put forward both in *Natural Capitalism* and *Walking the Talk*, sustainability is increasingly seen as a central corporate mission for TNCs. In this chapter we have especially focused on the manner in which TNCs have appropriated the harshest critiques in an effort to reshape SD.

In the subsection about Escobar's critique we have hinted at the ability of capitalism to coopt people into its own frame, especially through appropriating some of their concerns – for instance by positing these concerns as shared by all. More generally, capitalism can be presented as able to incorporate its strongest critiques. Agnew and Corbridge (1995) have shown how a strong opposition to hegemonic discourses and practices often ends up contributing to the growth of these discourses as well as their increased spatial reach. Baudrillard explains this phenomenon by pointing to the fact that capitalism is before all a sign system, and thus it can incorporate any opposition through 'the well known effect of recuperation, manipulation, of circulating and recycling at every level' (Baudrillard 1993: 4). For example, capitalism's incorporation of anti-capitalism works in the same way as 'the absorption of anti-art by art' (Doel 1999: 94). This suggests that not only can capitalism appropriate the discourses of sustainability, it is also always ready to refine its discourse so as to appropriate further critiques, including those that expose its appropriation of nature. Thus, we can say that O'Connor's and Escobar's critiques regarding the symbolic appropriation of nature are very much relevant to the discourse that the two books studied here convey, but at the same time we recognize elements of responses to (and appropriations/neutralizations of) the critiques that Escobar formulated about SD discourse in the mid-1990s.

Let us revisit the four aspects highlighted in *Encountering Development* (Escobar 1995: 194–6; as summarized in the first paragraph dealing with his critique) and analyze to what extent they have been addressed, and appropriated, in *Natural Capitalism* and *Walking the Talk*. To address the first critique, connected to the problematization of 'global survival', it is interesting to note that both books conspicuously show a concern with specific places and their local problems. Both books thus can claim to address the issue of the sustainability of the local, including local knowledge and sometimes even local (cultural) livelihoods: a way of appropriating the critique through 'glocalizing' the environment – also as a response to the glocalization of the struggles from the resistant groups (see Escobar 2001). Corporate capitalism thus can invest places more than ever – not only invest *in* them – in order to be present at the level where the meaningful struggles are now taking place.

Regarding Escobar's second axis of critique, it becomes evident that the poor are not presented as being at fault for the degradation of nature to the same extent as before. While both books continue to divert attention away from the big corporate polluters, they do so by blaming the problems on other forces that they also oppose to local communities, thereby showing that they are on the side of the people. These forces mainly are the dogmatic economists (guilty of being too narrow-minded and not understanding the necessary new market dynamics), the politicians and the states they represent (and especially the market-distorting subsidies they maintain), and even, in the most caricatured claims, nature itself, which, as we have seen, is at times depicted as though it was self-destructing. What remain hidden are all mentions of poverty and inequality in the home countries of TNCs.

As for the third critique, concerning the economicism behind SD, we posit that the same economic rationale has remained, but with a claim to the contrary. In both books, there is a strong criticism of the guardians of economic dogma, with an assertion that a radical change away from that economicist thinking has been occurring and is going to rein in natural capitalism, but, when looking closely at the economic system advocated, one can easily see that the market-based logic is still at the center of everything, and is even extended now to envelope new forms of capital.

Finally, a distinction has to be made regarding how the two books use the terms 'nature' and 'environment' (the fourth aspect that Escobar pointed out): *Natural Capitalism* reinstates 'nature' only to appropriate it more fully as natural capital, while *Walking the Talk* tends to stick to 'the environment' because of its more managerial relevance – in both cases, however, nature is to be taken care of, and will only be nature again if managed by man (mainly in the shape of corporate capitalism).

This discursive incorporation of the critiques should not be mistaken for a genuine move towards local communities and nature, but should rather be understood as an attempt to neutralize these critiques through reliance on the mode of seduction of natural capitalism. How is this seduction deployed in order to allow for the appropriation of 'glocal spatialities' – meaning, global space *and* local places, and also global space *through* local places, since both space and place can be understood to produce each other (see e.g. Escobar 2001[7])? The general discursive approach is characterized by 'optimism', 'ubiquity' and 'schizophrenia'. By optimism we wish to point to the overwhelming reliance on feel-good examples, whether in *Natural Capitalism*, where many problems are only loosely discussed at the global level if not avoided altogether, or in *Walking the Talk*, where the narratives are written by the companies themselves in a way that often exaggerates their beneficial action. There is an exclusive focus on 'win–win' examples, and even when they serve as inspirational examples, it would be equally important to discuss the more common 'win–lose' situations – and indeed the 'lose–lose' ones. This optimism is strongly connected to a deep Prometheanism, a belief in technology's ability to solve all problems, as there is 'nothing more ideologically powerful for capitalist interests to have at hand' (Harvey 1996: 149), although this is more apparent in *Natural Capitalism* than in *Walking the Talk*. By ubiquity we mean the abundance of examples referring to specific places that are meant to give the impression that each local problem can be addressed through natural capitalism; not only that this extended capitalist frame will be all-enveloping in order to address the issue of global survival, but also that it will be able to fit the particularities of all places and do so in a harmonious, *natural* way, thus preserving nature and sustaining local cultures. By schizophrenia we refer to the rhetorical tendency to write everything and its contrary so as to anticipate and appropriate all possible critiques, in order to neutralize their subversive potential. Examples of this recurrent rhetorical tactics abound: claiming to be radically opposed to mainstream economics while effectively promoting the exact same rationale, prescribing market-based systems while calling for true democracy, pretending to empower the local communities while dispossessing them of their basic free resources through full-cost pricing, and so on.

It should be clear that this schizophrenic ubiquity (or should we call it ubiquitous schizophrenia) does not prevent the selective exclusion of many actors in discourse deployed in the two books. There are those who are deliberately absent within certain contexts and those who are discussed but silenced in the process. The first group includes transnational corporations, which are always very present as agents of change but conveniently absent when it comes to identifying who is at fault regarding environmental degradation in particular. Central industries that are often targeted in sustainability debates, such as biotechnology, are not even mentioned in *Natural Capitalism*. National power, while debated at length when it comes to how detrimental state expenditure – especially subsidies – can be for global business, is also absent with regard to how the 'hidden fist' of its military force (see Ali, Chapter 6, this volume) often serves the agenda of big corporations, in ways that are euphemistically speaking deeply unsustainable. In addition, the third world within the first world – poverty in developed countries – is invisible. When convenient, environmental issues are mobilized to distract from social issues (and conversely), for instance when introducing the need for environmental taxes that seemingly should replace existing ones that cater for social needs. The local communities are easily silenced by the claim that the objective is to empower them: speaking in their name allows for the partial incorporation – and attempt at neutralization – of critiques from, for example, Escobar (1995). And nature itself, of course, is not given a voice. It is depicted as either largely passive or seemingly self-destructing.

CONCLUSION

In the closing chapter of *Natural Capitalism*, the authors review four worldviews 'on the emotional and intellectual frameworks that business, citizens and governments use to negotiate and choose about economics and the environment' (Hawken et al. 2000: 310). They discuss the *Blues* ('mainstream free-marketers' with 'a positive bias toward the future based on technological optimism and the strength of the economy', ibid.: 310), the *Reds* (representing 'the sundry forms of socialism', ibid.: 311), the *Greens* (who 'see the world primarily in terms of ecosystems' and 'want to bring about better understanding of how large the economy can grow before it outstrips its host', ibid.) and the *Whites* ('the synthesists', who 'do not entirely oppose or agree with any of the three other views' and have 'an optimistic view of humankind', ibid.: 312), before concluding that 'a successful business in the new era of natural capitalism will respect and understand all four views' (ibid.: 313), thus hinting that they do not take a particular stand. Our contention, on the contrary, is that the authors of both *Natural Capitalism* and *Walking the Talk* can be seen as *Blues* going into *Green* territory (appropriating their cause) by using *White* rhetoric (appropriating their style), and on most grounds remaining opposed to *Reds* (the only ones whose discourse does not need to be appropriated in any way, since they can be claimed to have been 'discredited by the downfall of the erstwhile Soviet Union', ibid.: 311).

Our endeavor here has been to expose how this optimism, ubiquity and schizophrenia proceed to seduce the reader and thus allow for a diversion from a more lucid understanding of the global and local environmental impacts of corporate capitalism. If corporations were to be made accountable for what they claim they can do through CSR to address environmental and social concerns, they would need to be dismantled because of their current legal status that makes them prioritize profit and value creation for shareholders above everything else. We hope that exposing this 'mode of seduction' (Baudrillard 1990a) can prove a way to subvert natural capitalism while avoiding a (bound to fail) head-on fight regarding its 'mode of production' (ibid.).[8] Preliminarily, our attempt to subvert natural capitalism discourse can be summarized as follows: while natural capitalism advocates, and in particular its corporate proponents, would claim it is possible to save the world while (or even by) making profits, our contention is that what they are doing is making the world while saving profits for themselves.

NOTES

1. GlobeScan surveyed 200 sustainability experts from five sectors: corporate, government, voluntary, institutional (e.g. academics), and service (e.g. consultants).
2. GRI is a guideline for globally applicable sustainability reporting.
3. Global Compact is a UN-led voluntary initiative network that works to advance sustainable development within the areas of human rights, labor, the environment and anticorruption.
4. This case, studied by Banerjee (2003), involves the exploitation of a uranium mine in Aboriginal territory in Australia.
5. Unless stated otherwise, citations and page numbers from this section refer to the paperback edition (2000) of the Hawken et al. book *Natural Capitalism: The Next Industrial Revolution*.
6. Unless stated otherwise, citations and page numbers from this section refer to the Holliday et al. (2002) book *Walking the Talk: The Business Case for Sustainable Development*.
7. As Escobar (2001: 147) puts it, 'place is certainly connected to, and to a significant extent produced by, spatial logics' and 'place-based dynamics might be equally important for the production of space'.
8. It is important to state here, however, that we do not intend to follow Baudrillard all the way to his 'fatal strategies' (Baudrillard, 1990b).

REFERENCES

Adams, William M. (2001), *Green Development: Environment and Sustainability in the Third World*, 2nd edn, London: Routledge.

Agnew, John and Stuart Corbridge (1995), *Mastering Space: Hegemony, Territory and International Political Economy*, London: Routledge.

Ali, Abbas J. and Robert C. Camp (2003), 'Risks of evangelical capitalism', *International Journal of Commerce and Management*, 13 (1), 1–10.

Ayres, Robert U. (1998), *Turning Point: The End of the Growth Paradigm*, London: Earthscan.

Banerjee, S.B. (2000), 'Whose land is it anyway? National interest, indigenous stakeholders, and colonial discourses', *Organization and Environment*, 13 (1), 3–38.

Banerjee, S.B. (2003), 'Who sustains whose development? Sustainable development and the reinvention of Nature', *Organization Studies*, 24 (1), 143–80.

Barchiesi, F. (2001), 'Transnational capital, urban globalisation and cross-border solidarity: the case of the South African municipal workers', *Antipode*, 33 (3), 384–406.

Baudrillard, Jean (1975), 'Design and environment, or how political economy escapes into cyberblitz', in *For a Critique of the Political Economy of the Sign*, St Louis, MO: Telos Press.

Baudrillard, Jean (1981), *The Mirror of Production*, St Louis, MO: Telos Press.

Baudrillard, Jean (1990a), *Seduction*, London: Macmillan.

Baudrillard, Jean (1990b), *Fatal Strategies*, London: Pluto.

Baudrillard, Jean (1993), *Symbolic Exchange and Death*, London: Sage.

Blaikie, Piers (1985) *The Political Economy of Soil Erosion in Developing Countries*, London: Longman.

Bryant, R. and G.A. Wilson (1998), 'Rethinking environmental management', *Progress in Human Geography*, 22 (3), 321–43.

Castree, N. (2003), 'Commodifying what nature?', *Progress in Human Geography*, **27** (3), 273–97.

Castro, C. (2004), 'Sustainable development: mainstream and critical perspectives', *Organization and Environment*, **17** (2), 195–225.

Chávez, W. (2005), 'Effervescence populaire en Bolivie', *Le Monde Diplomatique*, **March** (in French).

Club of Rome (1972), *The Limits to Growth: A Report for the Club of Rome's Project on the Predicament of Mankind*, New York: Universe Books.

Daly, Herman (1994), 'Operationalizing sustainable development by investing in natural capital', in Ann M. Jansson, Monica Hammer, Carl Folke and Robert Costanza (eds), *Investing in Natural Capital: The Ecological Economics Approach to Sustainability*, Washington, DC: Island.

Doel, Marcus (1999), *Poststructuralist Geographies: The Diabolical Art of Spatial Science*, Edinburgh: Edinburgh University Press.

Escobar, Arturo (1995), *Encountering Development: The Making and Unmaking of the Third World*, Princeton, NJ: Princeton University Press.

Escobar, Arturo (1996), 'Constructing nature: elements for a poststructuralist political ecology', in Richard Peet and Michael Watts (eds), *Liberation Ecologies: Environment, Development, Social Movements*, London: Routledge.

Escobar, A. (2001), 'Culture sits in places: reflection on globalism and subaltern strategies of localization', *Political Geography*, **20** (2), 139–74.

Frankental, P. (2001), 'Corporate social responsibility – a PR invention?', *Corporate Communications: An International Journal*, **6** (1), 18–23.

Friedman, Milton (1970), 'The social responsibility of business is to increase its profits', *The New York Times Magazine*, 13 September.

Gaines, A. (2003), 'The corporate paradox: corporate social responsibility in an age of corporate induced breakdown', *The Journal of Corporate Citizenship*, **10** (3), 28–35.

GlobeScan (2005), *The GlobeScan Survey of Sustainability Experts*, Toronto: GlobeScan International.

Haque, S.M. (1999), 'The fate of sustainable development under neo-liberal regimes in developing countries', *International Political Science Review*, **20** (2), 197–218.

Haque, S.M. (2000), 'Environmental discourse and sustainable development: linkages and limitations', *Ethics and the Environment*, **5** (1), 3–21.

Harvey, David (1973), *Social Justice and the City*, London: Edward Arnold.

Harvey, David (1996), *Justice, Nature, and the Geography of Difference*, Cambridge, MA: Blackwell.

Hawken, Paul, Amory Lovins and Hunter L. Lovins (2000), *Natural Capitalism: The Next Industrial Revolution*, London: Earthscan Publications.

Holliday, Chad, Stephan Schmidheiny and Philip Watts (2002), *Walking the Talk: The Business Case for Sustainable Development*, Sheffield: Greenleaf Publishing.

Jackson, Cecile (1994), 'Gender analysis and feminisms', in Michael Redclift and Ted Benton (eds), *Social Theory and the Global Environment*, London: Routledge.

Klein, Naomi (2000), *No Logo*, London: Flamingo.

Levitt, T. (1958), 'The dangers of social responsibility', *Harvard Business Review*, **36** (5), 41–50.

Nesmith, C. and S.A. Radcliffe (1993), '(Re)mapping Mother Earth: a geographical perspective on environmental feminisms', *Environment and Planning D: Society and Space*, **11** (4), 379–94.

O'Connor, Martin (1994), 'On the misadventures of capitalist nature', in Martin O'Connor (ed.), *Is Capitalism Sustainable? Political Economy and the Politics of Ecology*, New York: Guilford Press.

Olivera, Oscar and Tom Lewis (2005), ¡*Cochabamba! Water War in Bolivia*, Cambridge, MA: South End Press.

Pedynowsky, D. (2003), 'Science(s) – which, when and whose? Probing the metanarrative of scientific knowledge in the social construction of nature', *Progress in Human Geography*, **27** (6), 735–52.

Peet, R. and M.J. Watts (1993), 'Introduction: development theory and environment in an age of market triumphalism', *Economic Geography*, **69** (3), 227–53.

Peet, Richard and Michael J. Watts (1996), 'Liberation ecologies: development, sustainability and environment in an age of market triumphalism', in Richard Peet and Michael J. Watts (eds), *Liberation Ecologies: Environment, Development, Social Movements*, London: Routledge.

Proctor, J.D. (1998), 'The social construction of nature: relativist accusations, pragmatist and critical realist responses', *Annals of the Association of American Geographers*, **88** (3), 352–76.

Raco, M. (2005), 'Sustainable development, rolled-out neoliberalism and sustainable communities', *Antipode*, **37** (2), 324–47.

Robinson, J. (2004), 'Squaring the circle? Some thoughts on the idea of sustainable development', *Ecological Economics*, **48** (4), 369–84.

Sadler, D. (2004), 'Anti-corporate campaiging and corporate "social" responsibility: towards alternative spaces of citizenship', *Antipode*, **36** (5), 851–70.

Saha, Suranjit K. (2002), 'Theorising globalisation and sustainable development', in Suranjit K. Saha and David Parker (eds), *Globalisation and Sustainable Development in Latin America*, Cheltenham, UK and Northampton, MA, USA: Edward Elgar.

Shiva, Vandana (1988), *Staying Alive: Women, Ecology and Survival in India; Kali for Women, New Delhi*, London: Zed Press.

Shiva, Vandana (1997), *Biopiracy: The Plunder of Nature and Knowledge*, Cambridge, MA: South End Press.

Shiva, Vandana (2002), *Water Wars – Privatization, Pollution, and Profit*, Cambridge, MA: South End Press.

Smith, Neil (1984), *Uneven Development: Nature Capital and the Production of Space* (2nd edn 1990), Oxford: Basil Blackwell.

Smith, Neil (1996), 'The production of nature', in George Robertson, Melinda Mash, Lisa Tickner, Jon Bird, Barry Curtis and Tim Putnam (eds), *Future Natural: Nature, Science, Culture*, London: Routledge.

Swyngedouw, E. (1999), 'Modernity and hybridity: nature, regeneracionismo, and the production of the Spanish Waterscape, 1890–1930', *Annals of the Association of American Geographers*, **89** (3), 443–65.

Swyngedouw, E. and N. Heynen (2003), 'Urban political ecology, justice and the politics of scale', *Antipode*, **35** (5), 898–918.

Swyngedouw, Eric and Maria Kaika (2000), 'The environment of the city or . . . the urbanization of nature', in Gary Bridge and Sophie Watson (eds), *Reader in Urban Studies*, Oxford: Blackwell.

Velasquez, M. (1992), 'International business, morality, and the common good', *Business Ethics Quarterly*, **2** (1), 27–40.

Watts, Michael J. (1983), *Silent Violence: Food, Famine and Peasantry in Northern Nigeria*, Berkeley: University of California Press.

WBCSD (World Business Council of Sustainable Development) (2004), 'Doing business with the poor – a field guide', www.wbcsd.org/web/publications/sl-field-guide.pdf, 23 October.

WCED (World Commission on Environment and Development) (1987), *Our Common Future*, Oxford: Oxford University Press.

PART III

The political economy of knowledge

4. Contesting boundaries: the shifting borders of globalization

Diana J. Wong-MingJi

INTRODUCTION

Discussions of globalization often include frequent commentaries about blurring boundaries, which imply they are either diminishing in relevance or disappearing altogether. Ohmae (1990) described the increasing trend of globalization as ultimately leading to a 'borderless world' where boundaries essentially become meaningless. Mantras from convergence theories refer to declining trade barriers; free and rapid flows of peoples, goods, services, and ideas; integration of societies and economics; and alliance networks of new organizational forms, and rising tides of development and wealth proliferate many of the arguments in support of globalization (Dunning, 1995). In this context, boundaries are problematic obstacles that impede globalization and must be overcome in the interest of progressing with the agenda of economic integration and general societal well-being. More importantly, the projected images of globalization from such discourse create a sense of inevitability that cannot or should not be resisted or stopped, and to do so would be a foolhardy futile enterprise or backward looking.

Yet a growing chorus, albeit fragmented from different quarters, is questioning, resisting, and opposing the seemingly inescapable tsunami of globalization. The collection of voices comes from wide ranging and disparate perspectives that include trade unionists, environmentalists, farmers, blue-collar industrial workers, faith-based communities, human rights advocates, intellectual thinkers and researchers, and so on (Ancelovici, 2002; Cox and Jones, 1999). Their objections to globalization illustrate that boundaries as defined by blurring borders are not dissolving and giving way to a borderless world. Instead, boundaries are actually spaces where global contestations occur and, over time, boundaries become redefined until the next contest. Thus boundaries play a critical and central role in a turbulent age of globalization and, possibly, even more so than when they were taken-for-granted assumptions and mutually abided by, during an earlier stable period characterized by protectionism.

In the current period of globalization, dominant organization theories of organizational boundaries are too limited to explain more complex processes that create, negotiate and recreate boundaries. The shifting global context requires a more dynamic and radical perspective to explain how organizational boundaries are established, what processes enable boundary making, how boundaries shift on multiple levels, and who gets to decide. This chapter seeks to articulate a different direction to investigate organizational boundaries from the prevailing management orthodoxies. To support such an endeavor, I draw insights from human geography, which has developed an extensive body of research from multiple epistemological paradigms about boundaries. Recent studies in the political and cultural branches of human geography provide directions to rethink the notion of boundaries within processes of globalization as chaotic contested terrains of power between different actors (e.g. Murray, 2006; Newman and Paasi, 1998; Nicol and Townsend-Gault, 2004). Boundaries as spaces of struggles and tensions, where global actors negotiate to draw and redraw distinctions between memberships and territories, contrast with established notions in organization theory. Traditionally, boundaries are viewed as relatively static imaginary lines to be overcome or permeable membranes that facilitate the flow of information and resource exchanges between organizations and their environments (Leifer and Delbecq, 1978). This is also the case in earlier writings in geography. While traditional ideas of boundary may retain some validity, recent developments suggest a more complex active role for boundaries in organizations (Hernes, 2004; Yan and Louis, 1999). The rapidly changing global landscape amplifies the need for a more dynamic perspective on boundaries.

The questions raised about globalization are essentially questions of boundaries and the redrawing of new ones. Questions such as how boundaries are established, who gets to determine boundary location, and what kind of boundaries to set up have important implications for business organizations that require an understanding of the geographical underpinnings. The following discussion proposes a geographical approach to examine organizational boundaries as dynamic spaces of betweenness and then examines three interrelated contests of organizational boundaries with nation-state borders, intellectual capital, and e-commerce. Many other contests such as global workforce migration or environmental management can be explored but because of the limitation of space, these three will serve the purpose to illustrate how different global actors engage in processes of negotiating and constructing organizational boundaries. The chapter concludes with a pause in this dialogue of organizational boundary scholarship to create space for reflections.

PROPOSING ORGANIZATIONAL BOUNDARIES AS SPACES OF CONTESTS IN GLOBALIZATION

At the center of globalization is increasing international trade, where technological innovations enable people, goods, services, information, and ideas to transcend time and space. Economics, specifically economic growth to achieve competitive dominance, acts as a primary driver (Korten, 1995; Ohmae, 1990; Reich, 1991) for organizations going global. A plethora of evidence and fascinating anecdotal case studies are often brought forth to illustrate how dramatic changes in the flow of economic activities occur more rapidly and freely around the world than ever before. The ensuing predominant ideology is encompassed by theories of convergence where adoption of Western technologies, values, and managerial practices leads to adoption of organizational structures and values encased in free market capitalism (Dunphy, 1987; Eisenstadt, 1973; Hedley, 2002). Subsequently, the differentials in power to control boundaries on multiple levels are redefined and reconstituted. Before moving forward, a brief historical note about globalization needs to be made at minimum for recapturing the historical trajectory of developments and context setting.

An article in *The Economist* (1997) outlined some general characteristics symptomatic of globalization. It included the proliferation of technological innovations that gave rise to many new gadgets; changes in national border frontiers with the emergence of new countries in Eastern Europe and Central Asia; the ten wealthiest countries based on per capita GDP were 'offshoots' of Europe or in Western Europe; the remarkable growth of China's trade; Canada and the USA engaged in trade disputes over timber; the economic growth of Japan; the integration of Germany into one country; one undisputed superpower; and the image of a queen dressed in black for a royal procession to mark an untimely death. With the same set of characterizations, the interesting point was that the author referred to the state of globalization at two different points in time – 1897 and 1997. While there are marked differences between the late 19th and 20th centuries, memory lapses of the stark similarities in history occur when referring to the current rise of globalization as the pendulum has swung back and forth over time.

A key point about comparing and contrasting the two ages is not to take globalization for granted as often portrayed in the mass media. During the late 19th century, the rise of globalization certainly created and possibly blurred any existing national boundaries underneath various colonial powers, especially the colonial rule of the British Empire where the sun did not set on Britannia. But challenges to boundaries and the reconfiguration of new ones occurred through a number of global conflicts, including two world wars and a cold war, which led to the redrawing of different geo-political boundaries. This resulted in a decline in globalization, with several decades of isolationism and protectionism. The inevitability of globalization comes into question with a long enough historical lens that reveals its dynamic shifts.

Williamson (2006) provides a historical lens for three epochs of globalization as defined by the flow of people, goods and capital. The first one was from the late 19th century with the convergence of globalization; the second one was from 1914 to 1950 with deglobalization and last, in the late 20th century with the increasing convergence of globalization. The historical lens provides a dynamic perspective where people, goods and capital may ebb and flow over time in their movement around the world. The rise of protectionism entailed diminished boundary permeability along with new boundaries to restrict the flow of people, goods and capital with the subsequent decline in globalism.

With the rise, decline and rise again of globalization over the last century, the idea of organizational boundaries as static, natural, mutually acceptable and objective entities becomes highly questionable. Various military conflicts demonstrate how boundaries change over time. At the same time, the geo-political boundaries fundamentally shape organizational boundaries and visa versa. While sovereign powers regulate and limit the global flow of people, capital and goods, the economic interests in organizations act as a primary driver, through multilateral institutions such as the World Trade Organization (WTO), to dismantle trade barriers and facilitate free trade to expand markets. In 1817, Ricardo (1963) delineated the theory of comparative advantage in economics, which argues how each economy, even with various differences, should focus on producing what it does most efficiently and trade to achieve overall optimal gain for both to be better off than any other alternative combination of production. While comparative advantage, including its dynamic version (Klein, 1973), acts as a primary driver for globalization, the theory and its application neglects to account for political interests of sovereign states, the role of multinational organizations with powers that exceed some nation-states, and a new economic space with e-commerce. Furthermore, globalization based on the theory of comparative advantage neglects to address significant concerns over a growing inequality in the standards of living between the rich and poor, a superimposition of Western (primarily US) cultural values and practices, and increasing disparities within economies (Hedley, 2002). As a result, the dynamics underlying globalization through the different historical shifts and the various stakeholders lead to contentions over boundaries and reconfigurations of boundaries, regardless of whether they are geo-political or organizational boundaries.

In considering a boundary as a space where contests of globalization occur, Kellner (2002) provides an illustration with a critical theory of globalization that has a dialectical framework to consider 'globalization from below' and 'globalization from above'. Marginalized individuals organizing for social justice 'from below' can make use of social institutions, new technologies, and instruments from globalization to further agendas of democracy. Impositions by capitalism in 'globalization from above' provide channels for the very political struggles against it. These struggles take place in a bounded space of globalization for multiple stakeholders. Thus organizational boundaries become a much more complex phenomenon as space that is organized for global contests.

In sum, boundaries are not static lines found on maps, or simply demarcations between organizations and their environments that must be overcome. Boundaries are expressions of power in relationships regarding people, space, time and resources. The act of establishing boundaries is an exercise of power in negotiation and conflict resolution that could range from amiable collaboration to military aggression. During most of the 20th century, globalization was about organizations shifting, redrawing and redefining boundaries between different actors in the international community. This perspective of boundary making differs dramatically from the general approach in organization theories and international management research where boundaries are natural and taken for granted as objective and neutral organizational phenomena. But the rapid changes from globalization leave many mystified about changing organizational boundaries because the prevailing approach to boundaries as natural phenomena does not address why and how they come to be created, changed or dissolved. The following section takes a step back to examine boundaries in organization theory as a means to consider their historical development and the difficulties in explaining boundaries in a globalizing context.

BOUNDARIES IN ORGANIZATION THEORY

The concept of 'boundary' has an extensive history, starting with the earliest development of organization theory that includes the role of boundary spanners and boundary spanning activities (Galbraith, 1973; Levine and White, 1961; Thompson, 1962, 1967). Leifer and Delbecq (1978: 41) defined boundary as 'the demarcation line or region between one system and another that protects the members of the system from extra systemic influences and that regulates the flow of information, material, and people into or out of the system'. Boundary spanners and their inherent actions assume a boundary is an external entity to be overcome, while neglecting to consider how organizational members are constantly engaged in enacting and re-enacting in a space to construct and negotiate the boundaries. Organizational interfaces and interactions with the environment establish organizational boundaries (Spencer and Heinze, 1977/78) that result in considering organizations as open systems. Yet not all open systems have the same degree or extent of openness, also known as permeability. What the organizing mechanisms are in boundary making or how boundaries become more porous remain to be explained in the existing body of literature.

Recently, researchers began to take steps toward examining organizational boundaries as the intersection (Oliver, 1993) or demarcation (Santos and Eisenhardt, 2005) between organizations and their environments. Santos and Eisenhardt's (2005) development of boundaries with four distinct concepts – efficiency, power, competence, and identity – overlaps with Oliver's (1993) comprehensive review that identified six dimensions of boundary with five conceptual definitions. They are boundary as: (1) membership functions such as jurisdiction and purpose building that relate to the identity concept; (2) roles and activities such as monitoring and boundary spanning that relate to the competence concept; (3) a sphere of influence such as buffers and bridges to protect and connect the organization that relate to the power concept; (4) transaction cost dichotomy functions to assign transactions to hierarchies or arm's length transactions that relate to the efficiency concept; and (5) institutional filter functions such as isomorphic and image transmissions that relate to the power concept. Oliver (1993) outlines how the different boundary functions impact three boundary properties – openness to the environment, stability in relation with the environment, and information accuracy in exchanges with the environment – depending on the organization–environment interface.

In general, organization theorists consider the power of boundaries, boundary spanners and related activities by focusing on regulating and positioning the organization in its competitive context. Power in the transaction cost definition employs boundaries in a utilitarian function to control environmental factors. The use of boundaries based on membership and identity employs power through separation to elevate the status and legitimacy over outsiders. This is certainly evident in trading blocs as well as in branding processes. But how members with a shared identity accumulate power and deploy power to engage in boundary making entails a naturalness where the legitimating process generally ignores or assumes away questions about the boundary itself.

Future directions for boundary research point to the importance of a temporal dimension to address dynamic processes and multi-theoretical approaches to account for multiple realities that are inherent in globalization. After developing the four boundary concepts, Santos and Eisenhardt (2005: 504) identified the importance of the temporal dimension with dynamic processes where boundary concepts 'may lead, lag, or coevolve with another and causality is often bidirectional, tracking boundaries over time is critical'. This also requires considering a boundary as a space for the organizing processes of boundary formation. Oliver (1993) points to the importance of multi-theoretical perspectives, and pushed further with radical epistemological assumptions, for capturing a more comprehensive array of factors in boundary management. The demands of globalization requiring research agendas to examine such complexities need to account for dynamic shifts, power relations and the co-existence of multiple boundary realities.

Subsequently, Yan and Louis (1999) reviewed four significant functions of boundaries as lines of demarcation, perimeters, interfaces, and frontiers for transactions that extended prior research to examine boundary work at deeper levels of organizations. Compared to prior definitions, Yan and Louis (1999: 29) began to develop a more dynamic perspective to 'define boundaries as a system's domain of interactions with its environment in order to maintain the system and to provide for its long-term survival'. This integrates a number of earlier perspectives such as monitoring and boundary spanning, and legitimacy and credibility. The limitations of their focus on work unit levels from a unilateral perspective solve boundary problems without being able to account for multiple perspectives taking place within the interactions.

Boundary spanning refers to processes that are driven by motives related to the definition and functions of boundaries as outlined by Oliver (1993). She outlines the motives of boundary spanning as determining authority over membership, acquiring information, achieving autonomy and control, increasing efficiency and reducing costs, and gaining legitimacy and credibility. Boundary spanners are the decision makers, or filters, for determining flows in and out of the organization because they regulate the terms and conditions of the flow exchange (Miller, 1972). As a result, boundary spanners have the power to make inferences in their information processing task, engage in gatekeeping to manage resource and information flows, and leverage vital information for organizational survival (March and Simon, 1958). The space that boundary spanners engage in is actually between places rather than over a neutral and artificially drawn line. At the same time, how boundary spanners construct and change boundaries to legitimate their role in the space between organizations remains to be explored. Usually, vital information is related to non-routine boundary spanning tasks (Aldrich and Herker, 1977) such as environmental scanning for strategic planning among upper level managers or technological innovations. Tushman and Romanelli (1983) found that task and environment uncertainty was positively related to the influence of a boundary spanner.

From a different theoretical paradigm, Gilmore (1982) examined the boundary as a socially constructed phenomenon that places organizational leaders in not just performing boundary spanning tasks but also defining and redefining boundaries and questioning the existence of some boundaries. However, the discussion primarily focuses on a competence concept of boundary with little consideration for how the social construction of boundaries unfolds over time or how differential power positions socially construct boundaries. Recently, a more dynamic approach to organizational boundaries employs a composite of mental, physical and social factors to account for their central roles in interorganizational interactions (Hernes, 2004). Many of these interactions perpetuate globalization as they inherently facilitate connections and venues for the flow of people, goods and capital around the world. In particular with ideas and capital, the flows can be facilitated in a very compressed space and time with internet technology. Hence, boundaries become reconfigured in a different space that transcends the constrictions of physical geography and time into a different sphere – cyberspace.

Established organization theories of boundary help to examine issues such as types of boundaries (Rosenkopf and Nerkar, 2001) and coordination across organizations (Kellogg et al., 2006). Much of the research accepts the phenomenon with little question about what processes are involved in constructing boundaries, what assumptions underlie an organization's boundaries, and how shifts in organizational boundaries affect different stakeholders. The lack of critical analysis of boundaries sustains their static taken-for-granted nature and focuses attention on how boundary spanners solve boundary problems without recognizing that the process of solving boundary problems is in and of itself a process of reconstituting boundaries in the image of the organization's agenda. By recognizing boundaries as space for negotiating conflicts, processes of boundary making can be made more explicit. The next section proposes a more dynamic and complex approach to consider boundaries in a global context.

CONSIDERING BOUNDARIES AS CONTESTED SPACE

As actors question and challenge established organizational boundaries with overt actions, their engagement in the space to set about advocating for changes would lead to shifts of what become accepted as boundaries.

The competing interests engage in a space where negotiations take place to determine the nature, role, type and construction of acceptable arrangements of relationships between spaces – the boundaries. For example, the entry of a transnational corporation (TNC) into a local community often initiates a new set of boundaries related to different dimensions of what space it occupies in the community; who qualifies to work on its premises; who it serves; what influence it has on different stakeholders; and so on. While TNC boundary spanners determine many of these decisions, the process is rarely accepted in a unilateral manner. Stakeholders, including governments, communities, labor, suppliers and customers, could negotiate and challenge the creation of such boundaries as well as find ways to redefine, redraw and resist the development of boundaries (e.g. Luo, 2001; Murtha and Lenway, 1994; Shamir and Melnik, 2002). Thus negotiating boundaries involves multiple actors who often have unequal power positions and are equipped differently to engage in boundary negotiations.

A poignant example can be found in the 1999 Seattle protests at the World Trade Organization meeting. Between 40,000 and 100,000 demonstrators from a wide range of interests gathered to question and contest the boundaries of globalization concerning issues related to human rights, labor, indigenous communities, agriculture, environment, education, social justice, and other marginalized human concerns in the global economic and free trade negotiations. The precursor to the WTO was a series of negotiations for free trade under the General Agreement on Tariffs and Trade (GATT), which was primarily a multilateral international agreement regarding trade issues and not an organization. The initial agreement addressed reducing tariffs for about $10 billion US dollars in trade of commodities that made up 20 percent of the global market. Local markets and businesses primarily retained autonomy and control over their lives with little encroachment from globalization. However, as GATT expanded with the third phase of the Uruguay Round from 1986 to 1994, expansion of the agreement encompassed new areas such as agriculture, services, intellectual property and capital, and the trade agreement transformed into an organization, the WTO, with 165 countries as members today. The WTO did not only extend and consolidate power within its boundaries by becoming the arbitrating organization for global trade. Decision making is based on one country, one vote. However, an informal consensus-making process, with the strongest influence being the relative market size of a country, takes place. In this manner, the WTO itself constitutes a series of multiple boundaries of those whose voices count (the USA and the EU) versus those whose voices are excluded (developing countries) in constructing processes of global free trade. At the same time, the WTO employs its power to settle trade disputes to assert and protect free trade, which reinforces boundaries for free trade.

The most vivid and visceral expression of organizational boundaries to protect free trade also manifested itself as a large physical cordon of gas-masked and riot-shielded police who hauled protesters away to be locked up behind boundaries of metal bars. While ministers of developing countries negotiated free trade issues within the WTO, the contesting of free trade boundaries also involved a broad spectrum of stakeholders beyond TNCs and governments. The assertion of boundaries by means of police force separated what was deemed illegitimate by the WTO and governments. Boundaries were imposed through the exercise of sovereign state and economics powers. Protests against globalization continued at WTO meetings in Cancun in 2003 and in Hong Kong in 2005. In Hong Kong, a shift occurred when the WTO granted permission to the protesting groups to attend and address the ministerial trade negotiation conference. Although the security and police presence was very heavy, the invitation to protestors was a change in the WTO's boundaries that entailed a shift in who they consider as legitimate for at least minimal inclusion and/or exclusion. At the same time, some of the protestors' messages shifted from complete rejection of globalization to one of fair trade. The different actors brought multiple viewpoints and positions to the WTO sessions and their issues were multifaceted at different levels. Their engagement entailed competing values and perspectives, which led to contesting the boundaries. Ministers from developing countries attempted to negotiate global trade issues from within the confines of the WTO, but were excluded from the 'Green Room' informal negotiations where more powerful players engage in constructing agreements prior to formal meetings for negotiations. Thus physical and political economic boundaries shifted over time between 1999 and 2005 as protesters, trade ministers, and enforcing authorities negotiated different relationships and interactions with the global expanding governance into more local arenas, starting from amorphous commodities through to individual intellectual creative endeavors.

To examine boundaries in a global setting, an important field to draw on is geography because the field itself 'was founded as a tool for exploration of the globe, largely to support the needs of Western imperialism' (Murray, 2006: 21). Conceptualizing boundaries from a geographical orientation enables one to take a different direction and expansion to develop the dynamic conflicted nature of boundaries from multiple perspectives. By defining a boundary as a contested space between actors, the research agenda expands to account for the complexities of competing powers that seek to reconfigure boundaries and sustain temporal resolutions. In proposing this definition of boundary, the three interlinked components – space, power and time – require further clarification.

First, regarding space as existing between places, I start with Entrikin (1991: 16) who describes places as 'significant not because of their inherent value, but rather because we assign value to them in relation to our projects'. The projects of organizations have an assigned value that often revolves around maximizing economic well being. Boundaries exist at the margins of organization places of value. The space between places with differently assigned values depending on the actor's position becomes a contested one because of both ambiguity and conflict regarding which places' values prevail. An example of the space between places lies with borderlands, where sovereign boundaries are drawn but the point at which one sovereign state ends and another begins is an ambiguous space. For organizations, the space between where the organization ends and the environment begins is even more ambiguous. Membership in organizations with an outsourced function entails even greater ambiguities that are constantly renegotiated on a legal as well as on a daily basis. By accepting a space between the organization and the environment, the once invisible nature of boundary can come into sharper relief to explicitly surface the complexity of issues existing in the boundary space. Previous research on organizational boundaries related to membership and institutional filters is embedded in the idea of boundaries as contested spaces, because members from different places interact at the boundaries to establish their own platforms of legitimacy, control and interpretation.

Second, competing powers account for previous notions of roles, activities and spheres of influence in the degree of conflict and extent of engagement between unequally positioned actors. Both Oliver (1993) and Santos and Eisenhardt (2005) address the issue of power within the role of boundary spanners and how their influence shifts depending on contingent variables. Their reviews outline how the purpose of the power of boundaries is employed to reduce uncertainty and improve performance by buffering and bridging to protect the core functions of organizations. The existing difficulty of the current view of boundary power is the oppositional perspective from the organization's point of view, looking outward. This somewhat ignores the multiple complexities of the historical context of power accumulation among the actors to construct their boundaries and to supplant prevailing views while delimiting others in the same moment. But within boundaries as spaces, roles evolve within a context and through a series of activities that seek to influence spheres beyond each actor's place, and the meaning assigned to roles is likely to evolve throughout a complex series of trajectories of multiple interactions. Positioning in geographical places often endows actors with the power to exercise their role and sphere of influence at the boundaries that need to be acknowledged as part of unraveling the complexities.

Last, in addition to space and competing power in the proposed boundary definition, the third component is the temporal dimension of momentary resolution. When boundaries are considered during a specific period in time, they appear static, natural, and taken for granted, as is the case with most organization theory research on boundaries. Without inquiries into processes of how and who creates, reconfigures and dissolves boundaries, the scope of understanding such a central phenomenon constrains our broader understanding of organizations. Boundaries are mutually constructed by actors, however unbalanced in their power to influence, to meet particular social, cultural, economic and political conditions. Changing circumstances tend to challenge prevailing meanings of established boundaries and may require different ones.

The current trend of globalization expanding into increasing arenas of the local sphere over the last two decades has involved dramatic changes around the world with even more to come. The boundaries of globalization shifted from the multilateral agreement with GATT to the formalized institution of the WTO that not only expanded from indistinguishable commodities to arenas as unique as intellectual property and services but also consolidated power among members with relatively greater market power. Institutionalizing globalization meant increasing access into expanded arenas of the member countries. Yet as the expanded boundary impact of globalization unfolded into the different arenas, growing objections starting as isolated voices from disparate groups began to coalesce into a unified mosaic that attempted to push back the boundaries of globalization.

High profile global organizations such as Nike, Dell, eBay, and Wal-Mart have created global business models with outsourcing, network organizational structures, virtual organizations, supply chains, and the contingent labor force. The established concepts of boundaries in organization theory only elucidate part of their development. Most of the boundary concepts were based on monolithic organizations within stable environments. There was little need to address complex evolutionary processes of blurring and shifting organizational boundaries. Hence, in an environment of globalization, a focus on boundaries that examines the dynamics in the space where actors engage at global–local interfaces enables the use of a more comprehensive lens to account for the multiple realities that shape boundaries over time. The exercise of power among multiple actors has a very instrumental role in shaping and reconfiguring boundaries that appear to become ambiguous and hence blurry in the moment. By accounting for the temporal dimension, examining boundaries helps to untangle some of the complexities concerning what boundaries are created or shifted; what is driving the change; how they are evolving; and who are the stakeholders involved. Many of the deeper issues in these questions are beyond the scope of this chapter because the focus here is to expand the scope of boundary as an organizing concept.

The integration of space, power and time in a definition of boundary enables exploration of its dynamic and complex nature in a global context. Boundary as contested space between actors with competing powers to establish and sustain momentary resolutions addresses the dynamics of blurring boundaries. Discussions in the next section provide specific examples of how the proposed definition can assist in investigating and analyzing boundaries. The three cases of nation-state, intellectual capital, and e-commerce illustrate how the proposed definition of boundaries applies as an organizing mechanism for future research.

THREE CONTESTS OF BOUNDARIES

The following three contests of boundaries are minimalist sketches over broad swaths of histories and disciplines. The purpose is to focus on investigating the concept of boundary to examine how organizations manage boundaries to engage in globalization processes as well as how globalization processes shape organizations and their boundaries. Boundaries play a central role in each case. The types of boundary differ in each context but they are interrelated in terms of their contested space, competing powers and momentary resolutions.

Contesting Boundaries of Nation-states

Inherent in the rise of the modern nation-state is the conscious drawing of explicit formally recognized boundaries by multiple actors to separate one sovereign state from the others. Nation-state boundaries date back to 1648 with the Treaty of Westphalia, which established the function of sovereign rights over geographical locations in Europe to end 30 years of war. As a new concept of governing at the time, 'powers that were previously dispersed are now centralized; the very character of the modern state is historically unique' (Seidman, 1994: 296). The idea of nation-state severed the connection between religious and territorial control as well as fragmenting indigenous cultural communal structures in deference to relatively distant political systems. European imperialism furthered the diffusion of sovereign states around the world, which gave rise to the current system of international order. 'The drawing of state boundaries had the effect of creating national consciousness through exclusion' (Blake, 2005: 20). The exclusion

eroded established governance systems such as monarchies, tribal communities, feudal systems, and various indigenous communal systems. Over the
next three and half centuries, immeasurable numbers of lives were lost and
incalculable damage laid waste to many communities as a result of wars
that were fought in order to draw some of the nation-state boundaries. In
an apt comparison to organized crime, Tilly (1985) described how state
making asserted control over land, and then required resources to support
a military that could protect it and expand into more territory. In turn,
more military were required to protect the expansion and more resources
required to support the military. The difficult process of creating nation-
states continues to this day, as in the example of Tibet. The United Nations
provides the broadest forum for 192 nations to gather with the most recent
addition of Montenegro as a sovereign state in June 2006.

In a comparison of sovereign territories and boundaries between Europe
and Africa, Asiwaju (2005: 124) states that '[i]n Europe, as in colonial and
post-colonial Africa, state territories and boundaries share an essential
arbitrariness in their creation and their locally felt artificiality'. The stark
difference between the two was who had the power to create the boundaries. Colonial powers drew political boundaries in Africa with little regard
for existing indigenous cultures, socioeconomic patterns and ecosystems.
Chatterjee (1993) describes how anti-colonialist nationalists constructed
their own sovereign domain within the colonial society before engaging in
conflict with the imperial powers. His study of Indian society provides an
example of who has the potential power to recreate boundaries.

In the postcolonial period, many commentators refer to the same
boundaries as the source of contemporary political problems, crises and
wars in Africa. Compared to the European countries, the African nation-
state boundaries are relatively more entrenched, with central control and
greater distinction between nation-states. The existing political boundaries
in Africa demonstrate how problematic they can become when accepted
without questioning their existence, which in turn continues to reconstitute
their rigidity. From an organizational perspective, boundary spanners
such as foreign ministers perpetuate their sovereign boundaries with their
boundary spanning activities such as buffering and bridging with outside
constituents.

Creating boundaries is often a problematic process that may involve
long drawn-out conflicts such as the ones between Israel and Palestine,
India and Pakistan, North and South Korea, Turkey and Syria, Northern
and Southern Ireland, and Iraq and Kuwait. The boundary space is literally a contested one with military interventions. No clear line marks the
boundary. It is usually a space referred to as the borderland where conflicting engagements happen in a localized space, perpetuated by a distant

capital. The results of such conflict may include a substantial borderland zone for a boundary that is tens of miles wide.

Nation-states provide an important case to understand boundaries because the separation of nation-states entails a contested space that involves competing powers to create and establish boundaries. Sovereign contexts impact the development of boundaries in other arenas such as intellectual capital and e-commerce. Most nation-state boundaries are relatively stable and often taken for granted once they are created. The legitimacy of nation-state boundaries is based on a people supported in their quest for self-determination in a governing process until such time as challenges arise to question the legitimacy of these boundaries and seek to re-establish new ones. Today, about 70 dependent states continue to seek nationhood status.

Within the trend of increasing globalization, the current challenge to the boundaries of nation-states is the question of their relevance. Richardson (1990: 2) states that the 'concept of national sovereignty is being submerged by the flow of financial transactions and information exchanges which diminish the relevance of national boundaries'. Leading authorities in political science argue that clear demarcations between national and international relations and between domestic and international politics are increasingly outdated in a global age (Milner, 1998; Risse et al., 1999). The drive toward globalization by TNCs challenges the fundamental role of nation-states to provide for its citizens. Many TNCs have control of resources and revenues that surpass the size of many small states. The nation-state boundaries may not be able to rein in the influence of TNCs on a nation's citizenry because substantial resources can be brought to bear to override local objections. Computer and Internet technologies, telecommunication and transportation innovations enable the compression of space and time, which raises questions about the relevance and power of nation-states. Ohmae (1990) constructed one extreme image with the borderless world, which means the separation of sovereign states is somewhat meaningless in a global economy. He referred to strategic alliances between the metropolitan centers of the USA, the EU and Japan as primary launching positions for rapid deployment of competitive initiatives around the world and into the secondary markets of South America, Asia and Africa. The dismantling of trade barriers facilitates such mobility for business enterprises, and at the same time diminishes a fundamental organizing principle of the nation-state which is self-determination for its members.

In sum, activities of TNCs raise questions and challenge the relevance of nation-state boundaries to politically refashion regulatory regimes that facilitate trade flows. Few nations can resist or restrict the influence of TNCs within their boundaries. While TNCs are a strong force, an informed and organized citizenry can engage in acts of protests and resistance against the global imposition on the local. Korten (1995: 140) describes the actors with competing powers as 'the greater the political power of corporations and those aligned with them, the less the political power of the people, and the less meaningful democracy becomes'. Thus boundaries associated with nation-states are contested spaces where boundary definition, permeability and interpretation stem from local actions (governments and citizenry groups) in response to global processes (TNCs and associated foreign governments).

Contesting Boundaries of Intellectual Capital

Sovereign boundaries create meaning in conjunction with many other multilayered and hierarchical boundaries such as those related to knowledge, property, membership, social and racial identities, community, and so on. Establishing boundaries to construct modern nation-states needed the Enlightenment project, which entailed constructing boundaries to centralize decentralized knowledge dispersed in communal relationships and practices. Contesting the boundaries of intellectual capital centers on whether the project of Enlightenment with the social sciences is a humanitarian force to combat bigotry, fanaticism, corruption of excessive power of the church and the state or is an ideology of social progress. Hence, contesting boundaries would be used to justify domination and colonization of the 'undisciplined savage' lying outside the bounds of a rational social design. Between the two perspectives, a complex range of issues arise from different societal and industry sectors. Within the context of the modern nation-state system, boundaries of intellectual capital already excluded knowledge from local traditions, indigenous peoples, and non-Western communities as it was considered backward, primitive, superstitious and non-scientific.

Numerous barriers and infrastructures are drawn around what are considered relevant locally acceptable knowledge and ways of knowing. The assertions of such boundaries are manifested in established structures such as school walls and fences, grading and evaluation processes, educational degrees and certificates, titles of 'Dr' or 'Chief Learning and Knowledge Officer', and accreditation by institutions and agencies. The process of accumulating scientific knowledge has enabled the rise of experts who become documented with legitimacy through different institutional processes and designations. They become knowledge keepers and legitimating authorities to manage and control boundaries concerning requirements in educational curriculums, legitimate socially educated behaviors with rewards or punishments, and most importantly, governance structures and regulations of property rights including intellectual property. In addition to formal education, industries create a host of certification programs with hierarchical boundaries that sanction levels of expertise. In particular, the IT and healthcare industries offer a complex array of certification programs to recognize workers' legitimacy for certain knowledge tasks. Practitioners of traditional Chinese medicine whose knowledge is handed down through the generations would be excluded by external legitimating infrastructures.

Reich (1991) described a class of workers as symbolic analysts who engage in intellectual work such as problem identification, problem solving, experimentation, collaboration, and so on. The boundary identified by Reich and others who discuss knowledge workers has explicit separation from communities who are engaged in the same activities but without an externally validated formal educational infrastructure. Boundaries around experts, symbolic analysts and knowledge workers specifically focus on the Western scientific paradigm to the exclusion of many intellectual traditions (Ani, 1994). The scientific method rose to determine objective truth, which drew a boundary to exclude and dismiss non-scientific knowledge (Bauman, 1992). Hence, intellectual capital became the accumulation of expert knowledge that supported the development, management and legitimacy of the modern nation-state by gathering, organizing and disseminating information through various institutions such as schools, prisons, healthcare agencies, factories, and local and state agencies.

An important regulatory mechanism of the nation-state centers on boundaries for property rights including intellectual property with trademarks, copyright and patent laws. The principle of copyright law is for the 'encouragement of learning', and dates back to 1710 during Queen Anne's reign. In the USA, the 'encouragement of learning' principle is based on the rationale that profit is the primary motive for producers to search for and disseminate knowledge. Intellectual property rights, primarily driven by Western interests, are articulated and regulated through the WTO's Trade-related Intellectual Property (TRIP) agreement. In 1996, the World Intellectual Property Organization (WIPO) was created as one of 16 specialized agencies of the United Nations to help implement TRIP. The first two initiatives in 1998 and 2001 focused on helping developing and least-developed countries to conform to TRIP's intellectual property regulations.

Within the context of globalization, localized knowledge in traditional practices surfaced as having potential market value in the global marketplace. Resources and research scientists are deployed for scientific investigation and empirical determination for scientific goodness of fit and global dispersion within the global free trade infrastructure. As 'experts', researchers determine the scientific legitimacy of local traditional knowledge and then managers follow to create the business case for the global marketplace. Coupled with capitalist enterprises, intellectual property rights evolved to extract value for the producer where consumers require economic resources to gain access to intellectual property and in some instances, to regain access when a TNC asserts control over indigenous intellectual capital through patent regulations. Hence, the coupling of scientific knowledge and global economics acts to create boundaries around intellectual capital by disconnecting it from original sources for global dispersion.

The boundary becomes another contested space where the accumulation of intelligence and knowledge for market value conflicts with the creation of an informed and enlightened citizenry for self-determination within a nation-state. While the global market and self-determination may complement each other for international entrepreneurial activities, contested terrains and tensions arise when a citizenry faces restricted access to intelligence in order to make informed decisions and act in their own self-interest and well-being. Numerous examples exist that relate to environmental degradation and pollution, poorly informed consumer use of products and services, and political events. One of the most famous cases is Nestlé's baby milk formula being marketed to mothers in developing countries. More recent issues include genetically modified organisms in agriculture, nuclear testing by France in the South Pacific during the 1990s, and the US war on terror.

In sum, intellectual capital boundaries support complex structures to manage and control economic exchanges in the global market. The contested space centers on the legitimacy of knowledge and ways of knowing that support a TNC's ability to identify and detach knowledge from sources for distribution. Competition between different actors takes place within a regulatory framework established by the WTO and implemented by TRIP. While industry sector issues are negotiated by trade ministers from different countries, the overarching framework already established the foundational infrastructure that allows for the temporary resolution or stability of the regulatory boundaries. Gaining agency for resistance to challenge boundaries of intellectual capital will need to take place on multiple fronts to rebalance the intent of intellectual property rights for the 'encouragement of learning' versus the 'enforcement of global markets'. One access point of intervention could be in the contested spaces of e-commerce.

Contesting Boundaries of e-Commerce

The image of Ohmae's borderless world resonates almost naturally in cyberspace where information technology enables virtual organizations to conduct business in a seemingly frictionless fashion through time and space. Dismissing the idea of boundary almost eliminates the need for any further consideration of its related issues, especially when common rhetoric expounds on being able to connect and do business anytime, anywhere in the world. The basic idea of e-commerce is the conduct of business activities through information and communication technology (ICT) networks. Dutta (1997: 61) defined e-commerce as 'the sharing of business information, maintaining business relationships, and conducting business transactions by means of telecommunication networks'. However, boundary issues are significant concerns in e-commerce and they unfold on multiple levels that are interrelated to one another. E-commerce boundaries could be as prominent as the digital divide or as innocuous as spyware filters for protecting computers. The dissolution of geographical boundaries maybe simultaneously replaced by boundaries of preferences on different dimensions such as social, intellectual and economic, with the potential to be even more insular (van Alstyne and Brynjolfsson, 2005).

A prominent e-commerce boundary centers on the digital divide that refers to the bifurcation between the haves and the have-nots of ICTs. Research findings indicate that the diffusion of ICT on a global basis has a growing gap in the digital divide and that factors other than the state of economic development contribute to the growing trend. As of March 2006, North America had 68 percent population diffusion of Internet use, amounting to 22.2 percent of total usage in the world; Oceania/Australia had 53 percent population diffusion, amounting to only 1.7 percent of use in the world; Europe had 36 percent population diffusion, amounting to 28 percent of use in the world; Latin America/Caribbean had 14.4 percent population diffusion, amounting to 7.8 percent of use in the world; Asia had only 9.9 percent of the population diffusion, but makes up the largest portion of the world's Internet use at 35.6 percent (www.internetworldstats. com). In addition to economics, social factors such as political stability and the absence of violence, adult literacy, urbanization, and the popularity of television media have contributed to social learning processes that enable the diffusion of ICTs within nation-states (Liu and San, 2006). The social factors are often a complex array of interconnected forces. As a consideration, political instability pits different community factions against one another, which may lead to armed conflict that disrupts educational and media infrastructures as well as causing the migration of people. The physical development of ICT systems and the engagement of Internet users are not possible in such volatile contexts. However, the digital divide encompasses many other contested spaces that include struggles of class, race, age, education, and political systems. Hence, boundaries as contested spaces in the digital divide are social and economic composites that construct the access and distribution of necessary resources for the diffusion of ICTs and engagement in e-commerce.

The actors of competing powers in the digital divide are not Internet users versus non-users. Instead, the actors are the constituents who take up different positions in a contested space such as to provide computers for all students versus acquiring textbooks. The actors involved may include administrators, teachers, parents, students, textbook publishers, computer firms and professional staff members. The momentary resolution in the contested space determines which side of the digital divide the students will be situated. Yet, the digital divide is just one boundary set in e-commerce.

The context of nation-states shapes not only the digital divide but also the boundaries of e-commerce itself. Bingi et al. (2000) examined challenges to global e-commerce on four different dimensions – economic, social, technical, and legal. The nation-state has a strong influence in shaping the environment on all four dimensions. In addition to the intellectual infrastructure that contributes to regulating property rights over information as discussed above, sovereign states affect e-commerce by developing regulations concerning privacy, cyber crimes, technological developments, taxation, legal validity of transactions, and policing e-commerce conduct. While e-commerce may transcend time and geographical space, the lack of uniform international standards for e-commerce and different national infrastructures impose substantial obstacles to achieving expected and projected potentials of e-commerce (Frynas, 2002). ICTs like many technological innovations often move faster than socio-legal systems in creating the regulatory boundaries. Hence, boundaries as a contested space in e-commerce will likely continue to be ambiguous for the near future as various regulatory issues are debated through courts and different legislative systems across and within nation-states.

Organizations are the primary drivers of global e-commerce activities. The blurring of firm boundaries stems from evolving organizational design and structure with outsourcing, strategic alliances, network structures, supply chain management, and virtual organizations. The term 'post-Chandlerian firm' refers to the combined process of outsourcing some activities while increasing in-sourcing of other activities (Robertson and Verona, 2006). As a result, the impact of technological change, especially ICTs, may have conflicting outcomes for firm boundaries.

Cooperative firm partnerships in e-commerce take place at the level of intersecting firm boundaries. The contested space centers on developing viable economic interfirm relationships based on trust (Ring and Van de Ven, 1992) which is fundamentally a human endeavor that is more socially than economically or technologically based. The challenges to developing trust in virtual relationships of e-commerce stem heavily from a limited communication channel without the traditional rich non-verbal cues in face-to-face interactions. However, successful virtual organizations have managed to overcome obstacles in interfirm relationship development. The struggles in some cooperative firm partners lie in ambiguous boundaries. While moving forward into collaborative partnerships, managers engaged in creating trust must also guard against unwanted bleed through of competitive information and practices to partnering firms. Various computer security systems create safeguards with pre-approved access, firewalls and passwords to prevent unintended leakage of information. But they are not always foolproof and without established trust in the boundary spaces, competing actors may act in their own self-interest at the expense of their partner firms.

Global e-commerce influences organizational behavior within firms too. Two important considerations for e-commerce in overcoming geographical distance are boundaries related to the bounded rationality that limits human capacity for information processing (Simon, 1957), and the satisfaction of specialized preferences where local heterogeneity gives way to virtual homogeneity (van Alstyne and Brynjolfsson, 2005). Specialization allows for deeper development of expertise in a subject matter but the challenge is being able to reconnect into the larger scope of organizational operations. Boundaries of e-commerce within firms impact the workforce in different arenas that may include automated supervision, training and development, and the integration of work–family activities (e.g. when work is taken on vacation with access to emails) (Perlow, 1998). The contested space is work performance – where and when work gets done in conjunction with other spheres of life activities. ICTs allow for telecommuting but this diminishes serendipitous conversations by the water cooler and social contacts. Actors engaged in competing powers here may be found in a hierarchy of managers–employees and peers, where the span of control increases as a result of automation and peer oversight in addition to managerial oversight. E-commerce allows for more feedback loops from peers to impact the work space. Within organizations, the momentary resolutions in establishing boundaries in e-commerce are paradoxical in the sense that employees have many choices as to how to complete work but work has also encroached on many other aspects of their life because people can connect easily from many places 24/7. Thus work has a greater dominance in life, and organizational practices with ICTs enable greater monitoring and control over work.

In general, boundaries in e-commerce are very dynamic on multiple levels. While e-commerce on the surface appears to eliminate sovereign boundaries and geographical space, a critical factor is that new boundaries are being created in both the cyber space of e-commerce and the business context within which the e-business is taking place. Sovereign boundaries matter greatly in the borderless world of cyberspace. As some boundaries are dissolved, the focus needs to be on what boundaries are being constructed and at what level they are being imposed.

A PAUSE FOR REFLECTION

Boundaries in the current context of globalization are actually more important than prevailing rhetoric and belief about a borderless world. An important shift is from a static to a dynamic perspective of boundaries as illustrated by how boundaries related to nation-state sovereignty, intellectual capital and e-commerce matter more than ever. Furthermore, the boundaries in each forum are interrelated to the boundary sets in the other two forums. Boundaries in the nation-state construct the context of support and enforcement to develop intellectual capital and e-commerce. However, feedback loops from e-commerce activities and new frontiers in intellectual capital require nation-states to respond with configuring new boundary sets and/or revising established ones. While existing boundaries are questioned and debated concerning their relevance, the key lies in what new boundaries are created, defined and drawn. Determining new or altered boundaries is part of the precursor for developments that happen between two places or state of existence. As old boundaries are dissolved or dismantled, new boundaries are often simultaneously erected to reflect the positional powers of competing actors in a contested space.

The hope of this chapter is to expand the notion of boundary beyond a static and taken-for-granted phenomenon to include the dynamic chaotic processes of contestation in a space that is generated by competing actors in an era of rising globalization. While unequal distribution of power among the actors creates contests that are not fair, the layers of justifications and contradictions can still be brought forth for questioning with the possibility of redrawing boundaries. Globalization does not need to be accepted wholly as an inevitable process with its existing boundaries.

The pause for reflection in place of a conclusion here is to keep open this work in progress to explore future possibilities in recreating, redefining and reconstructing boundary studies as a dynamic globalization process.

REFERENCES

Aldrich, H. and D. Herker (1977), 'Boundary spanning roles and organization structure', *Academy of Management Review*, **1**: 217–30.

Ancelovici, M. (2002), 'Organizing against globalization: the case of ATTAC in France', *Politics and Society*, **30**(3): 427–63.

Ani, M. (1994), *Yurugu: An African-centered Critique of European Cultural Thought and Behavior*, Trenton, NJ: Africa World Press, Inc.

Asiwaju, A.I. (2005), 'Transfrontier regionalism: the European Union perspective on postcolonial Africa, with special reference to Borgu', in H.N. Nicol and I. Townsend-Gault, *Holding the Line: Borders in a Global World*, Vancouver, BC: University of British Columbia Press, pp. 119–41.

Bauman, Z. (1992), *Intimations of Postmodernity*, New York: Routledge.

Bingi, P., A. Mir and J. Khamalah (2000), 'The challenges facing global e-commerce', *Information Systems Management*, **17**(4): 26–34.

Blake, G. (2005), 'Boundary permeability in perspective', in H.N. Nicol and I. Townsend-Gault, *Holding the Line: Borders in a Global World*, Vancouver, BC: University of British Columbia Press, pp. 15–25.

Chatterjee, P. (1993), *The Nation and Its Fragments: Colonial and Post-colonial Research*, Princeton, NJ: Princeton University Press.

Cox, J. and D. Jones (1999), 'The weird jamboree: teamsters and turtle protectors on the same side', *USA Today*, 1 December.

Dunning, J.H. (1995), 'Reappraising the eclectic paradigm in an age of alliance capitalism', *Journal of International Business Studies*, **26**(3): 461–91.

Dunphy, D. (1987), 'Convergence/divergence: a temporal review of the Japanese enterprise and its management', *Academy of Management Review*, **12**: 445–59.

Dutta, A. (1997), 'The physical infrastructure for electronic commerce in developing nations: historical trends and the impact of privatization', *International Journal of Electronic Commerce*, **2**(1): 61–83.

The Economist (1997), 'The century the earth stood still', *The Economist*, **345**(8048): 65–7.

Eisenstadt, S.N. (1973), *Tradition, Change, and Modernity*, New York: John Wiley.

Entrikin, N.J. (1991), *The Betweenness of Place: Towards a Geography of Modernity*, Baltimore, MD: Johns Hopkins University Press.

Frynas, J.G. (2002), 'The limits of globalization – legal and political issues in e-commerce', *Journal of Management History*, **40**(9): 871–80.

Galbraith, J. (1973), *Designing Complex Organizations*, Reading, MA: Addison-Wesley.

Gilmore, T.N. (1982), 'Leadership and boundary management', *Journal of Applied Behavioral Science*, **18**(3): 343–56.

Hedley, R.A. (2002), *Running Out of Control: Dilemmas of Globalization*, Bloomfield, CT: Kumerian Press.

Hernes, T. (2004), 'Studying composite boundaries: a framework of analysis', *Human Relations*, **57**(1): 9–29.

Kellner, D. (2002), 'Theorizing globalization', *Sociological Theory*, **20**(3): 285–305.

Kellogg, K.C., W.J. Orlikowski and J. Yates (2006), 'Life in the trading zone: structuring coordination across boundaries in post-bureaucratic organizations', *Organization Science*, **17**(1): 22–46.

Klein, R.W. (1973), 'A dynamic theory of comparative advantage', *American Economic Review*, **63**(1): 173–84.

Korten, D.C. (1995), *When Corporations Rule the World*, West Hartford, CT: Kumarian Press.

Leifer, R. and A. Delbecq (1978), 'Organizational/environmental interchange: a model of boundary spanning activity', *Academy of Management Review*, **2**: 40–50.

Levine, S. and P.E. White (1961), 'Exchange as a conceptual framework for the study of interorganizational relationships', *Administrative Science Quarterly*, **5**: 583–601.

Liu, M. and G. San (2006), 'Social learning and digital divides: a case study of internet technology diffusion', *Kyklos*, **59**(2): 307–21.

Luo, Y. (2001), 'Toward a cooperative view of MNC–host government relations: building blocks and performance implications', *Journal of International Business*, **32**(3): 401–19.

March, J. and H. Simon (1958), *Organizations*, New York: John Wiley & Sons.

Miller, J.G. (1972), 'Living systems: the organization', *Behavioral Science*, **17**: 2–182.

Milner, H.V. (1998), 'Rationalizing politics: the emerging synthesis of international, American, and comparative politics', *International Organization*, **52**(4): 759–86.

Murray, W.E. (2006), *Geographies of Globalization*, New York: Routledge.

Murtha, T.P. and S.A. Lenway (1994), 'Country capabilities and the strategic state: how national political institutions affect multinational corporations' strategies', *Strategic Management Journal*, **15**: 113–29.

Newman, D. and A. Paasi (1998), 'Fences and neighbors in the postmodern world: boundary narratives in political geography,' *Progress in Human Geography*, **22**(2): 186–207.

Nicol, H.N. and I. Townsend-Gault (2004), *Holding the Line: Borders in a Global World*, Vancouver, BC: University of British Columbia Press.

Ohmae, K. (1990), *The Borderless World: Power and Strategy in an Interlinked Economy*, New York: Harper Business.

Oliver, C. (1993), 'Organizational boundaries: definitions, functions, and properties', *Canadian Journal of Administrative Sciences*, **10**(1): 1–17.

Perlow, L.A. (1998), 'Boundary control: the social ordering of work and family time in a high tech corporation', *Administrative Science Quarterly*, **43**(2): 328–57.

Reich, R. (1991), *The Work of Nations: Preparing Ourselves for 21st Century Capitalism*, New York: Alfred A. Knopf.

Ricardo, D. (1963), *The Principles of Political Economy and Taxation*, Homewood, IL: Irwin.

Richardson, (Hon.) E.L. (1990), 'Introduction', in R.T. Moran (ed.), *Global Business Management in the 1990s*, Washington, DC: Beachman Publishing, pp. 1–8.

Ring, P.S. and A.H. Van de Ven (1992), 'Structuring cooperative relationships between organizations', *Strategic Management Journal*, **13**(7): 483–98.

Risse, T., S.C. Ropp and K. Sikkink (eds) (1999), *International Human Rights Norms and Domestic Change*, Cambridge: Cambridge University Press.

Robertson, P.L. and G. Verona (2006), 'Post-Chandlerian firms: technological change and firm boundaries', *Australian Economic History Review*, **46**(1): 70–94.

Rosenkopf, L. and A. Nerkar (2001), 'Beyond local search: boundary-spanning, exploration, and impact in the optical disk industry', *Strategic Management Journal*, **22**(4): 287–306.

Santos, F.M. and K.M. Eisenhardt (2005), 'Organizational boundaries and theories of organization', *Organization Science*, **16**(5): 491–508.

Seidman, S. (1994), *Contested Knowledge: Social Theory in the Postmodern Era*, Cambridge, MA: Blackwell Publishers.

Shamir, B. and Y. Melnik (2002), 'Boundary permeability as a cultural dimension: a study of cross cultural working relations between Americans and Israelis in high-tech organizations, *International Journal of Cross Cultural Management*, **2**(2): 219–38.

Simon, H.A. (1957), *Models of Man, Social and Rational*, New York: John Wiley & Sons.

Spencer, G.H. and D.C. Heinze (1977/78), 'The testing of three dimensions in organizational space', *Organization and Administrative Sciences*, **8**(4): 145–54.

Thompson, J.D. (1962), 'Organizations and output transactions', *American Journal of Sociology*, **68**: 309–25.

Thompson, J.D. (1967), *Organizations in Action*, New York: Macmillan.

Tilly, C. (1985), 'War making and state making as organized crime,' in P. Evans, D. Rueschemeyer and T. Skocpol (eds), *Bringing the State Back In*, Cambridge: Cambridge University Press.

Tushman, M.L. and E. Romanelli (1983), 'Uncertainty, social location and influence in decision making: a sociometric analysis', *Management Science*, **29**(1): 12–23.

van Alstyne, M. and E. Brynjolfsson (2005), 'Global village or cyber-balkans? Modelling and measuring the integration of economic communities', *Management and Science*, **51**(6): 851–78.

Williamson, J.G. (2006), *Globalization and the Poor Periphery Before 1950*, Cambridge, MA: MIT Press.

www.internetworldstats.com, accessed 29 June 2006.

Yan, A. and M.R. Louis (1999), 'The migration of organizational functions to the work unit level: buffering, spanning, and bringing up boundaries', *Human Relations*, **52**(1): 25–47.

5. (How) Does knowledge flow? A critical analysis of intra-organizational knowledge transfer

Raza Mir, Subhabrata Bobby Banerjee and Ali Mir

In this chapter, we argue that the discourse of knowledge transfer in organizational studies fails to record the manner in which this transfer is implicated in the historical experiences of power differences and economic imbalances that undergird the international encounter. The chapter draws on an empirical study of several months conducted by the first author in India, an ethnographic examination of the work practices of the subsidiary of a large US-based multinational corporation (MNC), which we have named Chloron Corporation.[1] This chapter is a story of our attempts to make sense of the sea of data collected during this endeavor, through the analysis of a single episode of knowledge transfer.

The rest of this chapter is organized in three sections. In the first, we critically survey the representations of knowledge transfer in organizational research. We then present empirical research conducted at Chloron, to highlight the complete disjuncture between the theoretical descriptions of knowledge transfer and the empirical realities of corporate experience. In the final section, we theoretically analyze the research vignette to arrive at a different approach to knowledge transfer than that of mainstream research.

KNOWLEDGE TRANSFER AND ORGANIZATIONAL RESEARCH: A CRITICAL ASSESSMENT

The notion of organizational knowledge continues to be avidly researched in organizational theory (Coff, 2003; Rico et al., 2008; Sutcliffe and Weber, 2003). Of particular and continuing interest to organizational theorists is the study of the transfer of organizational knowledge (Tsang, 2008), specifically the transfer of relatively ambiguous knowledge across international boundaries (Inkpen, 2008), and even more particularly those regimes of knowledge transfer that occur within the boundaries of a specific firm (Monteiro et al., 2008). One of the biggest challenges for management theorists has been to offer an acceptable yet comprehensive definition of the term *knowledge*. Knowledge has been variously defined as 'information whose validity has been established through tests of proof' (Liebeskind, 1996: 94), as 'justified true belief' (Nonaka, 1994: 15), and in several other broad ways. In one of the more comprehensive definitions Davenport and Prusak (1998: 5) define it thus:

> Knowledge is a fluid mixture of framed experience, values, contextual information, and expert insight that provides a framework for evaluating and incorporating new experiences and information. It originates and is applied in the minds of knowers. In organizations, it often becomes imbedded not only in documents or repositories but also in organizational routines, processes, practices, and norms.

From this definition, a number of issues are immediately discernible. For one, knowledge is conceptualized as a higher order construct, one that involves an element of *judgment*. Also, the definition captures the dynamic character of knowledge, as a construct that is fluid. In other words, knowledge management by organizations would usually entail an explicit commitment to valuing fluidity, which is perceived as being incompatible with bureaucratic inflexibility.

It is also evident from the definition that knowledge is produced in individual minds. Consequently, much of the challenge of knowledge management has been to create processes whereby this individual knowledge is transformed into social knowledge (or appropriable corporate knowledge). The discourse of knowledge creation often is framed in terms of 'value', or its ability to deliver rent for the organization. Second, knowledge can provide value only if it is communicable across the organization (Bierly and Chakrabarti, 1996). This communicability across geographic boundaries is predicated on its codifiability, and its routinization, or at least an understanding of which elements of it can be codified and routinized, and which of them cannot. Finally, knowledge has been depicted as a construct that epitomizes the boundaries of the firm. It confers organizational identity on workers, and is the basis for an organizational culture and tradition (Bhagat et al. 2002). In other words, it has been argued that firms exist primarily because they are able to transfer knowledge within their boundaries.

One significant aspect of this research is that knowledge, which had hitherto been defined as a public good, is now being redefined as a *commodity*. If competitive advantage is seen as the construct that exists at the heart of a firm's performance (Porter, 1985: xv), knowledge is now perceived as the most dependable way to create and sustain this competitive advantage (Zack, 1999). Knowledge transfer has not only been subjected to theoretical examination, but has also been empirically measured (Poppo and Zenger, 1998).

Over the past few years, organizational theorists have been advancing the idea that the firm's entire identity should be based on the fact that it is an efficient carrier and distributor of knowledge (Teece et al., 1997). Despite occasional opposition from proponents of more traditional theories of the firm (Foss, 1996), these theories have found favor in organizational research. In particular, they are applied to MNCs (Inkpen and Beamish, 1997), and suggest that the inefficiencies of trade across geo-political boundaries can be transcended by a large, spread-out organization, which can then be a conduit for knowledge flows.

The arguments for the knowledge-based theory of the firm have traversed two distinct paths. The first view contends that 'firms exist because they provide a social community of voluntaristic actions that are structured by organizational principles that are not reducible to individuals' (Kogut and Zander, 1992: 384). Firms, they contend, derive their superiority over markets as a consequence of to their ability to offer 'higher order organizational principles' to their constituents. These higher order principles comprise 'shared coding schemes', 'values', and a 'shared language' (Kogut and Zander, 1992: 389).[2] Kogut and Zander (1996: 503) go on to suggest that 'a firm be understood as a social community specializing in the speed and efficiency in the creation *and transfer* of knowledge' (emphasis added).

The second path attempts to develop a reason for the firm that is independent of opportunism. These theorists point toward a variety of inter-firm and intra-firm transactions that are not dependent on opportunism, but are more dependent on flexibility, communication and learning (Conner and Prahalad, 1996). Significantly, they base their theory of the firm on a dynamic, flow-related concept, which they term the 'knowledge-substitution effect', which implies that firms exist because unlike in markets, knowledge flows within their boundaries can be taken for granted, and do not have to be forever renegotiated.

One could briefly summarize all the available theoretical positions on knowledge and the firm in the following 10 points:

1. Knowledge is now considered the most strategic resource of organizations (Zack, 1999).
2. Knowledge originates and primarily resides in the mind of individuals (Davenport and Prusak, 1998).
3. The challenge for organizations is to turn individual knowledge into social (organizational) knowledge (Nonaka, 1994).
4. Firms are the most efficient entities to coordinate such tasks (Hedlund, 1994).

5. There is a clear distinction between 'tacit' knowledge and 'explicit' knowledge. Tacit knowledge is often not totally expressible by the possessor of this knowledge (Cohen, 1998; Polanyi, 1966).
6. Just as individuals know more than they can say, there is more to organizations than their contracts. To understand knowledge, we need to re-evaluate our theories of the firm (Kogut and Zander, 1993).
7. Knowledge is usually embodied in organizational routines (Nelson and Winter, 1982).
8. In order to transfer knowledge, it needs to be codified. However, the more codifiable the knowledge, the easier it is to imitate. This is a very important challenge for organizations (Zander and Kogut, 1995).
9. The absorptive capacity of the recipient unit in organizations is a key contingency in knowledge transfer (Zahra and George, 2002).
10. Motivational and dispositional issues at the level of the source unit can affect knowledge transfer (Szulanski, 1995).

However, one must remember that such representations of knowledge transfer, if deployed unproblematically, tend to valorize the upper echelons of the corporation without ever examining the role played by lower level constituents (Huzzard, 2001; Marshall and Brady, 2001). Moreover, they conceive of organizational processes as moving toward a singular goal, thereby denying conflicts in the organization. To that end, such research is worthy of critique for 'universalizing sectional interests', or placing the interests of certain organizational subgroups (usually capital market stakeholders) as the interests of the firm itself (Shrivastava, 1985). The irony of theoretical representations of knowledge in the literature emerges precisely from the reality that in spite of a purported spectrum of theories addressing the issue of organizational knowledge, a consensus appears to emerge on the default assumptions of all theories, indicating that strategy scholars have dealt very similarly with the issue. This isomorphism stems directly from their reliance on an extremely reductive understanding of the concept of knowledge.

For example, consider knowledge-based theories that divide knowledge into two binary categories – tacit/explicit, procedural/declarative, or individual/collective or technical/mental (Chua, 2001). Typically, theorists who make this separation follow it up by representing declarative or explicit knowledge as relatively uninteresting from a research perspective, choosing to focus on the procedural or tacit dimension. Such parsing of the construct of knowledge into these specific categories is neither useful, nor indeed, innocent. This practice denies the reality that those who perform lesser, menial tasks are as implicated in the knowledge transfer process as organizational strategists and top managers. For instance, the transfer of declarative knowledge, a category that strategy researchers tend to dismiss as an unhelpful case of repetitiveness, forms the basis of 'the practice of everyday life' (de Certeau, 1984). It is this dull performativity that is the building block of discourse. It is only through these mundane routines, through the performance of routine tasks, through the storage and retrieval of unassuming documents in overflowing cupboards and hard drives, through conversations and meetings that subjects, cultures and discourses emerge, and create 'communities of practice' (Latour and Woolgar, 1986). As Becker (2001) has pointed out, while tacit knowledge has been the primary focus of research, the 'dispersedness' or distributed nature of knowledge has received less attention. The dispersedness of knowledge is identified as a significant economic problem because the division of labor is normally accompanied by a corresponding division of knowledge (Hayek, 1945; Tsoukas, 1996). One consequence of this is acknowledging the limits to the centralization of knowledge and that it is simply not possible to collect dispersed knowledge and manage it to achieve some organizational goal (Hayek, 1988).

Non-mainstream researchers of knowledge transfer have indeed picked on this aspect. As Tsoukas (1996: 14) suggests, 'to split tacit from explicit knowledge is to miss the point – the two are inseparably related'. In his analysis of the work of a stock controller in a warehouse (a rather mundane task, which would scarcely interest strategy theorists), Vickers (1983) suggests that even these mundane actions are part of a complex organizational grammar, which the stock controller learns performatively and through reference to organizational context. In other words, even simple acts such as updating organizational ledgers, sending routine messages, adhering to routine deadlines and such should be considered discursive practices. After all, those of us engaged in the performativity of organizational activity are agents, or 'subjects of representations; representations about the world outside and depictions of ends feared or desired' (Taylor, 1992: 49). This point is underscored by Alvesson and Kärreman (2001) in their critique of the 'ontological incoherence' of knowledge management where knowable objects can only exist as knowing subjects, thus creating confusion.

On examination of the various theoretical positions in organizational research that analyze the concept of knowledge, the following lacunae in the field are apparent:

1. A focus on 'procedural/tacit' knowledge at the expense of 'declarative/ explicit' knowledge does not allow us to adequately understand the 'performance' of knowledge-based routines in complex organizations. Despite the claims made by Nonaka and Takeuchi (1995), all tacit

knowledge cannot be converted into explicit knowledge (Tsoukas and Vladimirou, 2001).

2. Despite acknowledging the social character of knowledge transfer, organizational researchers continue to anchor their studies in individualist and cognitivist theories of knowledge. This functionalist perspective views knowledge as a discrete commodity and fails to recognize the continuous 'transformation and reconfigurations' that knowledge is subjected to (Lanzara and Patriotta, 2001).

3. If we place the resurgence of knowledge-based theories in context, we can see that there is a certain linkage between global macro-economic and political development and the development of knowledge-based theories. Such an act of contextualization is rarely attempted in the field (Banerjee, 2003). As Thompson et al. (2001: 928) point out, theories of knowledge management involve codifying and abstracting knowledge from workers thus enabling a rationalization of work that 'functions as a source of legitimacy and power for managers'.

4. There are several elements of the power relationships between nation states that underlie this knowledge flow. The acceleration of knowledge transfer across national boundaries is directly related to the exercise of power on 'recipient' nation states by those countries whose corporations constitute the sourcing of foreign direct investment (Keren and Ofer, 2002), and are mediated through international regimes such as the World Trade Organization (WTO) (Mir, 2001). However, none of this complex debate ever finds space in theories of knowledge transfer within organizations.

INTRA-ORGANIZATIONAL KNOWLEDGE TRANSFER: BETWEEN AUTHORITY AND DIALOGUE

In this section, we attempt to foreground some alternative theories of intra-organizational knowledge transfer, by presenting the results of an inductive ethnographic study conducted at the Indian subsidiary of Chloron, a large US-based MNC.[3] It is important to remember that the research presented herein is not meant to reflect an authoritative account of the goings-on at Chloron, or in MNCs in general. Rather, it represents our attempt to make sense of the sea of data collected during the research, and our political act of 'narrativizing' experiences within the contingent and colligative bounds of a 'story'. As Patriotta (2003: 350) argues, the received view of knowledge as a discrete, transferable commodity has resulted in the 'progressive consolidation of a managerialist epistemology' with its corresponding methodological choices. Our approach is consistent with Patriotta's call for a phenomenological approach to organizational knowledge, one that relies on the 'analysis of everyday organizational discourse as instanced by the construction of narratives in the workplace' (Patriotta, 2003: 350).

As the historian Sudipta Kaviraj (1992: 38) notes, 'the interstices of every narrative are filled with semblances rather than truth. Thus, the telling of true stories in history would not rule out the telling of other stories different from the first, which are also true.' However, we believe that this story is as authoritative as the mainstream accounts of knowledge flows in MNCs as alternative stories of knowledge transfer (e.g. Schulz, 2001; Tsai, 2002; Zander and Kogut, 1995). Indeed, we believe that this account provides an important counter-narrative. This alternative historicizing is a way of restoring the balance, and remaining true to what Gadamer (1975: 267–74) has referred to as 'the principle of effective history'.

Background

Chloron is one of the leading manufacturers of over-the-counter pharmaceutical products and consumer products in the world, with annual revenues in excess of $50 billion. It operates in over 100 countries, and its Indian subsidiary has been operational for over 50 years. It first began operations in India as an exporting house, and built its first Indian manufacturing plant in the 1950s. It was incorporated as a stand-alone corporation under Indian statutes in the late 1960s, and its shares were quoted on the Indian stock exchange. However, after the mid-1990s, these shares were no longer traded because Chloron-India was now fully owned by its parent company.

Chloron-India was designated as a 'fully integrated operating subsidiary', which meant that it manufactured most of the products needed for the domestic market in-house. It owned three manufacturing facilities, and also used around 20 third-party manufacturing locations in India. Outsourcing was a recent aspect of Chloron-India's business, since it was only since 1992 that MNCs had been allowed under Indian Company law to use contract-manufacturing facilities. This also explained the nature of Chloron-India's existing manufacturing operations. In two plants, they had the hardware necessary to manufacture over 25 products. Most of these facilities were far smaller in scale than Chloron as a corporation was used to, and therefore the cost of manufacture in those facilities was much higher. The stated objective of Chloron-India was to turn its manufacturing plants to large-scale facilities for a few strategic products, and outsource the manufacturing of many of their less critical products to contractors, which explained their growing interest in the Indian subsidiary.

Chloron-India was now a fully owned subsidiary of the parent corporation;

a recent development. A discussion of the context in which it became a fully owned subsidiary is important. Given the prevailing political and legal conditions in India in the past, only 39 percent of Chloron-India had been owned by the parent organization until 1995, and it operated as a 'stand-alone' business until 1995. This was primarily because India's Foreign Exchange Regulations Act (FERA) had stipulated various constraints on the investment of foreign exchange in the country; one of which had been that no foreign entity could hold more than a 40 percent stake in its Indian subsidiary. The rest of the equity had to be drawn from local investors. As a consequence, Chloron had relied on a variety of Indian entrepreneurs to provide the other 60 percent. Thus, the transformation of Chloron-India from a stand-alone corporation to a subsidiary was itself an artifact of globalization.

Beginning in 1991, the Indian government began an extensive project of liberalization, which, among other things, led to the relaxation of FERA (Chandrasekhar and Ghosh, 2002), making it possible for corporations like Chloron to increase their stake in their Indian operations. By 1995, Chloron had bought up all the available equity in its Indian operations, turning Chloron-India into a wholly owned subsidiary. The corporation then began an extensive reorganization process, where the accounting systems of the subsidiary were restructured to mirror the corporate structure. My research at Chloron-India coincided with a transition period, where the globalization of the subsidiary was underway, but incomplete.

Chloron-India had annual revenues of around $50m, which was very small by the standards of other national subsidiaries, but was growing at a rate of around 25 percent per annum, which was high by Chloron's standards. It employed around 1000 fulltime workers in its plants, offices and the sales force.

Enterprise Requirement Planning: A Story of Knowledge Transfer

It is extremely frustrating. Here is a perfectly serviceable UNIX system, which we have to dismantle and install this @#$% AS400 system. I could accept it if we were going to put in a much better system, like SAP or PeopleSoft's ERP. But now, in this day and age, we have to learn to use mainframes, when Springfield[4] itself has declared that it will phase out the AS400 by 2003. Our UNIX system is similar in architecture to the new system they have planned for the organization. So we are working to put ourselves back from 2000 to 1985! By the time we learn AS400 operations, we would have lost all our knowledge of distributed computing, and will have to go back with a begging bowl to Springfield, asking them to train us in networking and ERP. (Vijay Tendulkar, GM, Information Technology, Chloron-India)

The above quote represents a particularly poignant illustration of the absence of 'dialogism' in the knowledge transfer process. First, the story in brief. For a variety of political and contextual reasons,[5] Chloron-India had not been able to install the Enterprise Requirement Planning (ERP) system deployed by Chloron at the corporate level in the 1980s. Deprived of this centrally available knowledge, the subsidiary had developed an innovative system based on locally available hardware and software, which performed the ERP job adequately, and produced information in a format that was compatible with the requirements of headquarters. Now that the political constraints on hardware import had been lifted, Chloron-India was facing pressure from headquarters to change over to the centralized ERP system, at great capital and learning cost. The frustration embodied in the quote by Vijay Tendulkar arose from one important factor: the ERP system that Chloron-India was expected to install had itself been declared obsolete by headquarters a year ago. Now that the IT community was migrating from mainframe-based systems to distributed, networked and server-based systems, Chloron had embarked on an ambitious program to overhaul its corporate ERP system to a distributed system, albeit in a phased manner.

The new system proposed by headquarters for eventual global adoption ironically possessed many characteristics that were similar to the ones possessed by the *current* system at Chloron-India. However, the corporate IT team felt that it would be too long a wait if they let Chloron-India change over directly from its current system to the proposed future system, a process that could take 3 years. In the interim, they decided to make a change to the mainframe-based system right away. In effect, the headquarters decision to change the ERP system was pushing Chloron-India from the future into the past!

Tendulkar was particularly bitter because he felt that there were no institutional avenues by which he would be able to represent this information to headquarters. For one, as a 'promotee-manager', with a less-than-stellar educational background and a shaky command of English, he had been excluded from many of the interactions that Chloron-India's top managers had had with visitors from headquarters. For another, his boss Pinchoo Kapoor, the CEO of Chloron-India, was known to be more of a 'headquarters-man' than a champion of local initiative, having been transferred recently to Chloron-India as an explicit 'agent of globalization', presumably to counter the relatively intransigent stands taken against the headquarters by his predecessor. According to Tendulkar, Kapoor could scarcely position himself as an objector to the process:

> he makes constant speeches about how we should not be 'resistant to change'. He has been reprimanding people who do not keep the mission statement framed on their office walls. He is not going to go to Springfield (Chloron's headquarters) and say that we will not listen to their order.

Ultimately, as researchers, we were able to document the manner in which the new/older ERP system was installed in Chloron-India. Tendulkar was given the unenviable job of seeing this operation through, while simultaneously, S. Padmanabhan, a young MBA from an elite business school was appointed to an Asia-Pacific team that was drawing up a blueprint for the migration of Chloron's ERP systems to the distributed model by 2004. It was a matter of common knowledge in the corporation that Padmanabhan was being groomed to succeed Tendulkar as the GM of MIS at Chloron-India.

Of the many instances of knowledge transfer that we observed at Chloron-India, we have chosen to foreground the above incident because it fleshes out the manner in which the process of communication between the headquarters and the subsidiary is inflected with authority rather than persuasion, of a univocal rather than a dialogical process, and of an isolated rather than a contextual interpretation of organizational reality. We found Tendulkar to be almost like the figure of Oedipus in the Greek tragedy, whose will was completely subordinate to the determinism of circumstances, and who was doomed to participate in his own impending annihilation. Padmanabhan, on the other hand, found the position assumed by Chloron headquarters acceptable, despite its authoritarian streak. He found it convenient and expedient to accept their line lock, stock and barrel, because it suited his personal interests, and because in his worldview, he was more predisposed to see a global logic to it.

As a rhetorical device, we have structured the rest of this story as a set of two monologues, by Tendulkar and Padmanabhan. We must stress that these are not their actual words, uttered in sequence.[6] We have spliced these monologues together from observations of Chloron-India's operations at the headquarters, the plant, branch offices and the operations of Chloron-owned computer systems, conversations with people across the hierarchy of Chloron-India as well as with overseas visitors, and by reading various internal and confidential reports on the subject. This 'Rashomon' of interpretations gives us a clear idea of how different subjectivities in an organization tend to view the same phenomenon, and says much about the knowledge transfer process.[7]

*   *   *

Tendulkar's View

In early November last year, I was called into Mr Kapoor's office. He showed me a memo from Mike Clemente, the head of global IT. The memo said that our current computer system was unacceptable, and that we should consider using the system that was now in place at Springfield. 'What do you think?' he asked. I honestly thought that Mr Kapoor was asking me for my opinion, and since Mr Clemente also had only asked us to 'consider' the system, I was frank. I told him that this would be a foolish move. The corporate system runs on IBM AS400s, which are obsolete machines. Our UNIX-based system may not be state-of-the art, but it is actually much better than Springfield's system, and actually more suitable for future upgrades. The whole world is now going in for networking and there is no need to go back in time and get ourselves a mainframe-based data processing system.

Mr Kapoor began to get angry with me. 'The problem with you, Tendulkar, is that you are afraid of change. But I am not. Let me tell you that this is not [the old CEO's] time. You cannot begin every conversation with a "no" and get away with it! If we are to grow in today's environment, we will have to learn to look at markets in terms of regions, and not nations. We are not an Indian company; we are the Asia-Pacific subsidiary of a global company.'

I was puzzled. I said to him, 'Mr Kapoor, I am not disputing what you are saying. I am only giving you technical feedback. You can ask others as well. And anyway, Springfield has only asked us to "consider" it. What is the harm in giving them feedback?'

'You do not know how to interpret these messages,' Mr Kapoor said. 'This is a direct order.'

I knew then, that our goose was cooked.

In the next month, Mr Kapoor attended a strategy meeting at Lake Tahoe in the USA, and came back with the news that the mainframe system had been approved. He asked me to make an appropriation request. I hated the title he used for it; he called it the 'Chloron-India computerization project'. He was behaving as if we were not computerized already! My heart sank when I saw its scope. It involved the comprehensive computerization of all sites of Chloron-India in two phases. The first phase would encompass the financial module at the company head office, the distribution module at the Mumbai branch, and the manufacturing module at the Malegaon site. I was asked to install IBM AS400 computers and software at all these locations, which would be linked to one another through a communication network 'to provide a total integrated solution to our information needs'.

I was also extremely upset to read the budget figures. This project alone would end up costing over six times our entire annual MIS budget! Springfield was giving us nothing;[8] the entire cost was to be borne by us. Mr Kapoor told me that the project had been discussed with Mr Clemente during his last visit to India. The final blow to me was a statement co-signed by Mr Clemente and Mr Kapoor. 'The development of information systems at Chloron-India, both in terms of hardware and software, has been sporadic and need-based. It is essential that we change this into a total integrated approach across the organization. We believe that such an approach will significantly enhance our competitive advantage through speedier and actionable management information. We look forward to the installation of AS400s in India.'

I did not believe that the AS400 system was actually an 'integrated' one, or that it would make our operations speedier, but I had no option. As the head of IT, I had to spearhead this project. Now that the decision was taken, I decided to work on it in earnest. I put together my team, which consisted of seven of the best programmers and network managers we had. I was feeling bad, because I had handpicked these boys and girls. And if they continued to work on this project for 2 years, none of them would find good jobs in the market. After all, who wants to hire people with obsolete skills?

We worked hard on the project. You have yourself seen how we transmit the data now without much difficulty despite such limitations of the system. This was not an easy job. It is still a bit shaky, but in the beginning, it was worse. I remember how we used to work day and night. Even now, you were yourself here, and saw how all of us came even on Deepavali.[9] I had asked Mr Sidway if I could give my staff the day off on Deepavali. It is after all, a national holiday here, and everybody has religious functions at home. But he said, 'Our deadline here will be affected if you do not meet yours.' So we all came. Of course, when they have their holidays, we are automatically shut down. In late November, we had three days off because of Thanksgiving in the USA. This is our situation. We give thanks when corporate is thankful. Otherwise, our Deepavali remains thankless.

Anyway, when the first stage of the project had been conceptualized and the data flow had been modeled, we prepared a report that outlined the process for the installation of IBM AS400s in India, and invited Mr Clemente and Mr Jason Chow of Singapore to examine the proposal on site. Both came, along with Mr John Sidway and Mr Anthony Kwan of the Singapore Software Company that had written the software for the system. We went through the proposal in detail and also consulted the representatives of IBM in India. Our discussions in Mumbai ended with an uneasy feeling in my mind. When we met as a group at the end of the visit, I got the impression that although the plan was generally acceptable, the visitors were not comfortable with the installation of this system for manufacturing operations. Nobody, of course, said this in so many words. But I felt, if these guys themselves were so worried, we were going to have too many implementation bottlenecks.

To add to the above, I found out that IBM had come up with a new client-server hardware that Chloron Worldwide had adopted as a replacement for the very AS400 that they were making us 'consider'. I felt that even if we were to launch this new system, we should do so with the new server, at least it was more current. When I asked Mr Kapoor to raise it with the team, he was reluctant. Finally he raised it, but phrased it in a way that made my blood boil. He said, by way of preamble, 'we now need some firm advice on what we should do. To say that we are out of date with our computer systems is an understatement. It is obvious we will not be able to meet the future requirements of business and international reporting with systems that we have at the moment. We do not have the requisite expertise to take major decisions of this type, and we seek your guidance and through you, of the IT department of Springfield, about the next step to take.'

The response from corporate was typical. Mr Clemente sent an email report to Mr Kapoor saying that the problem was not with the hardware, but with us. He said that he was extremely unhappy with the proposal we had sent them, for it was too complex. He suggested that the computerization of our sites was not supportable by the current configuration. It would not be able to support so many facilities and so many production and distribution units at the same time. I could have told Mr Clemente myself that this system was inadequate. The only reason why I offered this proposal was because of the pressure that was put on me by my own CEO. In effect, he was blaming our operations because they were too complex for the reporting system. And I now realize why Mr Kapoor had 'generously' presented me as the author of the proposal, when I had not been involved at the system phase. So that when the shit hits the fan, I would be used as a scapegoat. There was nothing I could do. In any case, I reworked the proposal and emailed it to all the visitors who had come down and seen the first version.

After reviewing the new proposal, Mr Clemente suggested that I have it approved by the Singapore-based company that had written the software, to make the necessary modifications to support so many users and locations. He was understandably not equipped technically to evaluate our proposal, for our operations were far more complex than those at US, since the Malegaon site manufactured over 20 products, and no US site manufactured more than three.

I agreed to it, but also offered some suggestions of my own. Maybe we could begin by implementing the manufacturing module of the system, and persist with the local system for the financial and the distribution modules. That way, we would not risk overloading the system right away. Also, I mentioned that the telecom facilities in India were extremely underdeveloped and that should be taken into account as an important factor when designing the new system. I suggested this to Mr Kapoor, who finally saw the reasoning behind my suggestion and sent out a letter to Mr Clemente and Mr Sidway. He was promptly summoned to Springfield, and when he returned, he had bad news. Springfield had shot down our proposal. Mr Clemente claimed that it was unrealistic, that it was not cost-effective, and that we should hire a consultant to check into the matter.

At one level, I was relieved. While the new system was now delayed, at least we still had our UNIX-based stand-alone programs, which would do for now. I thought that if the consultant were a smart guy, he would see the logic behind what I had been saying. It would be better if they heard the story from a third party. For although there were real problems with the changeover, I had no credibility with Springfield. They would always behave as if I was resisting change, raising problems for the sake of stalling a perfectly good process.

The consultant arrived, studied the system, and made the exact recommendation that I had made to corporate. In his words on the memo, 'the manufacturing module should be delayed, and the finance and accounting modules should be the systems that are implemented initially. Given the tradeoff between the benefits it delivers and the constraints of the current telecommunication infrastructure in Mumbai, this would be a better place to test the system in India. I realize this is contrary to the thinking of the top management, but I feel that this is all the system should be burdened with for the time being.'

In the meantime, we received a quote from IBM for the AS400 system, which said that we should place an order for the hardware to be manufactured within 2 weeks. They said that if we failed to place the order, the next production run for AS400 would not take place for 12 weeks. This again, should give you an idea of how low the AS400 was in their manufacturing priorities! Then, I had an unexpected break! While our new proposal was being drafted, we received a sudden global note from Mr Steve Larson, the procurement head at Springfield, asking me to stall the entire project. A corporate decision had finally been made to move to an HP server as the preferred hardware, instead of AS400. Apparently, a new game plan was emerging for Chloron IT. You see, at the end of 1998, the old CIO at Springfield retired and Gary Lantz took over. Lantz had spent several years working for Sun Microsystems, and with his arrival, a UNIX-thinking came over Chloron. The corporation usually does an ABC analysis for its IT equipment. A are recommended items, B are items that should only be bought on a replacement basis, and C items are literally banned, for they are obsolete. Lantz had moved the AS400 from the B to the C list. I began to hope again. Maybe, instead of the AS400, we would get an upgrade to a Linux-based system right away.

Six months of planning for the AS 400 was going to be stalled. I felt a little angry at the wasted effort, but I also felt vindicated. I had been right all along. I have always told them that if we wanted to implement this system in India the way corporate wanted us, we would need six AS400s. That would be an impossibly high investment for our scale of operations. After all, our multi-facility operation was unique, and presented an open challenge to the computer system. My theory about why Mr Clemente and his team had pushed for the AS400 here is that when they heard of our earlier hardware, they though our operations were very basic. They could not realize how, in spite of our so-called confusing system, we had been able to innovate an extremely complex local system using older hardware, software, and competence that could outperform their system. Of course, they were not able to say that that this system could not work in India. So they said instead that Indian operations are screwed-up.

Unfortunately, my hopes were unfounded. The knowledge that India needs and can afford and can produce its own integrated system – such thinking will take a long time to trickle down. One day, I came to office and found an email from Mr Kapoor, where he had forwarded a message from Mr Lantz. Lantz basically said that he had approved the procurement of the AS400 for India on an exception basis, under advice from 'the Asia-Pacific team and the IT leadership'. Apparently, they had decided to go ahead with the system. Now, they planned to install the AS400 in India right away, and go for the distributed platform 3 years from now. Evidently, Mr Clemente had managed to convince Mr Lantz that we were OK in going ahead with the AS400-based system. I had finally lost.

Now the AS400 system is installed all over India. It is a slow and opaque system, and we constantly need to get upgrades from IBM. The company has stopped manufacturing the system, and we only get those pieces of hardware that are in their stock. The accounting and distribution modules are going to remain on the current system for a while. Now we are ninth in line as Asia-Pacific subsidiaries wait their turn to get an upgrade to Linux. Even then, we will have to work with the AS400s for a while. Only the finance module will be changed. The rest of the modules, God knows how long they will take.

What pains me is that we are again in the same boat that we were in 1995. The only difference is that while in 1995, there was a 'UNIX culture' in the IT department. By now, that competency has been eroded. In another year, it will be completely lost. Several old-timers have left, and the new people have worked only on an AS400 platform since their arrival here. We are becoming more and more backward. Linux and Windows XP have become the operating systems of choice all across corporate, but we still struggle with the AS400. I sometimes find it amusing. Mr Kapoor had been glad to pay the consultants who designed the project $1000 dollars a day to put this system into place. What he did not realize was that we are still paying for it.

* * *

Padmanabhan's View[10]

I am in charge of the Enterprise Requirement Planning project. I am truly proud of my position, because I am going to be an integral part of this company's future. UNIX was our past, the AS400 is our present, and SAP is its future. It is true that SAP is much closer to our older UNIX system from a programming perspective, but when we get it here, it will represent an important upgrade for us. I am so glad that I am not stuck with the AS400 system. The funny thing is, I think I was put on the SAP team after I had supported the AS400 project! When Mr Kapoor made it clear to me that we were going to go ahead with the project, and that he had agreed to Mr Clemente's suggestions, I decided to support it. No point in fighting losing battles like Tendulkar. His reputation now is one of a fighter against change. Why get saddled with that image? Frankly, I think it is time Tendulkar started mailing his résumé to recruiters. Once the AS400 project is wound up, he is not likely to have a job here.

I can say definitely that if I had been the decision-maker, I would never have purchased the AS400s. Between you and me, if I had been put on the AS400 team, I would be getting ready to post my biodata [mail my résumé] to recruiters right now. If Tendulkar had been given a free hand, we would have continued working with the existing older computers and then gone directly to networked 128-bit Pentiums running SAP. But unfortunately, because of the need for global standardization we had to go in for these AS400s, and we are not very good at using their system. New training, new hassles, it is all very dirty work. I am very happy that I was not sidelined into that project. Some of my colleagues now have to spend a lot of time getting trained on IBM AS400 machines. I think it is a very big waste of time. And if I was in their place, I would have really resigned and gone to another company. But I am doing very high-quality work here and it is very sad to see that the work they are doing will not really be of that much use in 5 to 6 years. But really, one must be practical. What is the point of fighting when corporate people like Mr Clemente, our big boss Mr Kapoor and the Asia-Pacific team, have all made a decision? It shows that Tendulkar does not understand human relations. He is too much of a technical man. He should have had an MBA like me, and he would have a better understanding of corporate culture.

Forget Tendulkar now; let me tell you about my project. SAP represents an important move for Chloron Worldwide. The entire information management division is now thinking of SAP as the ERP program of the future. It is as important as the transition we made from DOS to Windows. SAP is being tried out for the Consumer Division and the Asia-Pacific team is led by Shawn Wolf of IT Australia.

We are a group of 16 people – six of them are from the IM (Information Management) division. And the other ten are from various 'ops' – that is from sales, finance, from purchasing, from distribution, and from logistics. Nick Tallman, the Operations Director of the Asia-Pacific division, oversees the project. The world-famous consultants Elmer and Yardley (EY) guide this whole exercise. EY have pioneered an entire system by which a large and diversified corporation like Chloron can adopt SAP.

The first thing we plan to do when prototyping SAP in the chosen location is a Current State Analysis. In this process, what we do is document the 'As-Is'. We will then perform a Gap Analysis. It means we first develop what we feel are the ideal practices according to the ERP package. Then, we compare that with the existing practices and analyze what to do with the difference. Of course, there are a number of company-specific issues that one will have to incorporate. For example, if there are certain tax laws in a country that are different from others, we will have to write 'patch programs' to deal with that.

But, by and large, our team, in consultation with EY, is trying to develop a regional model of the ERP system that will work all across the Asia-Pacific region. In order to do that, we need top management support. Michael Miller himself – who is the boss of the Asia-Pacific region, heads the steering committee on SAP. Mike[11] has to authorize all company-specific requirements. And he does not agree easily to country heads that try to represent that a particular problem cannot be changed at the country level. So we do not plan to listen quietly if a subsidiary says a particular modification is necessary at their level. Our aim is to keep modifications down to a bare minimum, and have as uniform a system worldwide as possible. In fact, Mike will be making clear to the subsidiaries during the SAP project that he considers the number of modifications they request in the SAP project to be a good indicator as a resistance to change, and will not hesitate to report this information to corporate. That should slow down some of the demands on our team!

Standardization is the main objective of this process. EY plays a much wider role than you would expect from a traditional consultant. They are involved in the formulation of our entire strategy. We started the SAP project in July 1997. We will set up technological teams, infrastructure teams, and SAP expert teams everywhere. We will also give three sets of training to all personnel in the region. The first will be general overview training on SAP. The second will be more specific and will relate to how business practices will have to be changed as a result of SAP. The third training will be training with the actual configuration. We are also trying to go in for local language translation of some of the functionalities of the SAP program. We won't do that in India, because as you know, most of the Indian people are good at English. But we will be doing something similar in China.

In documenting current practices, we consider all subsidiaries in the Asia-Pacific region – that is the ASEAN subsidiaries, greater China, India, Japan, and Australia. Then we develop the regional model. And it has to be sold to the countries. The first implementation of SAP is scheduled to be in Hong Kong in the second quarter of next year. We in India had applied to be the company where the process would be initiated. We were hopeful that if we were selected, then we could bypass the AS400 installation altogether, and go straight from UNIX to SAP. But Springfield said that India would not be a good site for the first implementation for two reasons. First, we were too advanced in our understanding of UNIX and would, therefore, not be representative of the problems that may be faced in subsequent implementations. Second, because Indian operations involve the manufacture of so many products, that our complexity as a subsidiary would involve too much of a learning experience all at once. In a strange way, we got penalized for being too good! But I understand that for the global success of SAP, India must give up something.[12] And I am ready, especially since I am dealing with this future product.

Basically our job is much easier than what it must have been for the AS400 operators. We are finding that much of the standardization that we need in regional operations has already been done with respect to the AS400 project. Ultimately, AS400 has made all subsidiaries look the same from an ERP view. Only places like India are different. That was because India was not a global company, as it is becoming now.

One thing is certain, not everyone in the company reaps the benefit of standardization. In India, I feel that we will not get much benefit from standardization. But we have to do it because ultimately, corporate will benefit. The standardization process often makes all the products look exactly alike, so that they can be translated from one region to another. And we have so many products in India that are only suited to local markets, that we may lose the benefits of some of these products when we standardize. Also, standardization is best when coupled with automation. The more automated you are, the more the benefits of standardization. Compared to the other countries like Australia, we are not that automated. So the benefits of standardization will be a little low for us.

The SAP system has one major problem from the Indian view; it is too dependent on the system being up and running all the time. Once we go to SAP, if the phone lines are down, things will come to a grinding halt. And you know how bad the lines here are. In the earlier system, we had some backups, but in order to change the culture, it has been decided not to keep any backups to the SAP system. So, in order to be efficient, we literally have to build a parallel telephone exchange here! We already have a 256K leased line and we are asking for 1032K because once we go online, our data traffic to the Singapore server will become very high. We will become a subsidiary of Singapore, as well as Springfield! Also, since 1999, Chloron has developed an intranet system that connects 70,000 people. It is the default medium for financial reporting, application upgrades, everything. Unless we extend our telephone connectivity, we risk being completely shut out of the corporate intranet. In other words, we are out of the loop completely. I know the new infrastructure is costly, but in order to achieve full connectivity, we have to spend some money.

Soon, the SAP team is going to appoint a director of the software part, who will be in charge of Gap Analysis. That person is going to be selected from within the organization by EY themselves. I have been trying hard to get selected for that post. Mr Kapoor is supporting me. So even before I joined the international team, I have started some work. You saw yesterday how I had developed an in-house demo with payroll, with invoicing, with inventory planning, as well with international operations. Frankly, that model is the one we already have on the UNIX platform. The international team is unaware of it, because for 4 years, they have worked with an AS400 mindset. I, of course, have UNIX experience, so it is easier for me. All I have to do is to ask some of our people here to port the UNIX model on to a PC environment.

While the international team will have to change from an AS400 mindset to a distributed one, I have to make some key changes in my approach as well. Earlier, we at India always worked on a customization mindframe. So now it is a little difficult to change and I know I don't think of standardization all the time. Earlier the software we used, for example, was COBOL – which is not considered a very good piece of software, but which is very suitable for our activities. Even until 1991, we were COBOL-dominated. We had people with tremendous COBOL knowledge. And they can do so many interesting things with COBOL that the language does not look obsolete at all. It sometimes bothers me when the international team smirks when they find out that India is still using COBOL. But frankly, there is no need for me to defend a system that is earmarked for closure. I have to think ahead.

*   *   *

POURING TEA INTO A FULL CUP: AN ANALYSIS OF KNOWLEDGE TRANSFER AT CHLORON

Empirical research on knowledge transfer has tended to follow one of two assumptions. Either knowledge is perceived as flowing into a vacuum (Wheelwright and Clark, 1995), or it is depicted that knowledge flows play the role of agents of creative destruction, destroying old knowledge and replacing it with new (Dewar and Dutton, 1986; Tushman and Anderson, 1986). In this study, we have taken a more complex and contextualized view of knowledge, and attempt to move beyond these two perspectives. The focus of this analysis is to understand how the changes in organizational routines affect the lived experience of organizational members, and the troubled interactions between older and newer meaning systems.

'Knowledge flow' has been the term of choice used in strategy research to refer to various complex transfers of expertise in MNCs (Appleyard, 1996), but we find this to be a troubling legacy. The term 'flow' connotes the existence of a gradient, a movement that is natural, and involving a substance that is fluid. The *Merriam-Webster's Dictionary*[13] uses multiple terms to describe flow, such as 'to move', 'to proceed smoothly and readily', 'to have a smooth continuity' or 'to derive from a source'. Such descriptions exude a sense of desirability and inevitability that scarcely captures the complex, often coercive manner in which subsidiaries of MNCs are 'modified' according to the exigencies determined by their headquarters.

How then, does knowledge 'move'? Does it flow? If so, what furrows does it flow between, and what formulates the gradient of its flow? How is it stored after it has flowed? If it does not flow, what metaphors capture the dynamics of its movement? This metaphorical examination formed an extremely important cornerstone of our research.

In this analysis, we focus on three different elements of knowledge transfer that are relatively undertheorized in organizational theory, namely the coercive aspect of knowledge transfer, its failed attempt at achieving hegemony, and its relatively more successful attempts at creating an organizational subjectivity at the level of the subsidiary.

Knowledge Transfer and Coercion

Global change does not require so much a transfer of knowledge from one part of the globe to the other as it does the investment in different types of global dialogues that can create new knowledge contextualized in multiple sites. This requires investments in dialogues that can initiate localized creativity and imagination and foster newer meanings and texts. (Bouwen and Steyaert, 1999: 304–5)

The story of the 'upgrade' of Chloron-India from UNIX to AS400 offers us some important pointers. On one hand, we have the forces of globalization represented by Mike Clemente, the Singapore team, and partially, Pinchoo Kapoor and Padmanabhan, who force their logic on Tendulkar and his team. The absence of the dialogic process in this particular case is important. Padmanabhan is rewarded for his compliance, despite his off-the-record reservations. The executive team at India is used to apply pressure on Tendulkar. Interestingly, while Tendulkar is not fired, his punishment is very ironic and Sisyphean: he is forced to oversee the diminishment of his importance by giving him charge of the very process that he had opposed. While at times Tendulkar's position seems to find technological justification at the level of headquarters, the political process wins over the logic of technological rationality. We can only speculate about Tendulkar's assertion that the entire project was a case of escalated commitment based on Clemente's initial misreading of the complexity of Chloron-India's indigenous system, but it does seem quite clear that the process ran roughshod over local objections, which at times even found unlikely allies such as Kapoor himself.

In Padmanabhan's analysis of the situation, we can see the empirical representation of a corporate reality that the current theories of knowledge transfer are very well suited to describe. We have the consultant, the international team, the perils of standardization, the limits of absorptive capacity and infrastructure, cultural exchanges and a future focus. However, it is Tendulkar's story that is ultimately banished to the shadows of theory; the exercise of power, the loss of a valuable fund of local knowledge, and a subtle process of deskilling that is not even explored by labor process theorists.

The entire process of knowledge transfer at Chloron is of course driven by macro-economic changes. The intensification of Chloron's interest in its subsidiary, the changed ownership structure, and the facilitation of the integration of ERP systems through the re-entry of IBM (and the AS 400) into India are all artifacts of the triumph of globalization and neoliberal political reform in India (Chandrasekhar and Ghosh, 2002), which has radically different effects on the careers of Tendulkar and Padmanabhan.

Of particular interest to us in the above story are two quotes from Kapoor and Tendulkar that seem to be emblematic of a divergent understanding of globalization. The quotes are reproduced below:

> If we are to grow in today's environment, we will have to learn to look at markets in terms of regions, and not nations. We are not an Indian company; we are the Asia-Pacific subsidiary of a global company. (Pinchoo Kapoor)

> We give thanks when corporate is thankful. Otherwise, our Deepavali remains thankless. (Vijay Tendulkar)

It is interesting to juxtapose Tendulkar's sullen statement with the upbeat, yet measured and urbane statement made by Pinchoo Kapoor, the CEO of Chloron-India. Kapoor was indeed an urbane man. Educated in the prestigious Indian Institute of Management at Calcutta, he had spent two decades in the management cadre of Chloron. He had been rotated across several management functions and geographies, and his last stint was as the head of consumer marketing in Malaysia. He was an authority on teak furniture, and could speak informedly of the relative merits of French impressionist paintings and the Bengal school of paintings in India. And indeed, his statement could be incorporated seamlessly into such books on global corporations such as Kenichi Ohmae's (1990) *The Borderless World*. Postcolonial theorists have reflected on the emergence of the global subject among the third-world elite. From the perspective of postcolonial theory, we could make a linkage between this quote and another made over 200 years ago. Speaking in his capacity as the Legal Member of the Council of Indian Education in 1785, Lord Thomas Macaulay (Macaulay, [1782] 1972: 249) emphasized:

> We must at present do our best to form a class who may be interpreters between us and the millions we govern; a class of persons, Indian in blood and colour, but English in taste, in opinions, in morals, and in intellect. To that class, we may leave it to refine the vernacular dialects of the country, to enrich those dialects with terms of science borrowed from the western nomenclature, and to render them by degrees fit vehicles for conveying knowledge to the great mass of population.

Kapoor certainly fits the bill as one of the 'interpreters' in Macaulay's schema.

Tendulkar, on the other hand, was articulating his anger with Chloron in extremely local terms. For him, the peril of Chloron was that it devalued his local identity, which was expressed in this case as a religious affiliation. Thus Chloron's claim of being global rang hollow with him not just because he had to work on Deepavali, but also because of the Thanksgiving holiday he had to 'endure'. It appears that Kapoor, the global, postnational subject and Tendulkar, the local, national subject exist in uneasy proximity in Chloron-India. Globalization within Chloron, and indeed in all MNCs, is an extremely unfinished vision.

Knowledge Transfer and Hegemony

The absence of 'flow' in the knowledge transfer process at Chloron can be theorized thus: Modern complex organizations like Chloron are structured into hierarchies that create dominant and subordinate groups within the organization. The function of managerial practice is to exert control over the actions of the organizational subjects through the exercise of sanctioned power and dominance. This dominance is brought to bear through a combination of coercion and persuasion. Coercion refers to those managerial techniques that rely largely on overt supervision, surveillance and discipline. Persuasion, on the other hand, solicits the willful participation of its subjects.

We believe that we can make better sense of this idea by invoking the concept of hegemony (Gramsci, 1971; Guha, 1989; Williams, 1977). The analytical category of hegemony both includes and goes beyond the concept of ideology by pointing out that certain forms of dominance use persuasion over coercion in order to seek the active *consent* of the subordinate groups. This perspective allows us to understand that knowledge transfer can be better distinguished as a package of constitutive and constituting meanings, cultures and practices, which includes concessions by the headquarters that go beyond its own narrow and immediate interests. In a recent study of MNC–subsidiary relationships Geppert et al. (2003: 635) described the differences between 'home country rationalities' and 'host country rationalities'. They found that the global strategy of MNCs influenced decision making in host countries' subsidiaries by 'helping to shape local managers' decision-making power and resource dependencies'. Curiously, they did not attempt to frame this relationship in any theoretical framework of power; rather they chose to see the 'power resources' as 'contextual rationalities' that influence the formulation and implementation of global strategy.

The hegemonic project that undergirds knowledge transfer at Chloron does not dismantle the leadership of the dominant groups such as the managers at Springfield. However, it does manage to create a web of social relations, ideas and practices wherein some of the demands of the subsidiary (as articulated by Tendulkar's stubbornness) are met in the pursuit of a particular social order. While this order is maintained predominantly through persuasion, headquarters does not (and indeed, cannot) abandon its coercive apparatus. As Guha (1989) maintains, while steering us clear of this liberal-utopian conceptualization, hegemony is *a particular condition of dominance* where persuasion *momentarily* outweighs coercion. The concept of 'normative control' (Kunda, 1992) also appears to operate at Chloron, albeit with differing consequences for Tendulkar and Padmanabhan. As Kunda (1992: 11) argues, normative control is an attempt to direct the required efforts of members 'by controlling the underlying experience, thoughts, and feeling that guide their action. Under normative control members act in the best interest of the company not because they are physically coerced, nor purely from an instrumental concern with economic rewards and sanction.' Rather it is the particular type of subjectivities created that produce 'internal commitment' and 'strong identification with company goals' among employees. Both control and coordination are goals of MNCs that configure their relationship with subsidiaries. As Alvesson and Kärreman (2001: 1006) point out, these two modes of managerial intervention are enacted through social and technostructural mediums of interaction. At the social level MNCs attempt to exercise normative control ('prescribed interpretations') over their subsidiaries by persuading its employees to develop and sustain a distinct corporate identity (for example, Chloron's mission statement that says 'Powered by a diverse team of multi-talented people and technology, we strive to be a customer-driven, results oriented team'). At the technostructural level knowledge management becomes 'enacted blueprints' or 'templates for action' (Alvesson and Kärreman, 2001). This can occur through codification using information technology or personalization through normative control. At both social and technostructural levels, the aim is to increase the efficiencies involved in transforming inputs to outputs. However, as Alvesson and Kärreman (2001) argue, this often results in a loss of knowledge rather than a gain because of the reduced complexities, nuances and subtleties that are necessary for these efficiencies to occur. Thus, 'the technocratic and socio-ideological types of management are predisposed to operate in a way that eliminates and substitutes knowledge, rather than maintaining and creating it' (Alvesson and Kärreman, 2001: 1013).

Subsidiary responses to the regimes of empowerment therefore take forms that are subtler, even dialogical. Resistance to work practices often takes on a more passive, 'routine' dimension (Scott, 1985). Open confrontations are reduced, and replaced by 'subtle subversions', by acts of 'disengagement', and 'ambiguous accommodations' (Prasad and Prasad, 1998). For instance, instead of more confrontational practices such as work-to-rule, workers feign incompetence in carefully chosen arenas, thereby subverting organizational plans for a flexible workforce (Gottfried, 1994). For example, the invocation of the Deepavali festival by the workers under Tendulkar sent a signal to headquarters that while they would have their way, the disempowered employees at Mumbai neither appreciated having to work on their festival nor did they enjoy their day off for the US Thanksgiving. Headquarters had its way, but lost some of its legitimacy in the bargain.

A number of researchers have documented this phenomenon of how, in responding to large-scale organizational changes such as computerization (Prasad, 1992) or re-engineering (Diplock, 1997), workers periodically alter their level of enthusiasm for the process as a means of communicating their fears and expectations. Sometimes, workers in modern

organizational settings may play out their resistance through the invocation of ghosts, spirits, legends and religious deities (Ong, 1987). They
may choose to accentuate their separateness from the managerial class by
refusing to accept organizational gifts, thereby ceremonially disputing the
managerial posturing that there is more to the manager–worker relationship than a pact between wage and labor (Kondo, 1990). The everyday
relations at the workplace are the sites of class struggle, of alienation, of
the constitution of worker subjectivity, of the gendering of work and its
subversion, of intra-organizational bargaining, and sometimes of relations
of imperialism and cultural dislocation. In several instances at Chloron,
we encountered specific acts of resistance that were aimed primarily in this
direction – in that a number of employees as well as related groups such as
contractors and 'partners' at the subsidiary level engaged in acts that were
of minor consequence to the corporation, but were aimed at decentering
the legitimacy of headquarters in some small fashion.

Knowledge Transfer and the Organizational Subject

In the official narrative of knowledge transfer within Chloron, the corporation repeatedly utilizes the stubborn creativity of Tendulkar, but once it
becomes apparent that he is unprepared to become an ideal organizational
subject, he is summarily replaced in the organization by the savvy yet docile
Padmanabhan.

The loss of sovereignty by the subsidiary eventually leads it to a position
of submissiveness with respect to headquarters, exemplified by the willingness of Kapoor and Padmanabhan to toe the line of headquarters, even if
it does not tally with their convictions. Headquarters is able to microman-
age the subsidiary through the newer systems of control and coordination,
and is eventually able to make the subsidiary perform acts that are not
in its strategic interests, such as the case where Clemente and the global
team were able to use Kapoor as their agent to justify the AS400 project at
perhaps the most inopportune time, from the point of view of the Indian
subsidiary.

One of the important functions of the story of changing ERP routines
at Chloron is that it offers us a 'history of the present' and forces us to
ask: what are the modes by which Chloron tries to turn human beings
such as Tendulkar, Kapoor and Padmanabhan into 'subjects'? By way of
an answer, one could argue that relations of production operate within
a structure of relations of power. The stabilization of these relations is
effected through systems of signification. The project of knowledge transfer must be seen in this light, as a part of these systems of signification. For
example, the act of documenting manufacturing processes, of using outside

consultants to justify their actions, or even the acts of altering local reporting systems for global needs, can be viewed as systems of signification at Chloron.

Examining the knowledge transfer process at Chloron in isolation from an examination of the power differential between its headquarters and its Indian subsidiary that rendered it possible is disingenuous. It leads to a partial and a skewed analysis that runs the risk of leading us towards the unreflective celebration of knowledge transfer that has populated mainstream discourse. The value of our contextual analysis lies in its contention that the project of Chloron is concerned with the production of subjectivities at the subsidiary. This production creates a governable Chloron employee, and shapes their individuality in a new form that is determined by specific structures and patterns (for a theoretical elaboration of this point, see Dreyfus and Rabinow, 1982). Thus, by rewarding Kapoor and Padmanabhan, by punishing Tendulkar, by allowing Padmanabhan to take the credit for earlier UNIX-based achievements at Chloron, and by conferring on Tendulkar the dubious authorship of a document destined for failure, Chloron is undertaking the actual process of creating the governable Chloron-India employee, whose interests will mirror its own. Both the knowledge transfer process and the power differential between Chloron and Chloron-India simultaneously occupy a space within the discourse of organizational subjectivity, and headquarters, the subsidiary, and the larger institutions that create the ground for the unequal exchange between them, are all embedded within this discourse.

In an essay clarifying his reading of power, Foucault (1980: 222) writes that institutions bring the dual elements of 'tacit regulations and an apparatus' into play. In doing so, Foucault is pointing out the role of the creation of subjectivities in the process of governance, and the way in which the conduct of individuals is directed through both legitimately constituted forms of subjection and through considered and calculated modes of action intended to structure their actions. For Foucault, there is a reciprocal appeal in the relationship of power and the strategies of struggle. Relationships of power have the potential to generate an adversarial confrontation as well as provide a way in which the operations of the mechanisms of power can be put in place (Foucault, 1983: 114–18). Thus, when Tendulkar threatens to resign, Chloron does not throw him out, but rather brings an 'apparatus' of the manager/technical expert/consultant to bear in having its way. Similarly however, Tendulkar too does not always oppose Chloron through dissent, but sometimes through reference to contingencies, rules and 'logic'.

Knowledge transfer processes should not be dismissed easily by us either as innocuous processes by which MNCs coordinate mechanisms of efficiency, or contrarily as little more than a bald attempt by headquarters to exploit its subsidiary. It is true that some knowledge transfer routines may actually improve the quality of working life in the subsidiary. Indeed, these processes sometimes result in the improvement of the productivity and the quality of life of workers in the subsidiary in several instances, and at times, award them a certain role in the global decision making process. Also, many members of the subsidiary often support these initiatives both individually and collectively.

However, our empirical findings suggest that the discourse of knowledge transfer is incomplete unless we understand its consequences for the ongoing relationship between headquarters and the subsidiary. In order to do that, we have looked at the processes in a way that sees inanimate routines, but searches for, analyzes, and legitimizes signs of resistance as well as acquiescence, despair as well as eagerness. Mainstream representations of knowledge transfer often avoid the issue of resistance, constantly altering knowledge-based theories to suit the present exigencies faced by corporations. However, such theoretical work represents yet another part of a managerial device to recover the project of subjectification in different forms in response to continued dissatisfaction, alienation and, therefore, resistance at the lower levels of the organization. As Alvesson and Kärreman (2001: 1000) argue, knowledge can have negative and dangerous dimensions; knowledge can both enable and constrain and has 'the capacity to locate reality, to produce the institutions and subjects that it simply claims to describe and explain'.

The MNC often deploys the regime of knowledge transfer in an attempt to produce certain subjectivities. As a result, workers in these corporations do accept certain knowledge-transfer programs, and even demonstrate a significant degree of loyalty and commitment to their organization, thus imbricating their domain with that of the management. But as Hardiman (1996) points out, the operation of hegemony must be seen not just in the way in which some values are internalized as 'natural', but also in the resistance of subordinate groups. Persistent acts of defiance such as those by Tendulkar, and the inability or refusal of headquarters to abandon the right to control and police the subsidiary, all indicate that the hegemonic project is incomplete. The subject at the subsidiary level remains a contested domain. The failure of subjectification reflects not only a reluctance by headquarters to relinquish control but also a corresponding disinclination on the part of the subsidiary to fulfill its subjecthood. The endorsement of headquarter-supplied knowledge by people such as Kapoor and Padmanabhan, as well as the resistance of various people like Tendulkar to this knowledge, thus represents the resultant of various vectorial responses. On the one hand, we can surmise that knowledge transfer does work towards creating the governable subject at the level of the subsidiary. On the other, we can deduce that the partial sanction of this knowledge represents the subsidiary employees' partial attempts to accept this knowledge and these techniques only on their own terms. This equivocal position can perhaps be seen as a struggle for hegemony, a moment that highlights the contradictions of the organizational project.

These contradictions do not indicate that the project of subjectification in knowledge transfer is bound to be a failure. Such a claim would represent an impossibly optimistic illusion. The project of knowledge transfer and globalization proceeds, apparently inexorably. However, a critical analysis of this discourse tries in turn to articulate 'into a configuration different subjects, different identities, different projects, different aspirations' (Hall, 1990: 166).

CONCLUSION

As Stuart Hall (1990: 124) argues, in a power-laden dynamic, not only do material interests structure the dominant ideas of a particular culture, but also 'position in the social structure has the tendency to influence the direction of social thought'. Substitute the word 'organizational' for 'social' in the above quote, and we could well be summarizing the theoretical insights from this episode.

In this chapter, we have used the example of the power-laden and coercive character of knowledge transfer within an MNC to critique some of the celebratory and unreflective readings of this concept that populate recent organizational theory. We believe that the current framing of the theoretical constructs of 'knowledge' and 'knowledge flow' offer us no space to articulate the hybrid resistances that accompany knowledge transfer, especially among those who are the subjects of power.

It is important to reiterate that this study should under no circumstances be seen as a *repudiation* of the existing theories of knowledge transfer. Within corporations, the act of transferring expertise across divisions and geographies is often expedient and effective. Subsidiaries of corporations typically lobby headquarters to intensify the transfer process, and to be recipients of new knowledge. However, even while acknowledging this reality, this study seeks to highlight three elements of the process that have been curiously effaced by the generally accepted theories of knowledge transfer. First, for a variety of organizational subjects, the process is often inflected with coercion, and is devoid of dialogue. Second, the headquarters of the MNC attempts to render its perspective hegemonic, and passive resistance by the subsidiary continually subverts its attempt to achieve complete legitimacy. Finally, the success of intra-organizational knowledge transfer is predicated on the production by headquarters of the normalized organizational subject within the subsidiary, through routines of institutional and discursive control. The complete absence of any discussion of these elements in theories, accounts and empirical research studies of knowledge transfer also says much about the isomorphism that characterizes organizational theory.

It should be obvious that our own reading of knowledge transfer is not celebratory. We do not believe that these practices result in greater agency at the level of the subsidiary, nor do we think that the rhetoric of globalization, economies of scale and mutual benefits signals the advent of a more equitable or egalitarian MNC. On the contrary, these are mere catchphrases that try to refract contemporary work processes through an ideological lens and contribute to the hegemony, albeit contested, of a specific kind of corporate discourse. It is the responsibility of organizational scholarship to participate in the creation of counter-hegemonic discourses, to challenge sedimented wisdom and to subject the complacence of extant theorizations to critical scrutiny (Mir and Mir, 2002).

While many theorists have debated the phenomenon of knowledge transfer in the MNC, very few have addressed how these new imperatives of thought and action that constitute new knowledge are received in the terrain that constitutes the subsidiary of the MNC. It is easy to theorize that new knowledge flows into a vacuum of ignorance, but the reality is that there already exist complex and imbedded processes of learning at the subsidiary level, which new knowledges seek to displace. In the context of the proverb that we have used at the beginning of this section, this 'tea' is being poured into a full 'cup'.

In this context, therefore, we need a new research agenda in the field of knowledge transfer. Our new research questions may be articulated as follows: How are change demands communicated by headquarters of MNCs to subsidiaries? How are they internalized at the subsidiary level? How are they assimilated or resisted? More importantly, how do local interests hybridize, transform, and indigenize these alien demands so as to carve out a space of 'local' agency within the 'globalized' economy? And ultimately, what does this new story of knowledge transfer, of political economy, and the changing landscape of industrial accumulation have to offer to those researchers who try to write a different organizational theory, one that is sensitive to those subjectivities that are consigned to the periphery of mainstream organizing? Research that attempts to offer answers to these questions will be of great importance, and will join a small but growing body of research that offers a different understanding of organizations and their activities.

NOTES

1. The ethnography was supplemented with interviews of several executives of this corporation, and analyzed the data from a variety of documents, such as 'firewall-protected' FTP sites, public internet sites, internal memos, press releases and other public documents, and transcripts of executive speeches. Non-management labor and contract employees in this organization, trade union leaders and community activists were also interviewed. These data were juxtaposed with macro data on changing corporate laws in India and communiqués from trade federations and WTO representatives.
2. This idea is derived from the works of the sociologist Emile Durkheim, who while researching the loosening of human ties in modernizing societies, had suggested that 'since the division of labor becomes the chief source of social solidarity; it becomes, at the same time, the foundation of the moral order' (Durkheim, 1893, quoted in Kogut and Zander, 1996: 505).
3. In this chapter, we have substantially used material from two previously published works (Mir et al., 2008 and Mir, 2001), with permission from the copyright holders.
4. Springfield is the US headquarters of Chloron.
5. These reasons related to a policy of import-substitution adopted by the government of India in the 1970s, which led to the departure of companies like IBM from the country. IBM's AS400 mainframes were the systems on which Chloron's corporate ERP systems ran, and the absence of this key hardware led to ERP being unavailable in Chloron-India.
6. The following is a representation of research findings rather than a report on methodology. Our research followed the traditions of organizational ethnography (Kunda, 1992), including field notes, concept cards, semi-structured and unstructured interviews, thematic analyses, and follow-up of events over time.
7. The details described in the following excerpt may be a bit dense, but we feel that detail is necessary to convey the contestations that emerged around this system.
8. The choice of pronoun reflects the residual feeling (and the budgeting reality) that Chloron-India was a stand-alone company rather than an integrated subsidiary.
9. India's most important Hindu holiday, the equivalent of Christmas in importance.
10. It is important to contrast Padmanabhan's upbeat perspective, as well as his future-oriented project, with Tendulkar's sullen attitude and his dead-end assignment.
11. Padmanabhan's easy use of the informal first-name appellation contrasts with Tendulkar's relatively decorous forms of addressing his superiors.
12. Both Tendulkar and Padmanabhan come to the same conclusion. However, their attitudes to the result must be refracted through, among other things, their perceptions of their individual payoffs from the situation.
13. www.m-w.com.

REFERENCES

Alvesson, M. and D. Kärreman (2001). 'Odd couple: making sense of the curious concept of knowledge management'. *Journal of Management Studies*, **38**, 7, 996–1018.

Appleyard, M. (1996). 'How does knowledge flow? Interfirm patterns in the semiconductor industry'. *Strategic Management Journal*, **17** (Summer Special), 137–54.

Banerjee, S.B. (2003). 'Who sustains whose development? Sustainable development and the reinvention of Nature', *Organization Studies*, **24**, 1, 143–80.

Becker, M.C. (2001). 'Managing dispersed knowledge: organizational problems, managerial strategies and their effectiveness'. *Journal of Management Studies*, **38**, 7, 1037–51.

Bhagat, R., B. Kedia, P. Harveston and H. Triandis (2002). 'Cultural variations in the cross-border transfer of organizational knowledge: an integrative framework'. *Academy of Management Review*, **27**, 2, 204–21.

Bierly, P. and A. Chakrabarti (1996). 'Generic knowledge strategies in the U.S. pharmaceutical industry'. *Strategic Management Journal*, **17** (Winter Special Issue), 123–35.

Bouwen, R. and C. Steyaert (1999). 'From a dominant voice toward multivoiced cooperation: mediating metaphors for social change', in *Organizational Dimensions of Global Change: No Limits to Cooperation*. London: Sage, pp. 291–319.

Chandrasekhar, C.P. and J. Ghosh (2002). *The Market that Failed: A Decade of Neoliberal Economic Reforms in India.* New Delhi: Leftword Books.

Chua, A. (2001). 'Taxonomy of organizational knowledge'. *Singapore Management Review*, **24**, 2, 69–76.

Coff, R. (2003). 'Bidding wars over R&D-intensive firms: knowledge, opportunism, and the market for corporate control'. *Academy of Management Journal*, **46**, 1, 74–85.

Cohen, D. (1998). 'Toward a knowledge context: report on the first annual U.C. Berkeley forum on knowledge and the firm'. *California Management Review*, **40**, 3, 22–39.

Conner, K.R. and C.K. Prahalad (1996). 'A resource-based theory of the firm: knowledge versus opportunism'. *Organization Science*, **7**, 5, 477–501.

Davenport, T.H. and L. Prusak (1998). *Working Knowledge: How Organizations Manage What They Know.* Boston, MA: Harvard Business School Press.

de Certeau, M. (1984). *The Practice of Everyday Life* (Trans. S. Randall). Berkeley, CA: University of California Press.

Dewar, R.D. and J.E. Dutton (1986). 'The adoption of radical and incremental innovations: an empirical analysis'. *Management Science*, **32**, 11, 1422–33.

Diplock, P. (1997). 'Organizational change schemas: an empirical investigation of how health care managers make sense of organizational change', unpublished dissertation at the University of Massachusetts.

Dreyfus, L. and P. Rabinow (1982). *Michel Foucault, Beyond Structuralism and Hermeneutics.* Chicago: University of Chicago Press.

Foss, N.J. (1996). 'Knowledge-based approaches to the theory of the firm: some critical comments'. *Organization Science*, **7**, 5, 470–6.

Foucault, M. (1980). *Power/Knowledge: Selected Interviews and other Writings 1972–1977* (Trans. C. Gordon). New York: Pantheon Books.

Foucault, M. (1983). 'The order of discourse', in M.J. Shapiro (ed.), *Language and Politics.* New York: New York University Press, pp. 112–27.

Gadamer, H. (1975). *Truth and Method.* London: Sheed & Ward.

Geppert, M., K. Williams and D. Matten (2003). 'The social construction of contextual rationalities in MNCs: an Anglo-German comparison of subsidiary choice'. *Journal of Management Studies*, **40**, 3, 618–41.

Gottfried, H. (1994). 'Learning the score: the duality of control and everyday resistance in the temporary-help service industry', in J.M. Jermier, D. Knights and W. Nord (eds), *Resistance and Power in Organizations.* London: Routledge, pp. 102–27.

Gramsci, A. (1971). *Selections from the Prison Notebooks of Antonio Gramsci* (ed. trans. Quentin Hoare and Geoffrey Nowell Smith). New York: International Publishers.

Guha, R. (1989). 'Dominance without hegemony and its historiography', in R. Guha (ed.), *Subaltern Studies VI*. New Delhi: Oxford University Press, pp. 210–309.

Hall, S. (1990). *The Hard Road to Renewal: Thatcherism and the Crisis of the Left*. New York: Verso.

Hardiman, D. (1996). *Feeding the Baniya: Peasants and Usurers in Western India*. New York: Oxford University Press.

Hayek, F.A. (1945). 'The use of knowledge in society'. *American Economic Review*, **35**, 4, 519–30.

Hayek, F.A. (1988). 'The fatal conceit – the errors of socialism', in W.W. Bartley (ed.), *Collected Works*. Vol. 1. London: Routledge.

Hedlund, G. (1994). 'A model of knowledge management and the N-form corporation'. *Strategic Management Journal*, **15** (Summer Special Issue), 73–90.

Huzzard, T. (2001). 'Discourse for normalizing what? The learning organization and the workplace trade union response'. *Economic and Industrial Democracy*, **22**, 3, 407–31.

Inkpen, A. (2008). 'Managing knowledge transfer in international alliances'. *Thunderbird International Business Review*, **50**, 2, 77–91.

Inkpen, A. and P.W. Beamish (1997). 'Knowledge, bargaining power and international joint venture instability'. *Academy of Management Review*, **22**, 1, 77–202.

Kaviraj, S. (1992). 'The imaginary institution that was India', in R. Guha (ed.), *Subaltern Studies: VII*. New Delhi: Oxford University Press, pp. 1–39.

Keren, M. and G. Ofer (2002). 'The role of FDI in trade and financial services in transition: what distinguishes transition economies from developing economies?' *Comparative Economic Studies*, **44**, 1, 15–45.

Kogut, B. and U. Zander (1992). 'Knowledge of the firm, combinative capabilities, and the replication of technology'. *Organization Science*, **3**, 383–97.

Kogut, B. and U. Zander (1993). 'Knowledge of the firm and the evolutionary theory of the multinational corporation'. *Journal of International Business Studies*, **24**, 625–46.

Kogut, B. and U. Zander (1996). 'What firms do? Coordination, identity and learning'. *Organization Science*, **7**, 5, 502–18.

Kondo, D.K. (1990). *Crafting Selves: Power, Gender, and Discourses of Identity in a Japanese Workplace*. Chicago: University of Chicago Press.

Kunda, G. (1992). *Engineering Culture: Control and Commitment in a High-tech Corporation*. Philadelphia, PA: Temple University Press.

Lanzara, G.F. and G. Patriotta (2001). 'Technology and the courtroom: an inquiry into knowledge making in organizations'. *Journal of Management Studies*, **38**, 7, 943–71.

Latour, B. and S. Woolgar (1986). *Laboratory Life: The Construction of Scientific Facts*. Princeton, NJ: Princeton University Press.

Liebeskind, J.P. (1996). 'Knowledge, strategy, and the theory of the firm'. *Strategic Management Journal*, **17** (Winter), 93–107.

Macaulay, T.B. (1972). *T.B. Macaulay: Selected Writings*. Chicago: University of Chicago Press.

Marshall, N. and T. Brady (2001). 'Knowledge management and the politics of knowledge: illustrations from complex products and systems'. *European Journal of Information Systems*, **10**, 2, 99–112.

Mir, R. (2001). 'Migrating ideas: an empirical study of intra-organizational knowledge transfer', doctoral dissertation, University of Massachusetts, Amherst.

Mir, R. and A. Mir (2002). 'The organizational imagination: from paradigm wars to praxis'. *Organizational Research Methods*, **5**, 1, 105–25.

Mir, R., S. Banerjee and A. Mir (2008). 'Hegemony and its discontents: a critical analysis of organizational knowledge transfer', *Critical Perspectives on International Business*, **4**, 2/3, 203–27.

Monteiro, L., N. Arvidsson and J. Birkinshaw (2008). 'Knowledge flows within multinational corporations: explaining subsidiary isolation and its performance implications'. *Organization Science*, **19**, 1, 90–109.

Nelson, R.R. and S. Winter (1982). *An Evolutionary Theory of Economic Change*. Cambridge, MA: Harvard University Press.

Nonaka, I. (1994). 'A dynamic theory of organizational knowledge creation'. *Organization Science*, **5**, 1, 14–37.

Nonaka, I. and H. Takeuchi (1995). *The Knowledge-creating Company: How Japanese Companies Create the Dynamics of Innovation*. New York: Oxford University Press.

Ohmae, K. (1990). *The Borderless World: Power and Strategy in an Interlinked Economy*. New York: Harper Business.

Ong, A. (1987). *Spirits of Resistance and Capitalist Discipline: Factory Women in Malaysia*. Albany, NY: State University of New York Press.

Patriotta, G. (2003). 'Sensemaking on the shop floor: narratives of knowledge in organizations'. *Journal of Management Studies*, **40**, 2, 349–75.

Polanyi, M. (1966). *The Tacit Dimension*. London: Routledge & Kegan Paul.

Poppo, L. and T. Zenger (1998). 'Testing alternative theories of the firm: transaction cost, knowledge-based, and management explanations for make-or-buy decisions in information services'. *Strategic Management Journal*, **19**, 9, 853–77.

Porter, M. (1985). *Competitive Advantage: Creating and Sustaining Superior Performance*. New York: Free Press.

Prasad, P. (1992). 'Work computerization as symbol and experience: an inquiry into the meanings of technological transformation', unpublished dissertation at the University of Massachusetts.

Prasad, A. and P. Prasad (1998). 'Everyday struggles at the workplace: the nature and implications of routine resistance in contemporary organizations'. *Research in the Sociology of Organizations*, **15**, 225–57.

Rico, R., S. Sanchez-Manzares, F. Gil and C. Gibson (2008). 'Team implicit coordination processes: a team knowledge-based approach'. *Academy of Management Review*, **33**, 1, 163–84.

Schulz, M. (2001). 'The uncertain relevance of newness: organizational learning and knowledge flows'. *Academy of Management Journal*, **44**, 4, 661–81.

Scott, J.C. (1985). *Weapons of the Weak: Everyday Forms of Peasant Resistance*. New Haven, CT: Yale University Press.

Shrivastava, P. (1985). 'Is strategic management ideological?'. *Journal of Management*, **12**, 363–77.

Sutcliffe, K.M. and K. Weber (2003). 'The high cost of accurate knowledge'. *Harvard Business Review*, **81**, 5, 74–82.

Szulanski, G. (1995). 'Unpacking stickiness: an empirical investigation of the barriers to transfer best practices inside the firm'. *Instead Working Chapter*, November.

Taylor, C. (1992). *Malaise of Modernity: The Ethics of Authenticity*. Cambridge, MA: Harvard University Press.

Teece, D.J., G.P. Pisano and A. Shuen (1997). 'Dynamic capabilities and strategic management'. *Strategic Management Journal*, **18**, 7, 509–34.

Thompson, P., C. Warhurst and G. Callaghan (2001). 'Ignorant theory and knowledgeable workers: interrogating the connections between knowledge, skills and services'. *Journal of Management Studies*, **38**, 7, 924–42.

Tsai, W. (2002). 'Knowledge transfer in intraorganizational networks: effects of network position and absorptive capacity on business unit innovation and performance'. *Academy of Management Journal*, **44**, 5, 996–1004.

Tsang, E. (2008). 'Transferring knowledge to acquisition joint ventures: an organizational unlearning perspective'. *Management Learning*, **39**, 1, 5–25.

Tsoukas, H. (1996). 'The firm as a distributed knowledge system: a constructionist approach'. *Strategic Management Journal*, **17** (Winter Special Issue), 11–25.

Tsoukas, H. and E. Vladimirou (2001). 'What is organizational knowledge?'. *Journal of Management Studies*, **38**, 7, 973–93.

Tushman, M.L. and P. Anderson (1986). 'Technological discontinuities and organizational environments'. *Administrative Science Quarterly*, **31**, 439–65.

Vickers, G. (1983). *Human Systems Are Different*. New York: Harper & Row.

Wheelwright, S.C. and K.B. Clark (1995). *Leading Product Development: The Senior Manager's Guide to Creating and Shaping the Enterprise*. New York: Free Press.

Williams, R. (1977). *Marxism and Literature*. London: Oxford University Press.

Zack, M.H. (1999). 'Managing codified knowledge'. *Sloan Management Review*, **40**, 4, 45–58.

Zahra, S. and G. George (2002). 'Absorptive capacity: a review, reconceptualization, and extension'. *Academy of Management Journal*, **27**, 2, 185–203.

Zander, U. and B. Kogut (1995). 'Knowledge and the speed of the transfer and imitation of organizational capabilities'. *Organization Science*, **6**, 1, 76–92.

6. Evangelical capitalism and organization

Abbas J. Ali

The abatement of the Cold War and the eventual demise of the Soviet Union have resulted in a unipolar world. More importantly, it has deprived many countries of the relative freedom in choosing their political and economic systems. This point is crucial but organizational scholars often ignore it. Simply, the existence of a unipolar world enables the hegemonic world power to promote its new vision of an economic system to a vast number of developing nations. Faced with overwhelming social, economic, health, and other problems, these countries have found themselves in an unpleasant situation; forced either to follow the dictates of the hegemonic power or be a subject of its wrath. Consequently, their economic opportunities are constrained and their ability to choose an economic system that is relevant is largely curtailed. Some may argue that this situation might be a blessing for developing countries as they could get the necessary insight and assistance for avoiding economic pitfalls and dangerous minefields and, thus, ascend the path of prosperity and economic development.

This optimism, however, is unfounded. The rise of the new global power fiercely advocates a version of capitalism and economic organization irrespective of the cultural and economic conditions of other countries. Indeed, the zeal in promoting this new version appears similar in orientation to that of early colonization, but is more radical in its approach and its end game. Generally, the early European colonization of most of the world was primarily motivated by economic exploitation of the resources of the colonized countries. The European colonization sought to build a form of capitalism and stable market institutions that optimally served its economic and political game. Of course, there were some variations in how Europeans related to colonized subjects, as well as some serious cultural and political blunders. In fact, cultural and business blunders were common and some took place over a long period of time. The colonialists, however, worked diligently to conceal their true aims. In the current unipolar world, the ascending power elite promote conformity and uniformity across the board and the form of capitalism that is preached, as we see in the following sections, is different. Recently, Huntington (2004), in part, captured the new world reality. He stated that the new world great power defines itself as a 'crusader state' and seems to be determined to stamp its image on other peoples.

This chapter is designed to address the role of the firm in a changing world. The chapter is a genuine departure from the conventional coverage of the theory of the firm in that the role of the firm is examined in the context of a new form of capitalism – evangelical capitalism – a form of capitalism that celebrates unfettered freedom of corporations in the national economy and is zealously promoted to other nations as the Savior of humanity, with complete disregard for the desires of people in developing countries and their lawful rights over their resources and properties. For example, in its editorial on 30 October 2002, the *Wall Street Journal* clearly and assertively stated that the oil fields in Arabia must be taken over and that the location of the oil in the Middle East was an accidental geographic matter that ought to be dealt with. It urged the US government 'to take over Saudi oilfields, which would put an end to OPEC . . . [that it is] an accident of history and geography that nearly a quarter of the world's oil sits in these political backwaters'.

The chapter recognizes, too, that the existing theory of the firm does not take into account the reciprocal relationship between firm strategy and national policy. The chapter begins with an examination of the reason for the existence of the firm, with the focus on the evolutionary aspects of business organization, contrasting each stage of the evolution with a corresponding form of capitalism. In acknowledging the evolutionary aspects of the firm, we underscore the fact that there are various factors, including the market, which shape and determine organizational goals, in particular the forces that facilitate the emergence of evangelical capitalism.

WHY DO FIRMS EXIST?

In ancient societies and during the time of medieval empires, business organizations existed to perform economic and social functions. These economic organizations took the form of partnerships or of family owned businesses with little or no formal structure. In the medieval era, some types of sophistication were apparent, especially among businesses that conducted operations across countries and/or continents (Goitein, 1967). Undoubtedly, these business entities faced challenges in terms of risks and facilities, similar to today's problems, though their methods and techniques may have been different. Indeed, some business firms were innovative in their operations across continents. Their existence was mostly dictated by the quest to satisfactorily serve market and entrepreneurial needs. Rulers sought and encouraged market and trade activities and some were active participants in business ventures (Ali, 2005; Goitein, 1967).

In recent years, economists and organization scholars have attempted to seriously deal with the subject of the existence of firms. Two major approaches have dominated the discourse: transaction cost economics (cost minimization) and the knowledge-based (transformation) approach. Primarily, the emphasis of transaction costs is on market failure. That is, when the transaction costs of the market exceed the cost of handling the transaction within the organization (Dunning, 2003). Williamson (1975, p. 10) argued that the firm, rather than market, is better able to take the long view for investment purposes while simultaneously adjusting to changing market conditions in an adaptive, sequential manner. The knowledge-based view asserts that a firm is not a bundle of transactions but a specific bundle of resources and the underlying processes therein (Osterloh et al., 2002). Dunning (2003) organized several perspectives within each approach and viewed the firm as a coordinating unit of control that encompasses two major functions: exchange and value-added. Dunning asserts that the transaction and transformation approaches to the coordination function cannot be separated from each other and that both approaches provide insightful perspectives on the origin and growth of firms. Meyer (2003) reviewed the literature on the nature and existence of firms and concluded that most of the existing literature focuses primarily on how to better run businesses in terms of profits, and contributes relatively little to explaining and evaluating the role of firms, especially multinational corporations (MNCs), in society. He argued that a better understanding of the role of firms in society is a precondition for discussing policy in relations to MNCs.

Ioannides (2003) argued that firms are not only characterized by purpose, but also by the fact that they constitute command structures. That is, business firms should be viewed both as emerging from the market process and as being something distinct from the spontaneous market order. Ioannides specified three conditions for the existence of the firm: the continuity of the supply of specific services is more important for the continuity of the firm as productive organization than the continuity of the participation of specific agents; a firm must be thought of as coordinating the actions of others; and the firm must be accepted by the market – that is, the firm's products must find customers. These conditions are perceived as a set of interconnected processes. Ioannides argued that a business firm will retain its character as an organization for as long as purposeful direction is effectively exercised. In this context, the firm is viewed as a history-contingent process. This evolutionary approach to the firm constitutes an important perspective that may shed the light on the nature of the firm and its function in the context of market capitalism. That is, the firm has specific functions to perform in the market. These functions, however, are contingent on the interplay of various forces including governments and the power elite.

This chapter, therefore, presents a research agenda for clarifying the role of the firm in market capitalism. Its aim is to motivate scholarly research on the changing nature of capitalism and its direct and indirect influence on the role of firms and their possible impact on society. The chapter is an attempt to infuse political economy and sociological views into international business perspectives and to shed light on how the firm is intentionally used as an instrument for global domination and control. The current research on the role of the firm conspicuously focuses on how to maximize profit (see a thoughtful critique offered by Ghoshal, 2005) and on the essential roles that firms play in economic development, especially in the developing world (see Wilkins, 2005). In fact, academic research has become increasingly an intellectual exercise stripped of its political and social context. This is because some business scholars find this approach pays better and appeals to people with narrow ethical horizons (Buckley and Casson, 2003).

AN EVOLUTIONARY APPROACH TO BUSINESS FIRMS

In utilizing the evolutionary approach to the existence of the firm, we underscore the fact that the firm is an entity with a purposeful direction. Its goals and activities are not necessarily an outcome of primarily endogenous deliberation and consideration. Rather, these goals and activities are influenced by prevailing political forces and authority. It is important to mention that unlike firms in centralized economies, economic organizations in liberal economies have relatively vast latitudes of freedom in goal setting and action. Nevertheless, these firms are expected to act in accordance with national interests and foreign policy; otherwise, serious pressures, both by the state and the public, will eventually force the firm to reconsider its stance. These expectations, however, vary across the forms of capitalism. Despite repeated public pronouncements by leading politicians in the Western world that the state should not interfere in business conduct and that business globalization, rather than political domination, is the overriding goal, the global scene is still largely dominated by states, primarily by the global hegemonic one. State intervention in the business world, however, has varied considerably, ranging from minimum to intense intrusiveness. Most often, calls for a less intrusive state policy in business affairs are promoted by politicians of the hegemonic power (the USA) to convey to other governments, especially those in the developing world, the message that they should substitute their interests for those of the powerful state or its MNCs. In this case, the hegemonic state is expected to pursue its national interests aggressively. According to this notion, other states must not aspire to further their business or national interests. These aspirations are considered a violation of international norms and a manifestation of outdated 'nationalistic' tendencies. Indeed, in world business, like in politics, the hegemonic power follows what Moller (1997) termed 'multilateral unilateralism' – the hegemonic power pursues its own interests with vigor inside the framework of the economic system, but not in conformity with the intentions of the system. As alternatives, the hegemonic power may entertain coercive seduction and or forceful suppression and intervention. In recent years, both alternatives have been widely applied. The USA, for example, used economic sanctions against Libya and forced other countries to boycott it unless Libya complied with certain political and economic demands. As Libya has met the conditions specified by Washington, American executives have influxed, in large numbers, into the country to seize business opportunities. The *New York Times* reported that the newly 'opened American liaison office said it receives more than 200 inquiries a week from interested companies' (see Mouawad, 2005). The report quoted Clarence Cazalot, the chief executive of Marathon Oil, as saying, 'One of the most critical issues facing the oil industry today is access to oil reserves, and Libya represents tremendous resources.'

Luttwak (1997) made the argument that world politics is not about to give way to world business – the free movement of commerce governed only by its own non-territorial logic. Many international business scholars, however, appear not to agree with Luttwak. For example, Richard Cooper (1994) of Harvard University made an eloquent argument in support of the proposition that Western powers are not driven by political motives in the conduct of their foreign affairs. He asserted that in today's world (1) the notion that the primary role of government is to 'enhance the power of dominance of its state' is widely held by 'leaders in many developing countries' but not in the West; (2) military coercion 'will be non-existent among rich democratic countries'; (3) power is seldom used by Western nations as power 'has no useful meaning in today's world systems except with respect to governments that are physically aggressive against their neighbors or, increasingly, against their own population'; (4) 'political dominance among rich countries is not likely, and it is increasingly rare between rich and poor countries without substantial financial inducements'; and (5) conflicts result from religious or other ideological differences and thus, 'the historical basis for wars – conflict over resources – is gone'. Cooper's arguments and assertions ignore the fact that hegemonic powers are inclined to justify the use of force in pursuing their interests and that colonization of the most of the developing world was carried out by Western countries.

Current and past events, however, demonstrate that the state is still an important actor, though its role varies, in the world economy and that the global hegemonic power resorts to various methods and techniques to achieve its world objectives. Luttwak (1997) asserts that states always guide business firms for their own geo-economic purposes, or even select them as their chosen instrument. In either case, the state has 'been both user and used, and the companies both instruments and instrumentalizers'. In the literature there are two general views pertaining to the nature of the interaction between the state and the firm. The first perspective (neo-liberal) is promoted by Dunning (1995). He indicates that in the international market, firms are necessarily agents for their respective government. Dunning asserts that in the global market, the state's economic space 'is perceived more in terms of the markets exploited by its institutions than of its geographical boundaries' (p. 254). His proposition is that governments and firms are ultimately partners in the wealth-creating process. As such, both of them seek to reduce or circumvent undesirable market distorting practices of both firms and national governments. In this context, Dunning believes that the state has a fundamental role: to be an initiator and supervisor of the system by which all resources are created and deployed. Dunning appears to be overly focusing on the positive role of the state in protecting its national firms and in reducing market inefficiencies. Later, he made this clear when he stated (1997, p. 9):

> the need for increased government action to ensure that the social externalities of markets for dynamic goods are fully exploited; and that the social assets necessary for efficient upgrading and exploitation of the core competences of firms and individuals are adequately provided.

Within the neo-liberal perspective, there are those who assert the global logic and the ascendancy of international trade. This particular group promotes the proposition that globalization, rather than governments, is the ultimate arbiter in the global marketplace. Generally, this view states that in the era of economic interdependence and globalization, firms (MNCs) have become the sole engine for economic prosperity and world economic integration. Two views are common. The first is propagated by Reich (1990, 1991). According to Reich MNCs facilitate and accelerate global economic growth, development and integration. Reich views MNCs as an effective medium for investment and resource allocation, and for the transfer and accumulation of human skills. That is, MNCs create wealth, jobs, opportunities, and foster global outlooks. Consequently, the role of governments should be centered on developing national polices that reward MNCs. Attracting MNCs to invest in a country should be the primary objective of any government that is concerned with the welfare of its citizens. Reich (1991) suggests that in today's world the bonds between MNCs and countries are rapidly eroding. In fact, MNCs have become global webs with no particular affinity to a home country government. Their loyalty is to societies that offer them the best opportunities for growth and contribution.

Ohmae (1991) suggested that economic interdependencies have made traditional national borders a useless reality and have reduced government apparatuses to the state of virtual declining industries. His main proposition is that in today's borderless world, economic activity does not follow either the political boundary lines of the nation-state or the cultural boundary lines of 'civilization'. Consequently, MNCs are no longer conditioned by reasons of government and investments are not geographically constrained. Unlike Reich, Ohmae believes that MNCs should not purposefully seek government assistance. This is not only because governments do not understand the global logic but also because governments' intervention in the economy hinders the proper functioning of the global market. Thus, governments have no vital market-making role. Essentially MNCs are much better off following business instincts and locating their operations where the opportunities are more attractive.

In contrast, to the above neo-liberal perspective, the neo-Marxist perspective treats the state as an instrument for maintaining the cohesiveness and stability of a complex and multifaceted economic system. In another words, the state in a capitalistic system is committed to protect and preserve the essential position and power of the dominant classes (Solo, 1978). In this capitalist system, the firm is considered as part of the dominant classes that it exists to serve. Chase-Dunn (1999) asserts that, in today's capitalism, the hegemonic power is the instrument and the facilitator for the rise of MNCs. Chase-Dunn sees world capitalism as passing through various cycles. Nevertheless, he states that at any cycle of the world capitalist system, the hegemonic power exists to strengthen the role and position of MNCs and to facilitate their quest for 'global governance'. Under such conditions, the interests and aspirations of countries outside the 'core market' are marginalized. That is, the hegemonic power sets the tone for world economic integration and division of labor in a way that enhances the competitive position of its national MNCs and its own national advantage. So, the ability of other nation-states to independently pursue their national interests and the welfare of their citizens decreases substantially. While agreeing with this general orientation, Lefebvre (2001) suggests that the state can negotiate with MNCs if not resisting their pressure. Lefebvre believes the state is a prominent actor that manages the relations of 'the national market with the world market as well as with multinational firms'.

The preceding discussion demonstrates that the relationships between governments and business firms are complex and do exist in different forms. Indeed, it is impossible to imagine the existence of business firms without some type of government function, especially those of law and order, protection, and incentives. The government, as the most crucial entity within the state, performs regulatory and market roles in addition to its political and security function. The essence and depth of these roles differ significantly among democratic countries. The complexity of the relationships and the nature of interactions between the government and business firms, furthermore, vary across the evolution of the capitalist system and the interplay of national and global forces. These relationships can be positive or negative and both are subject to reciprocal manipulation (Luttwak, 1997). It is interesting to note that in distinguishing between positive (e.g. states seek to guide large companies for their geo-economic purposes) and negative (e.g. states oppose foreign companies that are believed to be the chosen instruments of other states), Luttwak implies that corporations are agents of their respective states, not vice versa. This view is similar to that of Dunning (1995), but not in line with the neo-Marxist perspectives on the firm.

Accordingly, in capitalism the relationships between firms and governments have been in a state of flux and the debate on whether the firm is an instrument of the state or vice versa is far from over. Early promoters of capitalism thought of it as an economic and social system that is based on property and individual rights, competition, and non-government intervention in the marketplace. Indeed, Adam Smith's vision of capitalism is based on voluntary exchange. Smith thought of free trade and of the market mechanism as a means to enhance people's welfare without the intrusiveness of the state. The state, in his view, has no business in the market and economy (Ali and Camp, 1999). In practice, however, capitalism has different faces and its evolution has been shaped by the cultural and national policies of the countries that espoused it. In fact, the literature is flooded with terms like popular capitalism, crony capitalism, collective capitalism, creative capitalism, democratic capitalism, and so on. In these and other forms of capitalism, the interface between government and the firm has not been simple. Dunning (1997) has attempted to map this relationship and highlight its complexity under different types of capitalism. He specifies three stages of capitalism: entrepreneurial (1770–1875), hierarchical (1875–1980), and alliance (1980–?). At the time of entrepreneurial capitalism, production was undertaken by small firms, mostly family owned, and the transactions were conducted at arm's length prices between independent buyers and sellers. The market was thought to be perfect and thus government intervention was not an issue: the emergence of the *laissez-faire* philosophy. The period of hierarchical capitalism experienced the emergence of multi-activity firms and relative internalization by these firms of a range of intermediate product markets. It is at this stage that government intervention was seen as necessary to correct market inefficiencies and facilitate economic development. Alliance capitalism has two distinct characteristics: emphasis on the partnership between the various organizational modes of resource allocation, and emphasis on the role that government plays as the overseer of the economic system and the ultimate arbitrator of the functions undertaken by both private and public institutions.

Dunning's typology is useful for understanding the nature of the economy and the various roles that a government plays in facilitating the function of business firms. Furthermore, it outlines the evolution of firms from simple form and function to more complex and dynamic entities across the three phases of capitalism. Nevertheless, Dunning's primary concern was with how governments facilitate MNCs' operations and subsequently improve the profitability of MNCs.

The issues of firms' influence on governments or vice versa, rivalry among firms and between firms and states, and the desires of the hegemonic state and its national firms to influence the cultures and economies of other countries have not been even remotely addressed. These subjects are vital for understanding the world of business, its prospects, and its challenges. More importantly, the quest for having an integrated and functional world economy demands an understanding of the forces that hinder or facilitate cultural dialogue. In fact, the financial health of the firm should not be separated from the cultural and economic well-being of the societies in which a firm operates. The health, prosperity, and the active economic involvement of the people of these societies positively influence current and future operations of MNCs and their overall performance, including financial ones. The emphasis on economic goals, irrespective of the socio-political and economic conditions of the societies where firms operate, often results in serious business blunders and inaccurate conclusions. In management and international business, there must be a realization that business and government interaction and processes are not value-free. Their outcomes may adversely affect people both as producers and consumers. Most of the existing literature on management in capitalistic societies, however, seems to overlook issues that affect humans at the deepest core of their existence (Mitroff, 1995).

In this chapter, four phases of capitalism (see Table 6.1) are identified: missionary (1600–1800), nationalistic (1800–1944), global (1945–89), and evangelical capitalism (1990–?). The assignment of the name to and the timing of the phases are intended to capture the essence and the main characteristic of each stage. We understand the possibility of an overlap and continuity of some aspects across the scheme. This by no means precludes the dynamic nature of capitalism and its capacity as a system for renewal and progression. The fact remains, however, that capitalism is a man-made system. It was envisioned and has been practiced to serve optimally the interests of those who benefit the most from it. It is across these four phases that the vision of and the mission attached to capitalism have varied widely. Both past evidence and current developments in many countries indicate that capitalism has shown flexibility in accommodating the demand of powerful actors such as governments, the power elite including senior bureaucrats, and business firms. Each actor has its own expectations and priorities and these in turn have shaped the nature of capitalism.

The emergence of missionary capitalism was associated with the emergence of the sovereign states in Europe and their appetite for trade in order to accumulate wealth and obtain power. In December 1600, Queen Elizabeth granted a charter to the Governor and Company of Merchants of London Trading to trade freely with countries in the East under the name of the East India Company. Other European countries followed suit. Companies were seen as important instruments with which to control new lands and markets, accumulate wealth, spread Christianity, and maintain military power. In the early 17th century, the United Provinces (Netherlands) dominated the seas and controlled most of the trade routes and The Netherlands competed with Britain, Spain and Portugal to dominate the sea trade routes. It was during that time the ruling families and their respective governments relied heavily on charter companies to advance their goals. On 3 June 1621, The States-General of the United Netherlands issued the charter of the Dutch West India Company. The charter gave the company the right to:

> contracts, engagements and alliances with the limits herein before prescribed, make contracts, engagements and alliances with the princes and natives of the countries comprehended therein, and also build any forts and fortifications there, to appoint and discharge Governors, people for war, and officers of justice, and other public officers, for the preservation of the places, keeping good order, police and justice, and in like manner for the promoting of trade; and again, others in their place to put, as they from the situation of their affairs shall see fit.

Table 6.1   Selected roles and activities of firms across forms of capitalism

Factor	Missionary (1600–1800)	Nationalistic (1800–1944)	Global (1945–89)	Evangelical (1990–?)
Root	Mostly colonial powers	Colonial powers and market competition	Market competition and globalization	Market competition and ideological power
Ownership	Mostly elite groups associated with or linked to powerful monarchies	Mostly publicly held, wealthy individuals linked to powerful political elite	Diverse ownership of private investors possibly from various countries	Diverse ownership but managed by ideologically committed managers
Management	Wealthy individuals connected to European royal families	Politically connected professional managers	Professionally oriented managers	Mostly professionally oriented and some are influenced by zealous beliefs
Goals	Maximizing profit by exploiting colonies' resources; promote Christianity	Nation-bounded; disregard for host country needs	Not bound to any nation; seize opportunities wherever are found	Influenced by the hegemonic power policies and priorities; profit maximization
Markets	Mostly colonies' markets	Markets that are linked to or sought by home government; follow the flag	Global markets	Global markets but investment choices and expansion strategies are influenced by the hegemonic power
Relations to the state	Directly linked to colonial power, extension of government	An instrument of the state but often exercise influence on the state	Relatively not bound to any state and appear to seek less state intervention in the market	Influenced by the hegemonic power and its policies; the state facilitates the interests of its major firms

Table 6.1   (continued)

Factor	Missionary (1600–1800)	Nationalistic (1800–1944)	Global (1945–89)	Evangelical (1990–?)
Involvement	Textile extraction industries, trade, and activities deemed essential to run colonies	Wide range of economic and non-economic activities essential to facilitate nationalistic goals	Wide range of activities stemming from and related to opportunities on a global scale	Wide range of activities with substantial consideration of the hegemonic power interests
Motivation	Exploitation of colonies' natural resources and reaping maximum profits in a short time	Exploitation of host countries' resources; maximization of profits	Taking advantage of global opportunities and utilize resources all over the globe	Economic and ideological goals that are influenced by beliefs and policies promoted by the hegemonic power
International role	Promote and promulgate the interest of the colonial power and ensure the submission of colonies; exercise territorial and political power	Work closely with the state and government to promote and reinforce its interests	Engage in a wide range of non-economic activities to reduce tension, political conflicts, and promote economic development	Engage in activities that are consistent with the hegemonic power's ideology and/ or serve its interests
Key resources	Military power; the state apparatus; natural assets; relatively unskilled workers	The state's support and infrastructure, financial capital and physical assets along with some know-how capital	Tangible and intangible assets, particularly knowledge capital and sophisticated networks	Tangible and intangible assets with relatively strong reliance on the state and its infrastructure

Table 6.1　(continued)

Factor	Missionary (1600–1800)	Nationalistic (1800–1944)	Global (1945–89)	Evangelical (1990–?)
Means to achieve goals	Military and the connection to powerful royal European families	Market competition and the home government	Competition, market liberalization; sophisticated global networks	Competition with direct/ indirect assistance from the hegemonic power
Concerns for host country	Pay no attention to the impact of their operations on local population or the environment	Pay little attention to the impact of their operations on local population but give attention to relationship with powerful elites	Pay considerable attention to their image and the impact of their operations on local population and environment	Selective in their attention to the impact of their operations on the welfare of the host country

Ottaway (2001) asserted that as the charter corporations assumed the task of spreading Christianity, they gained a sacred status far beyond their commercial and political duties. She quoted British statesman Edmund Burke as saying the powers of the East India Company have 'emanated from the supreme power of this kingdom . . . The responsibility of the Company is increased by the greatness and sacredness of the powers that have been intrusted [sic] to it' (p. 45). Charter corporations had a complete monopoly over the affairs and the businesses of the territories under their domain, and in their respective countries excluded others from trading with these territories. For example, the charter of the Dutch West India Company stated:

> whoever shall presume without the consent of this Company, to sail or to traffic in any of the Places within the aforesaid Limits granted to this Company, he shall forfeit the ships and the goods which shall be found for sale upon the aforesaid coasts and lands; the which being actually seized by the aforesaid Company, shall be by them kept for their own Benefit and Behoof. And in case such ships or goods shall be sold either in other countries or havens they may touch at, the owners and partners must be fined for the value of those ships and goods: Except only, that they who before the date of this charter, shall have sailed or been sent out of these or any other countries, to any of the aforesaid

coasts, shall be able to continue their trade for the sale of their goods, and cosine back again, or otherwise, until the expiration of this charter

By exercising territorial and political power in addition to their commercial duties, the charter corporations actually and legally were not an independent entity functioning independently of the state. In fact, it is impossible to ignore the fact that these companies were not only instruments of their states, but in the service of the official religion of those states. Their conduct had consequences that affected the lives of millions of people at home and abroad. And neither could the state nor the firm be treated solely as an economic actor. The missionary corporations were an integral part and essential force of the hegemonic power and helped to facilitate wealth accumulation, trade, territorial expansion, and colonization of the third world countries. Furthermore, they were essential instruments in promoting and strengthening capitalism. In their operations and conduct, however, they inflicted cultural, political and economic damage on foreign territories. The extent of the damage is not known and will never be assessed accurately. Nevertheless, it is possible to suggest that the capitalist system at that time was crude, constrained the freedom of trade as it limited rival countries and companies alike from pursuing their interests in the market, and was primarily driven by the narrow interests of the ruling elite and their allies. Missionary capitalism, however, contributed to an increasing awareness of the significance of foreign trade and the existence of the new world that offered opportunities beyond imagination. Consequently, it fostered economic development of the hegemonic powers and set the stage for the rising of new manufacturing and financial classes.

Around 1800, the continued existence of charter corporations was in doubt. The commercial monopoly of the Dutch West India Company came to an end in 1791 as its charter expired and was not renewed. Similarly, the trade monopoly of the British East India Company was broken in 1813. Ottaway (2001) suggests that the successes of the missionary corporations led to their demise. She explains that the colonial governments in Europe felt that it was prudent not to leave the administration of empires to private entities. Karl Marx (1853) viewed it differently. He suggested that the flourishing of trade with colonies led to the emergence of an industrial interest represented by manufacturers who exhibited confidence and maturity. Therefore, this new class decided to defeat moneyocracy and oligarchy that both exploited and dominated the trade with the colonies. Regardless of these two perspectives, the fact is that global trade and international interactions, at that time, generated a shift in class power, and the nature of alliances set the stage for the rising of a new form of capitalism; nationalistic capitalism. The new industrial class was more cosmopolitan than the previous one and more interested in seizing opportunities at home and abroad. Its appetite for colonial expansions, increasing production capacities, and investing growing financial surplus in other countries coincided with the interest of the ruling elite. The latter were interested in nationalistic glory and fame and economic opportunities. US Senator Albert J. Beveridge (1968, pp. 185–6) in 1902 succinctly expressed this fact when he stated:

> Hold what foreign markets we have; capture new foreign markets every year; push the advance of American commerce – that is one insistent task of American statesmanship at the beginning of the twentieth century. . . . Will retreat from our possessions in the Orients or the Gulf give us new markets? On the contrary, the getting of territorial footholds all over the world is one method by which every other commercial nation secures new markets with underdeveloped lands and peoples.

The political elite saw in the new emerging manufacturing corporations a means to translate their national vision into reality. Subsequently, they facilitated the expansion of the manufacturing activities. Rubinson (1978) called this era the second industrial revolution. This era was marked by the shift from textiles to capital goods industries based on coal, iron and railroads. Rubinson noted that as Britain shifted from textiles to capital goods, textile manufacturing in other areas such as Germany and Italy prospered. Free trade, therefore, was perceived positively and was actively promoted by the ruling elite. It was during this period that Britain's surplus capital was invested in industrial production in Europe and North America. Thus, it 'created large demands for food and new raw materials, which in turn led to the geographic expansion of the world-economy' (Rubinson, 1978, p. 43). Indeed, the search for new markets was deliberately pursued by dominating states. Writing in 1899, Flux (1998) underscored the significance of new markets in maintaining prosperity. He stated (p. 206): 'The manufacturing populations of Western Europe and of the United States of America are becoming increasingly conscious of the extent to which the continued development of their industries, on the present lines, involves a search for new markets for their products.'

The competition among hegemonic powers for new markets and their assistance for their own national companies in their quest for raw materials and markets encouraged the trend for free economy and market liberalization. British politicians and influential corporations thought of free trade as an effective cure for economic stagnation and as an instrument for increasing productivity and market expansion. Richard Cobden, a 19th century British liberal who dedicated his life to free trade, viewed free movement of trade as the grand panacea that would 'serve to inoculate with the healthy and saving taste for civilization all the nations of the world'. Cobden's remarks of 1860 seem as applicable today as when he wrote them (see Morley, 1988, p. 343):

> It is an economic error to confine our view to the imports or exports of our own country. In the case of England, these are intimately connected with, and dependent upon, the great circulating system of the whole world's trade. Nobody has fully grasped the bearings of Free Trade, who does not realize what the international aspect of every commercial transaction amounts to; how the conditions of production and exchange in any one country affect, both actually and potentially, the corresponding conditions in every other country.

The nationalistic attitude of the power elite of the colonial powers, the favor given by governments to national firms to the detriment of foreign corporations, and the strong alliance between governments and their national firms were the most common characteristics of that era. Flux, in 1899, captured this reality when he stated (p. 207):

> The demand for new markets needs no extended explanation, it is an obvious fact. Together with this demand comes the desire to control the new markets in the interest of the producers of some particular nation. The prevalent exclusion of foreigners, by discriminating customs duties, from the benefits of exploiting new markets in a colony or dependency, is at once a means of reserving trade for a particular group of merchants and a stimulus to others, belonging to other nations, to demand the control of any unoccupied portions of the earth's surface, so as to prevent them from falling under an influence which may prove exclusive in its operation. Even if the 'open door' be maintained in any particular case, there is a widespread confidence that 'trade follows the flag', and hence a desire that the flag which proclaims the controlling power may be that of the country of which one is oneself a citizen.

Capitalism, at that time, was closely associated with the nationalistic policy of the hegemonic power. Though free trade was promoted officially and its benefits were accentuated, the state was determined to produce tangible results for their own companies (e.g. new markets and obstructing the attempts of foreign corporations to enter colonies). These national companies were expected to create wealth and invest their profits from overseas operations and exploitation of the colonies in the home market. The nature of capitalism and the relations between the state and the firm was eloquently reflected in a statement made by Hobson (1919, p. 402):

> When after 1870 all the Great powers were advancing rapidly on the new industrial road, and most of them began to safeguard their home markets against importers in favour of their native goods, the backward countries of the world became areas of increasing solicitude to competing groups of traders and to the governments of their respective countries. . . . Moreover, the business methods

by which these schemes are financed and carried into operation involve the formation of powerful companies controlled by men of great influence, not only in
the world of business but in that of politics.

Unlike the first phase of capitalism, the second one experienced the
growing influence of manufacturing and financial firms that engaged in
multi-activities and were mostly managed by professional managers. These
firms, however, did not seriously attempt to differentiate themselves from
the policy of the home country government and some of them behaved
like an extension of the colonial power (e.g. oil corporations). In fact, they
benefited greatly from such an association, as it entitled them to certain
privileges that may not otherwise have been available to them (e.g. easy
access to influential actors, exemption from certain regulations, concession
from the colonies, etc.). This close association created a sense of superiority and a type of arrogance that prevented these corporations from being
sensitive to the demands and desires of the people of the Third World.
Thus crude exploitation of human and natural resources and the destruction of traditional cultures were undertaken with ease. Ottaway (2001)
indicates that corporations, especially oil, operated in the typical manner
of the time with little regard for the impact of their operations on the local
population or the environment (e.g. United Fruit model). Shenon (1995,
p. 3) explains how the Western colonization of the Pacific island of Nauru
made it possible for corporations to strip it of everything. At present, after
90 years of strip-mining, nothing is left for the islanders who are plagued
by bad diets and short life expectancies and who may have to evacuate
the island. He indicates that, culturally, during the German occupation
of the island from 1888 until World War I, the Germans 'banned native
dancing as pagan, and today only a handful of elderly Nauruans have even
the barest recollection of how the sacred dances should be performed'.
William Pfaff (1995) notes that the European colonial powers in Africa, for
example, uprooted ancient laws and destroyed Africa's existing social and
political systems and its customary institutions and law. He quoted (p. 4)
Robert Heilbroner who suggested that Western corporations in developing countries 'turned millions of traditionally self-sufficient peasants into
rubber-tappers, coffee-growers, tin-miners, tea-pickers – and then subjected this new agricultural and mining proletariat to the incomprehensible
vagaries of world commodity fluctuations'. Similarly, Koopman (1994, p.
74) asserts that the colonial powers proceeded with the mass violation of
human rights by destroying dignity and that an

> organizational design was imposed on Africa . . . regardless of the preappointed
> destiny theory of indigenous folklore. This scientific approach led to the differ-
> entiation of the Africa world view, destroying its dignity and self-respect, and

causing a cross-continental inferiority complex which further reinforced the sense of hopelessness amongst the mass.

After World War II a new type of capitalism was promoted on a world-wide stage; global capitalism. The emergence of the USA and the Soviet Union as the global superpowers inaugurated an intensive global ideological rivalry. The USA, in its quest to defeat the Soviet Union and communism, was determined to use economic and military powers, along with highly orchestrated media programs, across the globe to defeat communism. Capitalism was promoted as the system capable of eradicating poverty, improving economic conditions, and protecting individual freedom and private property. MNCs were considered instruments in spreading wealth and strengthening the cause of capitalism. The US encouraged Western-based MNCs to invest heavily in areas where the competition for political domination between the two rivals was critical. Friendly governments were subsidized and security was assured. Much of the economic assistance and investment took place in East Asia, and capitalism appeared to flourish in many parts of Asia (e.g. Singapore, Hong Kong, South Korea, Taiwan, etc.). Similar attempts were made in other parts of the world. Chemical, oil, and manufacturing corporations played significant parts in promoting capitalism and creating indigenous social classes whose futures, politically and economically, are now hinged on the success of the free market economy and capitalism.

During this phase, a profound political change took place in many developing countries: a rising nationalism and the quest for independence especially during the years 1950 to 1979. This development created a new pressure and risk for MNCs. In many parts of the world, people who had been subjected to foreign domination and control for many long years were determined to reclaim their future and shape their destinies. They espoused programs advocating complete political and economic independence. Many of the newly independent countries adopted centralized planning and attempted to constrain the MNCs' operations. Consequently, many MNCs found themselves obligated to distance themselves from the home country's colonial past and the legacy of colonization. In addition, they faced the risk of nationalization, extortion, and/or restriction of operations. In most of the developing countries, therefore, MNCs had to reconsider their strategies and approaches, as the issue of their nationality had become a liability rather than an asset. In general, MNCs had to carefully balance their approaches and reconcile the demands of their home country government with that of the host country.

The Soviet invasion of Afghanistan in 1979 and the election in the USA of Ronald Reagan in 1980 created circumstances hospitable for MNCs and

reinvigorated the spirit of promoting capitalism. Reagan's tireless efforts
to defeat the Soviet Union and spread the gospel of capitalism bolstered
MNCs' activities and increased their confidence globally. He built a political alliance to defeat the Soviet Union in Afghanistan and cooperated with
corporations to defeat the Soviet Union economically (see Norquist, 2001).
Both resulted in the withdrawal of the Soviet Union from Afghanistan
in 1989 and its eventual collapse in 1991. These events increased MNCs'
confidence in the merit of the free market economy and its causes. More
importantly, these events accelerated a worldwide trend toward liberalization of the economy, privatization, and market capitalism. This new development enabled MNCs to engage in global networking, pursue mergers
and acquisitions to improve their competitiveness position and managerial
prestige, rationalize production, and seize market opportunities in emerging markets. Furthermore, FDI in emerging markets increased substantially. At the same time, MNCs attempted to improve relationships with
host governments in developing nations without purposefully distancing
themselves from the policy of their home government.

The demise of the Soviet Union and the changing global political scene
has created an environment hospitable to aggressive foreign and economic
approaches (neo-conservatism) in the USA. In fact, these changes have
strengthened a rising economic philosophy; evangelical capitalism. This
form of capitalism is a mixture of mercantilism and Straussian philosophy
interwoven with religious idealism. This philosophy has produced a hybrid
political–economic orientation dissimilar to traditional American capitalism. It is promoted aggressively to other nations irrespective of cultural
orientations and socio-economic conditions. It advocates the uncompromising stance that this brand of capitalism is the Savior of humanity and
that salvation is possible only through the selfish pursuit of goals. That is,
evangelical capitalism is the only 'system that fully allows and encourages
the virtues necessary for human life' (Tracinski, 2002). Tracinski asserts
that acting selfishly is the true pursuit of happiness, because the first rule
of evangelical capitalism is that 'everyone has a right to dispose of his
own life and property according to his own judgment'. Policymakers in
Washington have often demanded wrenching reform for foreign governments, 'conflating the interests of the big banks with the financial health
of the world' and 'use[ing] huge loans to compel governments to sell off
companies they controlled . . . Aid was withheld if governments spent too
much money or protected key industries' (Kahn, 2002). Jackson Lears
(1999, p. 27) succinctly captures the mood in Washington:

> Good news from the frontiers of global capitalism: the magic of the market
> has rendered social conflict obsolete. The scramble for profits enriches us

all. Struggles between nations or classes for scarce resources are a figment of the fevered Marxist brain. The real challenge facing the world economy is the removal of archaic customs that inhibit 'growth'. Once that is done, the free-trading future promises utopian harmony.

This philosophy appeared in the 1980s but found acceptance in the new era of a unipolar world and the rising influence of biblical prophecies in public life. Unlike Nadesan (1999), who attributed the rise of evangelical capitalism to the growing influence of evangelical Christianity, Ali (1997) argues that American society and the American market experienced dramatic changes in the 1980s that facilitated the growth of evangelical capitalism. The rise of neo-conservatism ideology, the rising influence of religious fundamentalism in the public sphere, and the growing influence of financial and media corporations and their alliance with the political elite, have all created an environment that celebrates unfettered freedom of corporations in the national economy and aggressive promotion of national interests abroad. This form of capitalism shares in common some aspects with missionary and nationalistic capitalism. All are based on an aggressive promotion of national economic interests and exhibit a disregard for the national interests of developing nations and their lawful rights over their resources and properties. Differences, however, exist. In particular, there is the ease with which executives of major corporations move in and out of government and vice versa (e.g. several executives from Goldman Sachs recently served as US Secretary of Treasury, White House Chief of Staff, Governor of New Jersey, etc.). Furthermore, the line between secularism and messianic vision has become, in the context of hegemonic power, blurred. In fact, religious vocabularies have been consistently infused in political discourse and foreign policy. Consequently, it has become impossible to tell where policy ends and religion begins.

Ali and Camp (2003) argue that the most outstanding features of evangelical capitalism are an uncompromising stance (absolutism), economic inequality, a rigid pursuit of selfishness, and a conspicuous contempt of individual and property rights and sovereignty in the realm of international affairs. Under evangelical capitalism, MNCs may face more acute restrictions especially if they do not comply with the interests of the hegemonic power. Indeed, it is likely that in situations where MNCs fail to conform with the hegemonic power, their interests will be at serious risk. Certainly, in a unipolar world the hegemonic power is not inclined to tolerate what it perceives to be an unacceptable deviation.

Nadesan (1999) argues that in evangelical capitalism, the extension of multinational corporate capitalism is represented as a kind of manifest destiny. She asserts that the discourse of evangelical capitalism promotes individual and corporate rights, while resisting any government programs that strive to sustain women's reproductive rights and workers' rights and protections. Boje (2003) suggests that under evangelical capitalism, the US-based corporations have government support to spread their influence globally. Likewise, Kurtz (2004) asserts that the evangelical capitalism system allows unfettered freedom for large corporations to dominate national and global markets. Both Boje and Kurtz advance the proposition that, in the era of evangelical capitalism, MNCs, allied with the hegemonic power, exercise influence far beyond national borders and regions. They envision a situation where the interests of the rest of the world are overlooked and those of the powerful MNCs are pursued aggressively. These MNCs roam the globe to maximize profits while limiting benefits and freedom for workers and the rest of populations in developing countries.[1]

CHALLENGES FOR MNCs

Dunning (1993) underscores the complex relations between firms and the state when he acknowledges that, for most of the postwar period, the relationship between MNCs and the state has been more confrontational than cooperative. Nevertheless, Dunning raises an interesting and seemingly contradictory issue when he asserts that states have resorted to 'modify[ing] their laws, regulations, or even their entire economic systems' (p. 548) either to affect the behavior of MNCs or as a result of their increased presence in the global economy. This statement reveals that MNCs are influential actors in the global marketplace who, when necessary, flex their muscles to get their wishes. What is interesting to note is that MNCs usually exercise their power over developing countries with the help of their home government. The majority of these corporations are based in countries that are or were hegemonic powers. This may validate Modelski's (1987) proposition that the modern era's multinationals are a form of innovation characteristically linked to and originally associated with world powers.

The fact remains, however, that unlike previous phases or other forms of capitalism, evangelical capitalism poses certain challenges to MNCs. These challenges apply equally to MNCs, regardless of their home base. The evolution of MNCs and especially their expansion and outreach during the 'global capitalism' era have profoundly changed their global outlook and strengthened their global involvement. In fact, senior executives have voiced and exhibited extraordinary sentiments and commitment to societies and communities wherever their corporations operate. For example, Percy Barnevik (1991, p. 92), CEO of ABB, stated, 'We are not homeless. We are a company with many homes.' Similarly, Frank Popoff

(1994, p. 26), Chairperson of Dow Chemical, asserted that 'Companies must compete locally and view all major geographic markets, not as foreign markets, but as their home away from home.' These commitments manifest new founding realities in the global marketplace where national prejudices are treated as hindrances and obstacles to building an integrated and transparent world economy. These sentiments, however, are not encouraged or nurtured by evangelical capitalism. The tenets and pillars of evangelical capitalism appear to be contradictory to the cultivated global qualities and orientations that seek to foster global integration and citizenship. Thomas Friedman (1998, p. A27) interviewed managers in Silicon Valley and was dismayed at their lack of nationalistic attitudes and considered this development a 'disturbing complacency' toward 'Washington and even the nation'. Friedman appears to be offended by managers who disregard extreme nationalism and who espouse global orientations. He indicates that executives in Silicon Valley say things like 'We are not an American company. We are IBM US, IBM Canada, IBM Australia . . .' Friedman (1998) warned that the executives' global attitude is not conducive to national interests and reminded them not to forget that the hidden hand of the global market would not work without the hidden fist: 'The hidden fist that keeps the world safe for the Silicon Valley's technologies to flourish is called the United States Army, Air Force, Navy, and Marine Corps' (p. A27).

Since a large numbers of executives and MNCs have cultivated, in the last two decades, qualities that are attentive to and appreciative of global outreach and dialogue, cultural sensitivity, diversity of thinking and aspirations, and global outlooks, they are certain to have difficulties in accepting elements in evangelical capitalism that condone violation of the rights and dignity of others. More importantly, events associated with the rise and practice of evangelical capitalism demonstrate that an important pillar of capitalism, property rights, is often violated and market mechanisms are obstructed. Pisaturo (2003), writing in the *Capitalism Magazine*, urged that the US government has to

> use its military might, including its nuclear arsenal, to crush the evil governments, seize the oil properties . . . and make the territories of the Islamic Middle East into American colonies, thereby enabling American adventurers to exploit and civilize this new frontier just as American adventurers had exploited and civilized the American West in the 1800s.

These developments constitute a threat to optimal functioning of the market economy and are likely to alarm executives who appreciate free movement of goods and capital, openness and transparency. Subsequently, these developments will complicate the relationships between the state and the firm in a way that has seldom been experienced before.[2] New dynamics may emerge that further the interests and strengthen the market advantages of some firms, but generally adversely impact the viability of the majority of MNCs.

Likewise, managers of MNCs may find it offensive to espouse a position that discounts the patriotism and tradition of host countries. For example, in *The Pentagon's New Map: War and Peace in the Twenty-first Century*, Thomas Barnett (2004, p. 217) stated, 'When individuals can not find opportunity in life, they are reduced to fighting over what's left of the land and the cultural identity they attach to its history.' In this state of affairs, managers are confronted with a system of thinking that is irreconcilable with the teachings and practices of cultural sensitivity and the virtue of openness and pluralism. Certainly, some managers who do not appreciate such a call may find themselves at odds with powerful economic and political forces and have to spend considerable political and social capital to defend their companies and their rights to operate freely in the global marketplace.

Whether or not firms are instruments or instrumentalizers of the state, the fact remains that they operate on the assumption that the market economy functions optimally as actors observe and are guided by collectively accepted rules and norms. That is, the market is viewed as an open playing field where deception and fraudulent manipulation of the economy are not permitted. This assumption, however, is not valid under evangelical capitalism. This is because a cornerstone of evangelical capitalism is the necessity to promote only the good news while concealing the bad. In fact, advocates of this system believe that 'inequality is an ineradicable aspect of [the] human condition' and that truths are not intended for the 'unsophisticated general population'. Therefore, the elite have to master the 'art of concealment and secrecy' (Heer, 2003, p. H1). According to Heer the proponents of this philosophy assert that capitalism must not place 'the material well-being of the masses ahead of the cultivation of virtues among elite'. Thus deception, fraud and manipulation of market conditions may endanger the existence of some firms, while simultaneously strengthening the position of those that are inclined to undermine market competition.

The above challenges are a reminder that in operating in the marketplace, firms are influenced by various forces. Their conduct is molded by the interplay of diverse forces – political, social, cultural, and economic. Though firms are not passive actors, they have to function in a way that strengthens their performance through careful reconciliation and consideration of the conflicting demands of various players in the market, chief among them being the state. Historically, managers of these firms have coped with non-market challenges and seized opportunities to maximize their interests. Under evangelical capitalism, the challenge seems to be profoundly different and is often overtly dogmatic. It is not only immediate but also complex as it encompasses the market and a disciplined ideological stance.[3]

CONCLUSION

In this study, a typology of capitalism and the role of firms across four forms of capitalism have been discussed. The study attempts to infuse political economy and sociological perspectives into international business literature pertaining to firms. Recognizing that capitalism is a man-made system, various forms are expected to emerge. These variations differ substantially and are shaped by prevailing cultural, political and economic norms and conditions. In fact, the evolution of and the emergence of capitalism in Western countries, especially in the hegemonic power, evidence a dynamic interplay of vibrant socio-political and economic forces resulting in the formation of forms that are more likely culturally specific and historically bound.

In addressing the question of the existence of firms, this chapter reflects on two dominant views: neo-liberal and neo-Marxist. The transaction cost economics (cost minimization) and knowledge-based (transformation) approaches were briefly discussed within the first perspective. The neo-Marxist view is broad and is highly critical of the firm's role in society and its influences on governments at home and abroad. It is suggested, however, that in today's economy, firms' purposes and goals are not purely determined by endogenous and open deliberation. Rather, the firm is viewed as a history-contingent process. That is, firms are entities that essentially emerge from the market process and almost simultaneously retain something distinct from the spontaneous market order. As such, the firm has specific functions to perform in the market. These functions, however, are shaped by the interplay of various forces including government and the power elite.

It is in the context of capitalism that the nature of the relationships between the firm and state is examined. The two perspectives, neo-liberal and neo-Marxist, differ significantly in their outlook and treatment of the firm but both highlight the fact that firms are vital economic forces that exercise influence far beyond their economic sphere and could simultaneously play positive and negative roles in society. This is especially true as firms are not only economic but also social actors that seek to optimize interests, beyond the profit motive, by engaging in carefully orchestrated political and social activities. In this chapter, no attempt is made to validate any of the discussed perspectives or to mold ideas into sanctioned frameworks.

Most of the conceptualization and/or categorization of capitalism in international business literature is based on the assumption that firms are the primary actors in the economy and in subsequently shaping the form of capitalism. Instead, the perspective advanced in this study highlights the fact that national and cultural conditions facilitate the emergence of various actors, including the state and power elite, which shape and reshape economic reality and conditions at home and abroad. The priority and orientations of these actors and their weight in the power equation leave their mark on the nature and evolution of capitalism. Thus, four types of capitalism were identified: missionary, nationalistic, global, and evangelical.

The role of the firm, its purpose, alliances, and activities vary across these forms of capitalism. Under missionary capitalism, the charter firms were given autonomous authority in managing the political, military and economic affairs of colonies. These firms assumed a cultural role too, especially in prompting Christianity and institutionalizing Western norms where possible. The state, at that time, used its power and resources in the service of the firm and in preventing any rival from gaining a market advantage or establishing a foothold in the firm's designated market. Apparently, this state of affairs has not changed profoundly under the nationalistic form. What changed, however, was the state beginning to reassert itself in managing colonies and in viewing firms as an independent instrument essential for furthering and serving nationalistic goals. Viewing firms as actors who have a life independent of the State – autonomous, with constituencies, missions, and goals that separate them from the state and rivals alike – has been clearly articulated and embodied in the global capitalism stage. It is at this stage that the nationality of the firm appears to matter less than the firm's involvement and contribution to economic development and human capital formation.

The ascendancy of evangelical capitalism and the accompanying militaristic attitudes may change the complex relationships between the state and the firm. In fact, it may set the stage back and discount the view that firms are autonomous actors. Garten (2002) argues that, in this new era, power elites utilize trade in the service of political goals, not vice versa. That is, firms are expected to have less freedom in seizing global opportunities or in pursuing foreign investment than what was common under global capitalism. The hegemonic state grants or withholds favor to firms contingent on their commitment to declared policy. While the hegemonic power may still grant favor to its national firms, non-national firms are expected to observe its global hegemonic goals and act accordingly. That is, the practice of evangelical capitalism may endanger the principles of market economy, competition, equal and free access to opportunities, and social justice. Thus, firms may confront political hurdles that obstruct their ability to operate freely in a global environment.

In conclusion, the firm has specific functions to perform in the market. These functions, however, are shaped and molded by the dynamic interplay of various forces including government and the power elite. Instead of viewing the existence of the firm strictly from the perspective of profit maximization, the firm should be viewed as an entity with a purposeful direction. Its purpose and engagement in the marketplace are not necessarily an outcome of primarily endogenous deliberation and consideration. Rather, various forces including national politics shape these objectives and activities and the policies of the global hegemonic power. The intrusiveness and subtlety of the latter differ across the four types of capitalism, but are highly visible under evangelical capitalism.

NOTES

1. Writing in *Capitalism Magazine* (17 January 2006), Alex Epstein argued that companies have a right to charge whatever prices they choose. He stated, 'If we think we are spending too much on gasoline, we are free to drive less . . . or travel by bicycle or on foot. Gas station owners cannot *force* us to buy gasoline; they can only offer us a trade, which we are free to accept or reject.'
2. The *New York Times* reported (Myer 2006, p. A3) that local banks in the Palestinian territories abruptly stopped handling the transference of money to the Palestinian Authority when the US Treasury barred all financial dealings with it. The report stated that European banks did the same. The report quoted Molly Millerwise, a spokeswoman for the Treasury, stating, 'Generally speaking, if an organization or individual is facilitating direct fund-raising for Hamas [a political group that won a decisive victory in Palestinian legislative elections], they open themselves up to action by the United States.'
3. Both the US Department of State and the Treasury Department (May 2006) threatened to fine European banks if they did not curb their activities in Iran, even in the absence of a UN Security Council resolution (see Weisman, 2006 for details).

REFERENCES

Ali, Abbas (1997), 'Keeping faith in the free trade system', *Competitiveness Review*, 7 (1): i–ii.

Ali, Abbas (2005), *Islamic Perspectives on Management and Organization*, Cheltenham, UK and Northampton, MA, USA: Edward Elgar.

Ali, Abbas and Robert Camp (1999), 'Economic sanctions: obstruction or instrument for world trade?', *Managerial Finance*, 25 (3–4): 66–75.

Ali, Abbas and Robert Camp (2003), 'Risk of Evangelical capitalism', *International Journal of Commerce and Management*, 13 (1): 1–10.

Barnett, Thomas (2004), *The Pentagon's New Map: War and Peace in the Twenty-first Century*, New York: G.P. Putnam's Sons.

Barnevik, P. (1991), 'The logic of global business. Interviewed by W. Taylor', *Harvard Business Review*, March–April: 91–105.

Beveridge, Albert (1968), *Meaning of the Times and Other Speeches*, Free Port, NY: Books for Libraries Press.

Boje, David (2003), 'NeoCons: radical foreign policy for U.S. global empire', 10 April. Available at www.peaceaware.com.

Buckley, Peter and M. Casson (2003), 'The future of the multinational enterprise in retrospect and in prospect', *Journal of International Business Studies*, **34**: 219–22.

Chase-Dunn, Christopher (1999), 'Globalization: a world-systems perspective', *Journal of World Systems Research*, **V** (2): 187–216.

Cooper, R.N. (1994), 'Considerations for the future of the world economy', Remarks to annual meeting of the Academy of International Business, Boston, November on Prospects for the Future World Economy.

Dunning, John (1993), *Multinational Enterprises and the Global Economy*, Wokingham: Addison Wesley.

Dunning, John (1995), 'Trade, location of economic activity and multinational enterprise: a search for an eclectic approach', in John Drew (ed.), *Reading in International Enterprise*, London: Routledge, pp. 250–74.

Dunning, John (1997), *Governments, Globalization, and International Business*, Oxford: Oxford University Press.

Dunning, John (2003), 'Some antecedents of internalization theory', *Journal of International Business Studies*, **34**: 108–15.

Epstein, Alex (2006), 'The myth of "price gouging"', *Capitalism Magazine*, 17 January. Available at www. capitalismmagazine.com.

Flux, A.W. (1899), 'The flag and trade: a summary review of the trade of the chief colonial empires', in J. Foreman-Peck (ed.) (1998), *Historical Foundations of Globalization*, Cheltenham, UK and Lyme, USA: Edward Elgar, pp. 206–39.

Friedman, Thomas (1998), 'Techno-nothings', *New York Times*, 11 December, A27.

Garten, Jeffrey (2002), 'From economy to siege economy', Presentation at the World Economic Forum Conference, New York.

Ghoshal, Sumantra (2005), 'Bad management theories are destroying good management practices', *Academy of Management Learning and Education*, **4** (1): 75–91.

Goitein, S. (1967), *A Mediterranean Society*, Volume 1, Berkeley and Los Angeles: University of California Press.

Heer, Jeet (2003), 'The philosopher', *The Boston Globe*, 11 May, H1.

Hobson, J.A. (1919), *Richard Cobden*, London: Ernest Benn Limited.

Huntington, Samuel (2004), 'American creed', *The American Conservative*, **3** (7): 8–16.

Ioannides, Stavros (2003), 'Orders and organizations: Hayekian insights for a theory of economic organization', *American Journal of Economics and Sociology*, **62** (3): 533–66.

Kahn, Joseph (2002), 'A disaffected insider surveys globalization and its discontents', June. Available at www.nytimes.com/2002/06/23/books/review.

Koopman, A. (1994), *Transcultural Management*, Oxford: Blackwell.

Kurtz, Paul (2004), 'The free market with a human face', *Free Inquiry Magazine*, **24** (2). Available at www.secularhumanism.org.

Lears, Jackson (1999), 'Capitalism, corrected and uncorrected. The lobster and the squid', *The New Republic*, 15 February, 27.

Lefebvre, Henri (2001), 'Comments on a new state form', *Antipode*, **33** (5): 769–82.

Luttwak, Edward (1997), 'From geopolitics to geo-economics: logic of conflicts, grammar of commerce', *Foreign Affairs Agenda*, **4**: 177–86.

Marx, Karl (1853), 'The East India Company – its history and results', *The New York Daily Tribune*, 11 July. Available at www.marxist.org.

Meyer, Klaus (2003), 'Perspectives on multinational enterprises in emerging economies', *Journal of International Business Studies*, **35** (4): 259–76.

Mitroff, I. (1995), 'Review of the age of paradox', *Academy of Management Review*, **20** (3): 748–50.

Modelski, G. (1987), 'Long cycles', in G. Modelski, *Long Cycles in World Politics*, Seattle: University of Washington Press, pp. 7–63.

Moller, Orstrom (1997), 'The coming world governance', *The International Economy*, **May/June**: 62–7.

Morley, J. (1988), *Life of Richard Cobden*, London: Chapman & Hall.

Mouawad, Jad (2005), 'Libya is enticing U.S. executives with its abundant oil reserves', *New York Times*, 2 January. Available at www.nytimes.com.

Myer, Greg (2006), 'In new problem for Palestinians, banks reject transfers', *New York Times*, 4 May, p. A3.

Nadesan, Majia (1999), 'The discourse of corporate spiritualism and evangelical capitalism', *Management Communication Quarterly*, **13** (1): 3–42.

Norquist, Warren (2001), 'How the United States used competition to win the Cold War', *Journal of Global Competitiveness*, **9** (1): 1–27.

Ohmae, K. (1991), *The Borderless World*, New York: Harper Perennial.

Osterloh, M., J. Frost and B. Frey (2002), 'The dynamics of motivation in new organizational forms', *International Journal of the Economics of Business*, **9** (1): 61–77.

Ottaway, Marina (2001), 'Reluctant missionaries', *Foreign Policy*, **125**: 44–53.

Pfaff, W. (1995), ' A new colonialism?', *Foreign Affairs*, **74** (1): 2–6.

Pisaturo, Ron (2003), 'The age of invisible virtue', *Capitalism Magazine*. Available at www.capmag.com/article.asp?ID=2417.

Popoff, F. (1994), 'Issues management. Interviewed by S. Ainsworth', *C&EN*, 23 March, 25–7.

Reich, R. (1990), 'Who is us?', *Harvard Business Review*, **January–February**: 53–64.

Reich, R. (1991), 'Who is them?', *Harvard Business Review*, **March–April**: 71–89.

Rubinson, Richard (1978), 'Political transformation in Germany and the United States', in Barbara Kaplan (ed.), *Social Change in the Capitalist World Economy*, Beverly Hills, CA: Sage, pp. 39–73.

Shenon, P. (1995), 'A Pacific island nation is stripped of everything', *The New York Times*, 10 December, 3.

Solo, Robert (1978), 'The neo-Marxist theory of the state', *Journal of Economic Issues*, **XII** (4): 829–42.

Tracinski, Robert W. (2002), 'The moral basis of capitalism', *Capitalism Magazine*, July. Available at www.capmag.com/article.asp?ID=1701.

Wall Street Journal (2002), 'The Saudi contradiction', Editorial, 30 October, p. A22.

Weisman, Steven (2006), 'Pressed by U.S., European banks limit Iran deals', *New York Times*, 22 May. Available at www.nytimes.com.

Wilkins, Mira (2005), 'Multinational enterprise to 1930: discontinuities and continuities', in A.D. Chandler and B. Mazlish (eds), *Leviathans*, Cambridge: Cambridge University Press, pp. 45–80.

Williamson, Oliver (1975), *Markets and Hierarchies: Analysis and Antitrust Implications*. New York: The Free Press.

PART IV

Power, subjects/subjectivities and identity

7. Flexible careers in a globally flexible market

Suzette Dyer

INTRODUCTION

The development and implementation of organization and labour flexibilities in the 1980s transformed the structure, nature and composition of paid employment. By the end of the 1980s and throughout the 1990s, these flexibilities were being theoretically and practically embedded in two emerging, yet quite distinct, discourses of globalization and of career management and development. These discourses share certain liberal assumptions about freedom and individuality and converge in the metaphoric space of organization. Collectively they capture, describe, endorse and prescribe changes to global political, economic and sociocultural arrangements, the nature and composition of paid employment, and what it means to have a career.

Proponents of liberalization argue that this socioeconomic and political framework improves business profit, social wellbeing and personal choice. Critics point to disparate outcomes associated with workplace change and the extension of liberalization through globalization with the benefits accruing to particular powerful elites. In this chapter I argue that the three discourses of globalization, organizational and labour flexibility and career represent macro, meso, and micro level aspects of the extension of neo-liberalism as an organizing principle for all aspects of life. My focus in this chapter is on the disciplinary function of career management and development within this framework.

My argument is presented in four sections. In the next section, the disciplinary analysis offered by Foucault (1977), Rose (1990) and Deetz (1992) is briefly reviewed. Their combined work helps make visible links between the seemingly disconnected macro, meso and micro level phenomena described by the discourses of globalization, organizational and labour flexibility and career. To this end, the next section presents a discussion on the development of organizational and labour flexibility and globalization and the impact these changes have had on the shape and conditions of work. Throughout the 1990s, the changes to work were being embedded in emerging career metaphors, the more popular of which are described in the fourth section, along with a typical prescription of career management. These sections provide the framework for discussing the disciplinary relationship between globalization, flexibility and contemporary career discourses. Thus as citizens become re-fabricated through career discourse to match requirements of flexible organization structures, they simultaneously become assimilated within the system associated with global neo-liberalism.

THE PANOPTIC GAZE, THE PSY-SCIENCES AND DISCIPLINING DIFFERENCE

The theorizing of discipline offered by Foucault (1977), Rose (1990) and Deetz (1992) illuminates the invisible processes involved with fabricating individuality in modern and postmodern society. Foucault's (1977) analysis of Bentham's panoptic prison highlights the usefulness of confined metaphoric spaces to train and produce docile utilizable bodies that fit the needs of the wider metaphoric space of society. Power–knowledge relationships are embedded in the circular and panoptic processes of hierarchal observation, normalizing judgements and examination (Foucault, 1977). Hierarchical observation places the worker, inmate, child or the sick under the panoptic gaze of the manager, warden, parent, teacher or doctor. Behaviours, symptoms and so on are measured, recorded, codified, graphed and located along a continuum. During examination individuals provide information and in return receive an assessment, score, statement or picture of the self. Normalizing judgements are made on the basis of the location of an exam score along the fabricated continuum. Discipline is achieved as individuals constrain their behaviour to become (or appear to become) normal as defined within their space of reference. By learning to become normal, a community of individuals becomes docile (Foucault, 1977). While a compliant, docile citizenship may lead to community improvement, Foucault suggests these improvements are often at the expense of individual autonomy. As such we lose the ability to make meaning for our self, simultaneously losing our ability to question meanings given to us.

Rose (1990) draws on and extends Foucault's analysis to make visible the links between the political agendas of governments and their engagement of organizations and experts to manage citizens at a distance. Rose's analysis illustrates the fluidity of the metaphoric disciplinary space by illuminating how discipline permeates the macro level political spaces, through the meso spaces of complex organizations, into the seemingly private spheres of our inner selves. He points out that governments, irrespective of political persuasion, seek to manage the subjective capacities of citizens by first making abstract speculations about issues concerning the population, for example, unemployment, crime or health, and articulating these concerns as public policy. Governments then create or instruct existing organizations, institutions and bureaucracies to administer public policy, often through the engagement of 'experts in subjectivity' (Rose, 1990, p. 2). These experts include the growing professional categories of, for example, psychologists, social workers, personnel managers, probation officers, occupational psychologists and so on.

Rose (1990) contends that experts in subjectivity use panoptic techniques to create governable knowledge. Thus the panoptic gaze of the manager, warden, teacher or doctor has shifted to become the psychological gaze of the expert. Rose (1990) maintains that the citizen subject 'is not to be dominated in the interests of power, but to be educated and solicited into a kind of alliance between personal objectives and ambitions and institutionally or socially prized goals or activities' (p. 8). He goes on to say that experts achieve this through intervening and acting on the 'choices, wishes, values, and conduct of the individual' (Rose, 1990, p. 10). In this sense, Rose contends the management of subjectivity can be better thought of as disciplining difference. Individual behaviour, values, habits or capacities are to be compared to desired norms and values; the variance disciplined, rewarded, sanctioned or punished. Compliance is sought by offering an image of a desired life that can be achieved by simply being willing (and presumably able) to amend the self in accordance with a new set of norms. Interventions that have the aim of reshaping human capacities are legitimized and indeed justified based on an apparent scientific knowledge base. Thus organizations provide the metaphoric space and experts provide the intervention to manage citizens' subjective capacities from a distance. Indeed experts have also come to alert government of social concerns witnessed within their fields of practice and have sought political responses.

Deetz's (1992) interpretation of the interrelated processes of colonization and deinstitutionalization (e.g. Habermas, 1984, 1989) further deepens our understanding of disciplinary processes. Deetz (1992) emphasizes that increasingly what are deemed to be desirable norms, standards, values, beliefs and behaviours are created within the corporate context. These new normalities uphold and support corporate goals and agendas. Colonization occurs when the activities carried out in other institutions (e.g. the family, the church, the state and so on) come to support the activities of the corporate world. The process of deinstitutionalization is signified as corporations become primary-meaning institutions; at the same time the influence of family, church and so on weakens. As part of the process of deinstitutionalization the individual must make sense of the world, and is increasingly doing so by turning to the psychologist, the human resource manager, or the therapist to help create meaning and self-identity.

DEVELOPING ORGANIZATION AND LABOUR FLEXIBILITY AND GLOBALIZATION

Many Western nations implemented Keynesian macro level frameworks in the post-Second World War era. Various analyses concluded that international trade difficulties, unregulated market activity and Taylorist low-wage mass-production structures contributed to creating and sustaining the Great Depression of 1929 (Boyer, 1995; Drache, 1996; Giddens, 1998). Keynesianism was viewed by many as a means to protect businesses and citizens from future market fluctuations and failures (Lipietz, 1983). Applied to the international level, regenerating and stabilizing international trade was considered integral to smoothing out market fluctuations. To this end, the Bretton Woods institutions, created at the closing of the Second World War, were charged with creating a system to facilitate international trade (Driscoll, 1998). The General Agreement on Trade and Tariffs (GATT; later to become the World Trade Organization) was to generate international goods trade; the International Monetary Fund was to develop an international financial system, and The World Bank was to facilitate infrastructural and economic development, initially in post-Second World War Europe, and later in transition economies and developing nations (Kelsey, 1999).

At the national level, market regulation, managing budget deficits and initiatives, employment creation, and public expenditure on welfare, healthcare, education, housing and public works were deemed key government responsibilities (Kelsey, 1999). At the firm level typical employment legislation legitimized unions, encouraged union/employer wage bargaining and created productivity linked wage rises; in exchange, employers could maintain control over work process (Drache, 1996; Lipietz, 1983). Paid employment was understood as involving secure, full-time jobs, relational employment arrangements, and life-long employment with the same employer (Hall and Associates, 1996). Underpinning this was a concerted effort to facilitate women returning to the home after the Second World War. This was manifest as a largely gender-segregated workforce, reinforced by the continuance of gendered pay differences and the creation of minimum wages and 'the family-wage' accorded to male workers (McClure, 1998). Such government regulation and intervention was legitimized based on the dual intent to enhance citizen wellbeing and to generate conditions conducive to business and sustained economic growth (Giddens, 1998).

Between 1950 and 1973 most Western industrialized countries experienced annual growth and low unemployment, enabling the maintenance of welfare and social security measures (Boyer, 1988). By the late 1960s however the post-Second World War economic boom gave way to rising inflation and unemployment, monetary instability and balance of trade difficulties (Piore and Sabel, 1984). The neo-liberal analysis and solutions to this gained favour, and from this perspective the economy was portrayed as being in crisis because of Keynesian welfare intervention (Humphries, 1998). The solution was to deregulate and liberalize national economies.

Similarly, bureaucratic organization structures and protectionist employment legislation were implicated in the 1970s' economic decline (Lipietz, 1997). High fixed costs, excessive union power, restricted management prerogative and inflexible organizations and workers were all in some way viewed as contributing to decreased firm productivity (Thompson and McHugh, 1990). Business leaders and members attending the Big Seven Summit of 1980 proffered that organizational and labour flexibility were necessary if the industrialized West was to remain competitive in the rapidly developing international marketplace (Lipietz, 1997).

In harmony with the above analysis, a number of organizational and labour flexibility models were put forward throughout the 1980s as offering the solutions to rigid organization structures and inflexible workers, and hence to enhance international competition. The more popular models included the flexible firm model (Atkinson, 1984), flexible specialization (Piore and Sabel, 1984), lean production (Womack et al., 1990), and the Total Quality Management system (Perry et al., 1995). This interest in organizational and labour flexibility continued throughout the 1990s, by which time it was held to be the solution to growing global competition (Ehrensal, 1995; Felstead and Jewson, 1999). While the models differ in the finer points, each addresses perceived rigidities of organization and labour. For many, flexibility became a euphemism for downsizing, mass redundancies and work intensification. For others, flexibility became synonymous with the development of core and periphery workers, with an increase in precarious forms of employment including contractual, part-time, casual and temporary work, and the rise in unemployment (Bruhnes et al., 1989; Campbell, 2002).

Pollert (1991) argued that the implementation of organizational and labour flexibilities throughout the 1980s is directly linked to the development of globalization; liberalization of the political economy being the precondition for both. The extensive liberalization of the United States of America, Great Britain and New Zealand in the late 1970s and early 1980s has been well documented (Kelsey, 1995). Throughout the 1990s, other nations began to liberalize their economies and privatize state assets, diminish welfare spending, downsize state employment, and deregulate industry, labour, finance and capital markets (Brook Cowen, 1997). These neo-liberal values became embedded in the agendas of the World Trade Organization (WTO; formerly the GATT), the International Monetary Fund (IMF), and the World Bank. Together, these institutions have sought to expand neo-liberalism and a free trade agenda to the global level by initiating structural adjustment programmes and insisting nations liberalize their economies to gain access to IMF or World Bank loans, and as entry criteria to the WTO. Similarly, the liberal rhetoric became mirrored in the regional alliances and trading blocs (e.g. the Organisation for Economic Cooperation and Development (OECD) and the North American Free Trade Agreement) (Kelsey, 1995). This convergence of liberalization is signalled by the expansion of cross-border movement of finance, goods and services, and the use of international manufacturing sites and labour supplies. Within the liberal framework, globalization has become a socio-political and economic system that operates on the basis of governments simultaneously decreasing market interference and increasing protectionist legislation for capital (Cerny, 1999).

Voluntary or coerced adoption of structural adjustment programmes and the concomitant extension of globalization based on neo-liberal values have not gone unchallenged. Some have expressed concern over the weakening of national sovereignty caused by government policy reflecting the interests or dictates of international institutions and alignments and the needs of global capital (Crane, 1999 Washington; 1996). Similarly, others are concerned about diminished democratic participation as decisions about technology, labour and resources are increasingly made by non-elected managers within the confines of corporate board meetings and under the guise of commercial sensitivity (Deetz, 1992). The exclusion from negotiations in the international arena and the boardroom makes it difficult for meaningful debate or opposition to occur.

Loss of sovereignty and democratic participation is believed to be exacerbated for certain indigenous groups who have lost ownership rights to land and resources as their governments have privatized state assets (Kelsey, 1999). Private and often foreign owners possess the liberal notion of natural rights to retain profits and to conduct business according to the laws of the land (Brook Cowen, 1997). However, in some instances the health and safety of workers and citizens have been compromised where multinational companies have taken advantage of minimalist protection legislation. Such exploitations have been recorded in Mexico (Global

Trade Watch, 1998), India, (Cassels, 1993), and Indonesia, China and Vietnam ('Shoes giant', 1998). Despite these evidences, this privatization process is endorsed by many Western governments, the World Bank and the IMF (Kelsey, 1999).

Concerns over the impacts of organizational restructuring on the shape and conditions of employment have also been raised. Some categories of workers have experienced longer working hours, which are linked to increased stress, accidents and injury, decreased family and leisure time, and restricted access to organizational hierarchies for those (primarily women) with family responsibility (Ehrensal, 1995; Leka et al., 2003; Moss Kanter, 1990). In contrast, Grawitzky (2000) points out that nearly 900 million people worldwide are underemployed or unemployed, many of whom are seeking more hours or more secure forms of work (Pawson et al., 1996; Rosenberg and Lapidus, 1999; von Hippel et al., 1997). The creation of peripheralized workers has seen increased occurrences of contractual exclusion from sick leave, holiday entitlements and lower wages (Humphries, 1998; Rosenberg and Lapidus, 1999; von Hippel et al., 1997; Watts, 1997). Unemployment is linked to social withdrawal, anxiety, stress, physical and mental illness, alcoholism, drug abuse, family violence, child neglect, poverty entrapment, 'hate group' participation, suicide and crime (Ehrensal, 1995; McBride, 1999; Uchitelle and Kleinfield, 1996). Of concern is Watts' (1997) observation that unemployment becomes concentrated in particular households and communities.

Many authors (e.g. Bruhnes et al., 1989; Clegg and Dunkerley, 1980; Humphries, 1998) argue that the threat of downsizing and contracting-out and the existence of unemployment acts to discipline remaining employees to accept diminished pay and conditions. Resistance has been met with redundancies (Ehrensal, 1995; Global Trade Watch, 1998; Watson, 1999). Re-employment has often been at lower wages and conditions or in the growing yet traditionally low-waged service sector (Morris and Western, 1999; Perkin, 1996; Uchitelle and Kleinfield, 1996). Indeed, globalization based on liberal ideals and the concomitant establishment of organization and labour flexibility have been accompanied by growing gaps between rich and poor, both within and between nations (Gutkin, 2000; Mander, 1996). Income polarization is partially explained by increased compensation for executives and higher income earners coupled with declining real wages for low income earners (Morris and Western, 1999; Perkin, 1996). Downward pressure on the incomes of some categories of workers has resulted in the expansion of the working poor, some of whom are in fulltime employment (Kossek et al., 1997), others with precarious attachment to the labour market (Uchitelle and Kleinfield, 1996). Kossek et al., (1997) note that children living in poverty are less able to gain tertiary (or any) education and are forming a new 'under-class'. Such children are more likely to be restricted to low-pay positions, competing directly with lower paid international labour forces (Nevile and Saunders, 1998).

Gendered segregation of employment and women's lower wages relative to men's is also implicated in the downward pressure on incomes and working conditions. Western women have lost their secure manufacturing jobs to less expensive female labour in developing nations (Bianchi, 1999; Mies, 1998). More recently, women in developing nations are losing their jobs to even less expensive women living in China and in transition economies (Rosen, 2003). Western women are over-represented in the low-paid, insecure and peripheral jobs, and are reconstituted as reproducers and consumers of affordable imported products (Bianchi, 1999; Global Trade Watch, 1998; Walsh, 1997). Women in Third World, developing and transition nations have been reconstituted as producers as they shift their productive capacities from subsistence work providing for families to poorly paid employment producing export goods (Global Trade Watch, 1998; Mies, 1998; Waring, 1996, 1988). Women and their children throughout the world are over-represented in poverty and working poor statistics. Ironically, the World Bank advocates that Third World women's poverty will be relieved through education enabling them to access jobs in the global economy (The World Bank Group, 2000). Such rhetoric is underpinned by the persistent non-valuing of women's unpaid and poorly paid productive work that effectively obscures their contribution to family, business and the economy (Burgess and Strachan, 1999; Mies, 1998; Waring, 1996). Similarly, this advice ignores the critical issue of downwards pressure on incomes for some categories of jobs requiring education and training (Nevile and Saunders, 1998), the use of international contracting-out to create this downwards wage spiral (Mies, 1998), the difficulty for those living in poverty to gain access to education (Kossek et al., 1997), and the role that the creation and global extension of low-cost female labour has in this process (Fuentes and Ehrenreich, 1983; Mies, 1998).

By the late 1980s, and more so throughout the 1990s, the changes to the structure of work resulting from organizational downsizing and restructuring gained the attention of a new generation of career theorists. They began to recognize that the ensuing reconfigurations of employment undermined tenure, stability and upward mobility, conditions central to the bureaucratic and traditional notions of career. Gaining ever higher positions, pay and status within one organization, they argued, was no longer feasible in this turbulent environment (Greenhaus and Callanan, 1994; Moss Kanter, 1990). Moreover, they observed changing attitudes, behaviours and values towards career, and that career was being enacted in new ways. Meanwhile responsibility for managing and developing career was being transferred from organizations to individuals. At the same time, employer/ employee loyalty and relational employment arrangements were eroding, with transactional employment contracts becoming more evident (Hall and Associates, 1996). These observations formed the basis of a number of career management and development models that gained favour during the late 1980s and throughout the 1990s.

CHANGING CAREERS

As noted above, in harmony with structural changes, throughout the 1980s and 1990s a number of career researchers began articulating new metaphors for career management and development. For example, Moss Kanter's (1990) description of internal and external entrepreneurial and professional careers captures job expansion and reduced managerial layers resulting from corporate downsizing during the 1980s. The internal or organizationally bound entrepreneurial career is typified by gaining responsibility for developing a new product line or service; career growth is signified by the expansion of support roles beneath the entrepreneur. Moss Kanter notes that while the entrepreneurial careerist may have greater responsibility, freedom, independence and control over the product or service, their employment and hence career is not guaranteed. One way, she suggests, to manage this instability is for managers to support internal entrepreneurs to set up business so they may contract their services back to the corporation. Indeed, this practice of creating external entrepreneurs to supply once in-house services reflects the creation of periphery labour markets as suggested and prescribed by earlier commentators (e.g. Atkinson; 1984; Bruhnes et al., 1989; Handy, 1989).

Similarly, the professional career is achieved by possessing a valued skill or knowledge base (Moss Kanter, 1990). Career develops as skills and reputations are enhanced. Again, career is signified by job expansion or by gaining new contracts, and is reminiscent of the constant downsizing and rolling redundancies experienced throughout the 1980s. Having a career is dependent on the careerist developing generic and portable skills and being flexible to respond to changes in the external environment (Moss Kanter, 1990).

Handy (1994) links his description of the portfolio career to his earlier work on organizational restructuring. Handy (1989) used the 'shamrock firm' metaphor to describe new organizational structures that involve the contracting-out of non-core business activities. The portfolio career captures and legitimizes multiple and simultaneous work arrangements of wage work, fee work, homework, and community work. Such a career requires updated marketable skills and individual flexibility to move to new contracts, wage or fee work.

Brousseau et al. (1996) describe four distinct career patterns. Their descriptions of the expert and linear careers reflect aspects of the core workforce, as these forms grant limited relational employment arrangements to core workers. The expert career is built on gaining more knowledge and technical skill in a particular occupational field or speciality. The linear career involves limited upward movement within reconfigured and flatter organization structures. These theorists hold that organizations need to provide tenure as an incentive for some individuals to invest in furthering their knowledge and skill base, and to ensure the development and retention of business knowledge. They suggest that tenured staff are more likely to commit to and identify emotionally with the organization, all of which drives innovation and change essential for long-term survival in a competitive market.

The 'spiral' and 'transitory' careers reflect transactional employment arrangements associated with different categories of the peripheralized labour force. The spiral career involves shifts that build on current knowledge, for example moving from engineering to product development. In-depth competence is gained in an area but moves are made every 7 to 10 years and before mastery is achieved (Brousseau et al., 1996). In contrast, the transitory career is characterized by constant change or movement from one job or field to an unrelated area every 3 to 5 years, requiring new and different skills with each move.

Hall and Associates' (1996) protean career model is characterized by constant job and organizational moves facilitated by continuous learning and self-reflection. Within this model, the organization is deemed only one of many spaces in which a career may be enacted. The protean careerist is deemed a 'free agent' who is willing and able to learn new skills and morph into another self in preparation for each move. Moreover, preparing for job change is as much about identifying and fulfilling self needs. To this end the protean career may be signified by working from home, taking career breaks, raising children or caring for the elderly. As with the previous career models, the protean career reflects changes to the structure and security of employment and locates the responsibility for career management with the individual.

These emergent career metaphors imply a different definition of career that is in harmony with organizational restructuring and changes to the nature of paid employment. Greenhaus and Callanan (1994) offer a typical definition of career as '*the pattern of work-related experiences that span the course of a person's life*' (p. 5, emphasis in original). Anyone engaged in work-related activity is engaged in a career. Objective elements of career include job positions, duties or activities and work-related decisions. Subjective elements of career may include interpretations of work-related events and 'work aspirations, expectations, values, needs, and feelings about particular work experiences' (Greenhaus and Callanan, 1994, p. 5). In a subsequent edition of their book, Greenhaus et al. (2000, p. 9) explain:

> the definition's omission of advancement in the corporate hierarchy as a defining characteristic of a career meshes well with the limited mobility opportunities within today's flat organization. Similarly, to require that a career provide stability within one organization – or even one career path – is unrealistic in today's world of downsizing, contingent workers, and constantly changing jobs.

Greenhaus et al. (2000) argue that individuals must plan their own career in this environment. They offer a prescriptive career management model that according to them 'describes how people *should* manage their careers' (p. 24, emphasis added). In this model, key tasks of the 'career exploration' phase are to evaluate the self and the environment. Thus we should explore our interests, talents, strengths and weaknesses, and work values. Similarly we are to explore the employment environment by reviewing occupations, companies and industries; and assess the kinds of skills needed for various job types. This self and environmental awareness enables the formulation of realistic career goals. The remaining tasks of the career management model require the development and implementation of a personalized career strategy to achieve the realistic career. Because of the uncertainty in employment, they argue their model is circular, thus one must continuously review the self and the external environment, (re)generate appropriate career goals and where necessary make adjustments to the self, goal or career strategy.

While it is believed that most individuals are capable of designing their own career, a plethora of assistance is now available within the public and private sectors via self-help books (Garsten and Grey, 1997), the World Wide Web, and in the growing professional body of careers practitioners. Indeed, 'career' has morphed into an academic discipline in its own right as indicated by careers streams at international conferences (Greenhaus et al., 2000). Career has also captured the imagination of many Western governments and the OECD as a means to facilitate welfare, education, training and labour market policies (Boyd et al., 2001; OECD, 2003). Governments from nations as diverse as New Zealand (Oakes and von Dadelszen, 1999), middle-income and transition economies (Watts and Fretwell, 2003), European Union nations (Sultana, 2004) and acceding European Union nations (The European Training Foundation, 2003) are providing publicly funded career services. The nature of these services differs from nation to nation, however many are integrated with welfare-to-work programmes seeking job placement with a central feature being to help individuals to 'future proof' themselves through becoming 'career resilient'.

DISCUSSION

A number of features can be discerned that render career discourse as an extension of the disciplinary apparatus. First, Grey (1994), Fournier (1998) and Savage (1998) provide insight into the disciplinary relationship between the discourses of contemporary career metaphors and organizational and labour flexibility. Grey's (1994) findings from his research in an accounting firm reveal the disciplinary use of performance appraisals to determine which of the intern trial employees would be retained and which would be dismissed. These employees were offered a desirable image of career, that of attaining tenure, should they meet performance standards. What was unclear to these candidates was what constituted standard performance. Moreover, Grey found that career became a central organizing theme for all aspects of an employee's life; thus family, friends and leisure time became harnessed in the pursuit of career. Moreover, employees began to align personal attitudes and values with (limited) organizational scripts. Similarly, Fournier (1998) noted that the construct of career could simultaneously be drawn on as evidence of career success and career failure within a newly restructured organization. Employees who had normalized job expansion and extended working hours following the restructure perceived themselves to have successful careers. Employees who articulated these same changes as work intensification and exploitation became embedded in organizational narratives of career failure. Their ensuing lack of progression in the organization provided visible examples to others about what could happen to those who do not conform to organizational values and norms. Indeed Savage (1998) concludes that discipline has been a central theme in the construction of career from the outset; bureaucratic rules providing cues for self-management. These organizational examples are similar to Deetz's (1992) articulation of colonization of the life world. Individuals are left responsible for the task of managing themselves, including the possibilities of harnessing or subordinating all aspects of life in order to fit an organizationally shaped career.

Grey, Fournier, and Savage provide insight into the disciplinary aspects of career within the organizational context; however career is no longer to be understood as being embedded within any given organization. Thus the second disciplinary feature is associated with the shift of rules and prescriptions guiding career management from organizationally located job descriptions, training requirements, and so on to externally sourced career service providers and the proliferation of self-help books (Carson and Phillips-

Carson, 1997). In this context the 'career consultant' becomes a new addition to the family of experts in subjectivity as articulated by Rose; and individual willingness to seek such help supports one aspect of Deetz's theorizing around the notion of deinstitutionalization. Career experts facilitate the fabrication of citizens to accept personal responsibility for creating an employable self and the normalization of new employment patterns as natural, inevitable and indeed self-manageable. Similarly, Garsten and Grey (1997) argue that self-help books suggest individuals can reflect on the self and make meaningful changes, yet typically such books ignore the environmental constraints within which people live their lives. Thus they claim these books promote the individualization and de-politicization of citizens, at the same time encouraging individuals to create a self that is desirable to organization needs.

Third, while many contemporary career theorists make explicit links to changes in paid employment, little attention is given to the less optimistic outcomes of these changes (e.g. casualization, part-time and fixed-term employment arrangements, and downward pressure on some incomes). Moreover, there is little mention of how structural issues that diminish life outcomes for individuals may be overcome. Rather, individuals are merely advised that these less optimistic outcomes can be avoided for themselves through a properly managed career. Even if this were the case for a specific individual, there is no sense of a collective responsibility for the affects of 'the system' on the lives of fellow human beings.

Finally, career theorists give no attention to the concerted political intent behind the development and implementation of globalization and organizational and labour flexibility. Yet career instruction entrenches the ensuing changes to the structure and conditions of paid employment. In this context government provision of publicly funded career services aimed at harnessing individual capacities to fit the reconfigured employment environment must be understood in terms of Rose's (1990) analysis of managing citizens from a distance. Indeed, the focus of teaching individuals to manage themselves according to the reconfigured structure of paid employment fits neatly with the neo-liberal assumption that atomized individuals ought to take care of the self through attachment to the labour market. Thus the lexicon of the seemingly disparate discourses of globalization, organizational and labour flexibility and career is embedded in neo-liberal rhetoric.

CONCLUSION

In the context of greater individualization and atomization of humanity, together with the loosening of bonds to other institutions, career can be viewed as an organizing principle. Individuals can use this career principle to guide and manage themselves and all aspects of their lives to better fit the context of global neo-liberalism. The disciplinary features of career described here facilitate the re-shaping of individual understanding of work and workers. Acting on the self to become employable helps assimilate individuals to wider sociopolitical and economic structures. This individualized approach to making sense of workplace change obscures the political intent behind developing economic frameworks that have resulted in disparate outcomes for many, and hence obscures the potential to negotiate an alternative framework. In this sense, career facilitates the creation of a docile utilizable individual who is equipped to maintain particular power relationships embedded in global neo-liberalism.

REFERENCES

Atkinson, J. (1984), 'Manpower strategies for flexible organizations', *Personnel Management*, **16**(8), 28–31.

Bianchi, S. (1999), 'Feminization and juvenilization of poverty: trends, relative risks, causes and consequences', *Annual Review of Sociology*, **25**, 307–33.

Boyd, G., B. Hemmings and E. Braggett (2001), 'A career education program for gifted high school students: a case study', *Australian Journal of Career Development*, **10**(2), 6–10.

Boyer, R. (1988), 'The evolution of wage/labour relations in seven European Countries', in R. Boyer (ed.), *The Search for Labour Market Flexibility: The European Economies in Transition*, Oxford: Oxford University Press, New York: Clarendon Press, pp. 3–25.

Boyer, R. (1995), 'Capital–labour relations in OECD countries: from the Fordist Golden Age to contrasted national trajectories', in J. Schor and Y. Jong-Il (eds), *Capital, the State and Labour: A Global Perspective*, Aldershot, UK and Brookfield, USA: Edward Elgar, pp. 18–69.

Brook Cowen, P. (1997), 'Neo-liberalism', in R. Miller (ed.), *New Zealand Politics in Transition*, Auckland, NZ and Oxford, UK: Oxford University Press, pp. 341–9.

Brousseau, K., M. Driver, K. Eneroth and R. Larson (1996), 'Career pandemonium: realigning organizations and individuals', *Academy of Management Executive*, **10**(4), 52–66.

Bruhnes, B., J. Rojot and W. Wassermann (1989), *Labour Market Flexibility: Trends in Enterprises*, Paris: Organisation for Economic Co-operation and Development, pp. 11–36.

Burgess, J. and G. Strachan (1999), 'The expansion in non-standard employment in Australia and the extension of employers' control', in A. Felstead and N. Jewson (eds.), *Global Trends in Flexible Labour*, Basingstoke: Macmillan, pp. 121–40.

Campbell, I. (2002), 'Extended working hours in Australia: the importance of working time legislation', in I. McAndrew and A. Geare (eds), *Celebrating*

Excellence, Proceedings of the 16th AIRAANZ Conference, Queenstown, New Zealand, 5–8 February, pp. 77–87.

Carson, K.D. and P. Phillips-Carson (1997), 'Career entrenchment: a quiet march toward occupational death?', *Academy of Management Executive*, **11**(1), 62–75.

Cassels, J. (1993), *The Uncertain Promise of Law: Lessons from Bhopal*, Toronto: University of Toronto Press.

Cerny, P. (1999), 'Globalising the political and politicising the global: concluding reflections on International Political Economy as a vocation', *New Political Economy*, **4**(1), 147–62.

Clegg, S. and D. Dunkerley (1980), *Organization, Class and Control*, London, UK and Boston, USA: Routledge & Kegan Paul.

Crane, G. (1999), 'Imagining the economic nation: globalization in China', *New Political Economy*, **4**(2), 215–32.

Deetz, S. (1992), *Democracy in an Age of Corporate Colonization: Developments in Communication and the Politics of Everyday Life*, Albany: State University of New York Press.

Drache, D. (1996), 'From Keynes to K-Mart: competitiveness in a corporate age', in R. Boyer and D. Drache (eds), *States Against Markets: The Limitations of Globalization*, New York: Routledge, pp. 31–61.

Driscoll, D. (1998), 'What is the International Monetary Fund?', www.imfsite.org/operations/driscoll998.html (Accessed 19 January 2009).

Ehrensal, K.N. (1995), 'Discourses of global competition: obscuring the changing labour processes of managerial work', *Journal of Organizational Change Management*, **8**(5), 5–16.

Felstead, A. and N. Jewson (eds) (1999), *Global Trends in Flexible Labour*, Basingstoke: Macmillan.

Foucault, M. (1977), *Discipline and Punish: The Birth of the Prison* (Trans. Allan Lane), Harmondsworth: Penguin Books.

Fournier, V. (1998), 'Stories of development and exploitation: militant voices in an enterprise culture', *Organization*, **5**(1), 55–80.

Fuentes, A. and B. Ehrenreich (1983), *Women in the Global Factory*, Cambridge, MA: Southend Press.

Garsten, C. and C. Grey (1997), 'How to become oneself: discourses in subjectivity in post-bureaucratic organizations', *Organization*, **4**(2), 211–28.

Giddens, A. (1998), *The Third Way: The Renewal of Social Democracy*, Cambridge: Polity Press.

Global Trade Watch (1998), 'School of real-life results', www.citizen.org/pctrade/nafta/reports/5years.html (Accessed 3 January 2000).

Grawitzky, R. (2000), 'Globalization: the plight of billions stressed', *Business Day (Johannesburg)*, 30 March, www.igc.apc.org/globalpolicy/globaliz/econ/benefic.html (Accessed 30 December 2000).

Greenhaus, J. and G. Callanan (1994), *Career Management*, 2nd edn, Fort Worth, TX: Dryden Press.

Greenhaus, J., G. Callanan and V. Godshalk, (2000), *Career Management*, 3rd edn, Fort Worth, TX: Dryden Press.

Grey, C. (1994), 'Career as a project of the self and labour process discipline', *Sociology*, **28**(2), 479–97.

Gutkin, S. (2000), 'Rich–poor gap as wide as ever in Latin America', *Times India*, 5 September, www.igc.apc.org/globalpolicy/inequal/2000/latinam.html (Accessed 23 December 2001).

Habermas. J. (1984), *The Theory of Communicative Action, Volume 1: Reason and the Rationalisation of Society* (Trans. Thomas McCarthy), Boston, MA: Beacon Press.

Habermas, J. (1989), *The Theory of Communicative Action, Volume 2: Life-world and System, a Critique of Functionalist Reason* (Trans. Thomas McCarthy), Boston, MA: Beacon Press.

Hall, D. and Associates (1996), *The Career is Dead: Long Live the Career*, San Francisco, CA: Jossey-Bass.

Handy, C. (1989), *The Age of Unreason*, London: Hutchinson Business.

Handy, C. (1994), *The Empty Raincoat: Making Sense of the Future*, London: Hutchinson Business.

Humphries, M. (1998), 'For the common good: New Zealanders comply with quality standards', *Organization Science*, **9**(6), 738–49.

Kelsey, J. (1995), *The New Zealand Experiment: A World Model for Structural Adjustment?*, Auckland, NZ: Auckland University Press/Bridget Williams Books.

Kelsey, J. (1999), *Reclaiming the Future: New Zealand and the Global Economy*, Wellington, NZ: Bridget Williams Books.

Kossek, E., M. Huber-Yoder, D. Castellino and J. Lerner (1997), 'The working poor: locked out of careers and the organizational mainstream', *Academy of Management Executive*, **11**(1), 76–91.

Leka, S., A. Griffiths and T. Cox (2003), *Work Organization and Stress: Systematic Problem Approaches for Employers, Managers, and Trade Union Representatives*, Protecting Workers Health Series, No. 3, Switzerland: World Health Organization.

Lipietz, A. (1983), *The Enchanted World: Inflation, Credit and the World Crisis* (Trans. Ian Patterson), Paris: New Left Books.

Lipietz, A. (1997), 'Economic restructuring: the new global hierarchy', in P. James, W. Veit and S. Wright (eds), *Work of the Future: Global Perspectives*, Melbourne: Allen & Unwin, pp. 45–65.

Mander, J. (1996), 'The dark side of globalization: what the media are missing', *The Nation*, 15–22 July, 9–32.

McBride, S. (1999), 'Towards permanent insecurity: the social impact of unemployment', *Journal of Canadian Studies*, **34**(2), 13–30.

McClure, M. (1998), *A Civilised Community: A History of Social Security in New Zealand 1898–1998*, Auckland, NZ: Auckland University Press.

Mies, M. (1998). *Patriarchy and Accumulation on a World Scale: Women in the International Division of Labour*, London: Zed Books.

Morris, M. and B. Western (1999), 'Inequality of earnings at the close of the twentieth century' *Annual Review of Sociology*, **25**, 623–57.

Moss Kanter, R. (1990), *When Giants Learn to Dance: Mastering the Challenges of Strategy, Management and Careers*, London: Unwin Paperbacks.

Nevile, J.W. and P. Saunders (1998), 'Globalization and the return to education in Australia', *Economic Record*, **74**(226), 279–85.

Oakes, L. and J. von Dadelszen (1999), 'The New Zealand policy framework for career information and guidance', paper presented at the International Symposium on Career Development and Public Policy: International Collaboration for National Action, 2–4 May, Ottawa, Canada.

OECD (2003), *Career Guidance and Public Policy: Bridging the Gap*, Paris: OECD.

Pawson, E. and others (1996), 'The state and social policy', in R. Le Heron and E. Pawson (eds), *Changing Places: New Zealand in the Nineties*, New Zealand: Longman Paul, pp. 210–46.

Perkin, H. (1996), *The Third Revolution: Professional Elites in the Modern World*, London: Routledge.

Perry, M., C. Davidson and R. Hill (1995), *Reform at Work: Workplace Change and the New Zealand Industrial Order*, New Zealand: Longman Paul.

Piore, M. and C. Sabel (1984), *The Second Industrial Divide: Possibilities for Prosperity*, New York: Basic Books.

Pollert, A. (1991), 'The orthodoxy of flexibility', in A. Pollert (ed.), *Farewell to Flexibility?*, Oxford, UK and Cambridge, MA, USA: Blackwell, pp. 3–31.

Rose, N. (1990), *Governing the Soul: The Shaping of the Private Self*, 2nd edn, London: Routledge.

Rosen, D. (2003), 'How China is eating Mexico's lunch: the Maquiladora system's comparative advantage is being challenged head on', *The International Economy*, 17(2), 22–5.

Rosenberg, S. and J. Lapidus (1999), 'Contingent and non-standard work in the United States: towards a more poorly compensated, insecure workforce', in A. Felstead and N. Jewson (eds), *Global Trends in Flexible Labour*, Basingstoke: Macmillan, pp. 62–83.

Savage, M. (1998), 'Discipline, surveillance and the "career": employment on the Great Western Railway 1833–1914', in A. McKinlay and K. Starkey (eds), *Foucault, Management and Organization Theory: From Panopticon to Technologies of the Self*, London: Sage, pp. 65–92.

Sultana, R. (2004), *Guidance Policies in the Knowledge Society: Trends, Challenges and Responses across Europe*, Malta: CEDEFOP.

The European Training Foundation (2003), *Review of Career Guidance Policies in Eleven Acceding and Candidate Countries Synthesis Report*, Viale Settimio: European Training Foundation.

The Waikato Times (1998), 'Shoes giant faces civil suit over Asia sweatshops', 21 May, p. 10.

The World Bank Group (2000), 'World Bank programs', www.worldbank.org/html/extdr/about/programs.html (Accessed 25 January 2002).

Thompson, P. and D. McHugh (1990), *Work Organizations: A Critical Introduction*, Basingstoke: Macmillan.

Uchitelle, L. and R. Kleinfield (1996), 'On the battlefield of business: millions of casualties', *The New York Times*, 3 March, www.nytimes.com

von Hippel, C., S. Mangum, D. Greenberger, R. Heneman and J. Skoglind (1997), 'Temporary employment: can organizations and employees both win?', *Academy of Management Executive*, 11(1), 93–103.

Walsh, P. (1997), 'From arbitration to bargaining: changing state strategies in industrial relations', in B. Roper and C. Rudd (eds), *State and Economy in New Zealand*, Auckland, NZ: Oxford University Press, pp. 183–201.

Waring, M. (1988), *Counting for Nothing*, Wellington, NZ: Allen & Unwin New Zealand.

Waring, M. (1996), *Masquerades*, Auckland: Auckland University Press.

Washington, S, (1996), 'Globalization and governance', *OECD Observer*, 199(April/May), 24–7, www.oecdobserver.org/

Watson, M. (1999), 'Rethinking capital mobility: re-regulating the financial markets', *New Political Economy*, 4(1) 55–75.

Watts, A. (1997), 'The future of career and of career guidance', Keynote Speaker at *Career Planning: Signposting the Future Conference*, Career Services Rapuara, Wellington, New Zealand, 15–17 January 1997.

Watts, A. and D. Fretwell (2003), *Public Policies for Career Development: Policy Strategies for Designing Career Information and Guidance Systems in Middle-income and Transition Economies*, Washington, DC: World Bank.

Womack, J., D. Jones and D. Roos (1990), *The Machine that Changed the World*, New York: Macmillan.

8. Cultural mimicry and hybridity: on the work of identity in international call centers in India

Diya Das and Ravi Dharwadkar

he no longer recognizes the distinction between waking and dreaming states; he understands now something of what omnipresence must be like, because he is moving through several stories at once. (Salman Rushdie, *The Satanic Verses* 1988: 457)

INTRODUCTION

The concept of 'identity' in organization studies, in both its noun and verb (to identify) forms, has been an extremely 'integrative and generative' one that has been able to travel at multiple levels of conceptual analyses (Albert et al., 2000). Many of the studies on this concept have sought to explain the phenomena of self-definition that are associated with an individual's experiences within the workplace. The foci of these studies have tried to explain a variety of issues such as the process of role identifications or organizational identifications (and disidentifications), the processes by which management fosters such identifications, and the benefits (or not) derived from that, and so on (for a review, see Whetten and Godfrey, 1998). Some studies within this field have tried to understand the complications that can arise in the process of identification. For example, researchers have studied the complications that arise within racially diverse organizations, and how employees constantly negotiate their specific racial identity stereotypes and professional identities within the workplace (Bell, 1990; Chattopadhyay et al., 2004; Ellemers et al., 2002; Roberts, 2005). Other studies have also explored the complications that arise when there is ambiguous organizational membership, as in the case of contract workers (George and Chattopadhayay, 2005). In spite of their diverse theoretical orientations, however, the extant scholarship on identities in organizations seems to be predicated on one basic assumption that might be surmised as follows: all identities such as those of certain professions, organizations, race, gender,

181

ethnicity, or nationality are stable, constant and corporeal; that is, they can be traced to a person (Latin *corpus*) – who then has to negotiate with the implications of such embodied identities (Chattopadhyay et al., 2004; Roberts, 2005). However, globalization of work is mandating other different kinds of identity imperatives where employees are being required to mask their personal and social identities completely – the ones that have so far been thought to be rather stable and corporeal – and consciously enact 'other' social identities. One interesting site where this has been widely observed is in the Indian international call centers that have sprung up as a result of the process of a recent international move to offshore different kinds of service work, mainly from the USA, the UK and Australia.

The unique imperative of such call center work for the Indian employees consists of being able to impersonate the cultural identity of the client in order to create an impression of seamless customer service from across the globe. They accomplish this by adopting a 'Western' name, a different accent, and by pretending to be located somewhere in the customer's country. Such kinds of enactments reveal the contingent/provisional nature of all identities and the complicated identity dynamics generated therein, and thus cannot be completely understood by the existing frameworks of identity theories in organizations. For this, we turn to the recent developments in postcolonial theory that urge us to go beyond the originary, essentialist narratives of identity. In general, within organization studies, postcolonial theory has begun to be employed to understand different dimensions of power, control and resistance within organizations and the continuing trends of (neo)colonial domination therein (for a review see Prasad, 2003). Commenting on the intersections of postcolonial theories and globalization studies Simon Gikandi, a postcolonial theorist, offers

> [that while] diverse writers on globalization and postcolonialism might have differing interpretations of the exact meaning of these categories, or their long-term effect on the institutions of knowledge production in the modern world, they have at least two important things in common: they are concerned with explaining forms of social and cultural organization whose ambition is to transcend the boundaries of the nation-state, and they seek to provide new vistas for understanding cultural flows that can no longer be explained by a homogenous Eurocentric narrative of development and social change. (2001: 629)

While Gikandi is of course specifically concerned with one of the most enduring of such originary and stable identities, namely national identity, these theories come together around all the different uses of the concepts of 'hybridity' and 'difference'. Postcolonial theory has also recently been used to explore the effects of globalization within organizations, as in the study of ICTs and new technology by Gopal et al. (2003), the study of identities in international mergers (Aihlon-Souday and Kunda, 2003), and on cross-cultural training by Jack and Lorbiecki (2003).

An engagement with postcolonial theory is therefore relevant to our analysis of these call centers as a postcolonial Indian variant of the globalization of work. In this we draw on the formulations of hybridity as propounded by Homi Bhabha, a renowned cultural theorist. Bhabha shows that the colonial mimicry practiced by 'English educated' Indians created 'a subject of a difference that is almost the same, but not quite' (Bhabha, 1994: 86). This mimicry of the British colonizer and thereby the creation of 'almost the same' was in turn enabled primarily through the introduction and institutionalization of systems of English education/socialization (Viswanathan, 1989).[1] It emphasized, among other things, the need and importance of the ability to speak properly the language of the colonizer, in this case English (Fanon, 1967). Through the lens of this theoretical, philosophical and political framework one can then start conceptualizing the dynamic identities that are being produced 'in excess of' and 'in between' the conditions of corporate globalization. In the case of the Indian call centers we can see a similar process through which the ability to speak English is emerging as the currency for success and new socialization into 'Western' ways of life.

The overall aim of this chapter is to try to understand how new identifications are being produced by particular processes of corporate globalization such as the offshoring of service work. We have tried to record the experiences of these 'call center agents' through the narratives of their work experiences and hope to attain an emic perspective on the complex identification processes that are being produced. We attempt to understand how the employees in these call centers are being trained into these new identity orientations through processes of mimicry, and how they negotiate these enactments with their other salient identities. The other crucial aspect of such identity work is the responses they receive from the customers (especially the hostile ones), and how that affects their sense of self, and how they reconcile this. These experiences of call center executives lead us to also raise questions, via postcolonial theory, about the notion of 'Anglicization'[2] and the concurrent ambivalence that comes with it in the contemporary global workplace. To build this understanding, one of the authors spent about six months in various international call centers in Kolkata, in eastern India. We chose this city because the industry is now moving to Kolkata, after saturation at the initial sites of Delhi in the North and Bangalore in the South. The author had immersed herself in the industry to develop a close understanding of the process through ethnographic observations of the various recruitment and training processes and life on the work floor, and conducted interviews with the employees of these call centers.

THE INTERNATIONAL CALL CENTER INDUSTRY IN INDIA

Call centers are a relatively new industry that has been growing at a very fast pace in the last few years around the world (Deery and Kinnie, 2004). It has become a cornerstone of the service industry in the developed world. The unique attributes of this kind of workplace are that there is a dual focus of the management of cost efficiency on one hand and customer service quality on the other. Because of such seemingly contradictory require- ments and the practices generated therein, there is an ongoing debate on the nature of work in call centers. Some scholars have noted the tremen- dous control that is exercised here over the employees and have called these workplaces 'electronic sweatshops' (Garson, 1988), and 'twentieth century panopticons' (Fernie and Metcalf, 1998). Others like Frenkel et al. (1998), have argued that the call centers typify jobs with greater challenge and interest, and a clear recognition of the value of frontline personnel. Batt and Moynihan (2002, 2004) show that despite an increasing predominance of the production-line model in the service sector, call centers that have high-involvement work practices and invest in employees tend to generate greater revenues (2004). Call centers in India are a direct result of the glo- balization of work enabled by new communication technologies. This can be concluded from the fact that about 75 percent (approximately) of this industry caters to international markets (Batt et al., 2005). They are part of the overall business process outsourcing (BPO) industry and produce about 70 percent of its revenue. There is tremendous growth being expe- rienced by this industry – having started in the 1990s it is now projected to employ 1.2 million young Indians by 2008 (Nasscom estimates). A tremendous acceleration in the industry happened around the turn of the century with the bursting of the bubble in the software industry in the USA (Friedman, 2005). And the reason for this large exodus of call center work from developed countries has been directly attributed to the availability of a low cost, good quality, English-speaking workforce in India (Dossani and Kenney, 2003).

The call centers in India have been shown to be substantially different from those in the USA in their HR practices, with the Indian ones char- acterized by higher levels of education and training, significantly lower employee discretion and problem-solving, and very high levels of surveil- lance (Batt et al., 2005). It is precisely here that it is interesting to note some other important work-related modifications that are being made in this industry to ensure the smooth global transactions that the employees carry out, and what existing identity theories in organization studies fail to account for. To begin with, the Indian call center employees work mainly at night times that correspond to the daytime business hours of the client country (Taylor and Bain, 2005). The second aspect is that of the intensive 'Voice and Accent' training, through which the employees are required to eliminate or at least significantly reduce their mother tongue influence (MTI) and are encouraged to adopt the accents of the client countries. They are also given cultural training, where they are indoctrinated to understand and imitate the social and cultural life-styles of their clients in the USA, the UK or Australia (Mirchandani, 2004). The third such interesting variation in the job is that these employees usually undergo a 'naming ceremony' (Sitt, 1997) where they adopt a 'Western' name that they use in their interactions with their clients. They are often asked to 'pretend' to be living in the client country, and also in their conversations they have to appear to be employed by the company they are representing at that time (who are often not their employer but have subcontracted the work to their employers). Thus, very often, the employees actually impersonate and enact a whole different 'self' in their workplace – a person from a different country, with a different name and working with different social identities for a different company. The main reasons behind such active concealment of one cultural identity and enactment of another have been attributed to two factors – (1) first and foremost, to prevent a backlash from the customers who may not find it acceptable that 'their jobs' are being sent away to other countries, and (2) to increase efficiency and customer satisfaction (Sitt, 1997).

To capture this dynamic of identity formation and identity negotiation, we trace the organizational initiation process through a set of ethnographic accounts where the employees are systematically trained into the performance of such new identities. We then develop on the different themes of experiences and identity negotiations that come up in the interviews conducted.

RESEARCH METHODS

To understand the identity negotiations and experiences, here we employ two different methods: a method of an ethnographic immersion, and that of semi-structured interviews with the call center executives and HR/training personnel. One of the authors spent about six months in the industry – visiting the firms, sitting through the training programs, interviewing the agents, commuting with them, and also sometimes accompanying them to after-work parties and social events. The ethnography of the initiation process was carried out by the author by sitting through the entire recruitment process, followed by a 3-week generic training program in one mid-sized (about 700 employees) call center in Kolkata. The ethnography comprised of observations and informal conversations with the trainers and the trainees.

We also conducted over 100 interviews with agents and HR/training personnel in seven different call centers in Kolkata. All the interviews were conducted on a one-to-one basis. These interviews were semi-structured in nature and were aimed at understanding the attitudes and emotions of the agents toward the different dimensions of their work-life through a narration of their experiences. The interview time ranged between 25 minutes to an hour and a half with an average of about 35 minutes. The researcher approached the organizations and asked for permission to interview the employees and the managers. The interviewees were then randomly selected by the researcher from the different campaigns of the organizations where she was allowed to interview on the premises. In some cases, a snowball method was used to approach call center agents of organizations where the researcher was not granted access to the employees on the floor.

PRELIMINARY TRENDS

A preliminary analysis of the ethnographic accounts and interviews shows us interesting trends that can be read with a postcolonial lens in an attempt to capture the experiential reality of such identity work. In the following section we use the data to draw the HR processes of selection and training in this industry. We then provide an analysis of the narratives of the call center employees obtained through the interviews and try to identify some of the trends in their identity-related experiences.

INITIATION

The recruitment process of this organization (one medium-sized call center of about 700 employees) involved three rounds. The first round was when the prospective candidate met with a junior HR professional who would ask him/her some basic questions on why he or she wanted to join a call center, about his/her previous work experience, and so on. The HR person would also give a small reading in English to test the fluency of the candidate in the language. The next stage included a round of interviews with one of the generic trainers and the Assistant Vice-President – Human Resources (AVP-HR) where the candidate was asked 'situation questions' and future plans. Here the person was also asked about his/her shift preference. The last round was an interview with the COO (Chief Operating Officer) of the organization. According to Banani Chowdhury, the AVP-HR of the firm in question, 'the key skill in this industry is that of English language – if a person can speak good, fluent English with very little MTI [mother tongue influence], we will take that person. English speaking is the basic thing we are looking for – they are hard to find these days.' Most call centers follow the same mode of recruitment. They may have more or fewer rounds of interviews but the key skills for the industry are the knowledge of and ability to speak 'proper English'. In some of the organizations the first round also involves a written test of English grammar and a 'cultural test' on general knowledge about the USA and the UK. For example, in one organization, the HR manager explained that 'knowledge of American movies and politics show that the person has some good exposure and can be a better caller.' Some firms also conduct an additional listening and comprehension test on the lines of the Test of English as a Foreign Language (TOEFL). Thus, the centrality of English and the affinity and exposure to client country ways of life are established right in the beginning of the employer–employee relation. In fact, there is a boom in independent training institutes in India now where call center aspirants enroll to develop their English speaking skills and to learn about 'Western' cultures. Certificates obtained through training are also valuable for getting jobs in call centers.

TRAINING

In most call centers the training process is divided into two different parts – the 'Generic' training and the 'Process/Product' training. The generic training is usually the longer training program, and involves voice-and-accent training, soft-skills training and cultural training. The process or product training initiates the employees into the specific process or campaign for which they will work. Here they learn about the product, the pricing, the services provided, the competitors, the competitive advantage of the product they need to sell, and other aspects of their sales pitch. They are also trained into specific 'rebuttals'; that is, they are trained to answer specific questions about their location, and the weather, geography and cultural aspects (such as sports teams) of that area.

Right at the beginning of the training program, the employees are given an 'alias' – a 'Western' name. Each organization has its own set of rules about what names can be taken by the employees. In many organizations, they insist that the aliases have the same initials as the real name of the employee. In some others, they have a set of names generated by the training department and the employees are asked to choose from that. Others give a free hand to the employees to take up any name that they feel comfortable with. In one organization, where the researcher observed the entire training program, the last name for the specific training group was given by the trainers and the trainees were free to select their first names. For example, the training group the author observed had the last name of 'Hill' and was referred to as the 'Hill family' or the 'Hill batch'. Over the course of the training they learn to live with this name at work and respond to this name. Initially they make mistakes in their mock calls when they confuse their name or stutter in saying it, but by the end of the training they usually get it right. They also begin to stay up during the night – times that correspond with the day times of their customers – and consequently get 'lunch breaks' at 11 in the night, learn to speak in pounds and dollars, move between Celsius and Fahrenheit, kilograms and ounces, cricket and baseball, and so on. The adaptation to new names and time schedules is also accompanied by a simultaneous process of learning to conceal their real location and real name. To make this possible, the trainers try to de-familiarize the employees from their native way of speaking. There is, for example, a very common practice of doing a fairly long session on 'Indianisms.' 'Indianism' is used to refer to the manner in which English is spoken in India, and this session usually provokes a lot of laughter. It is supposed to be funny because the session is premised on a mockery of the so-called 'Indian' way of speaking English, with the expressed intention of inculcating a sense of shame at the agent's own native way of speaking English. Instead the 'neutral', British, American and Australian accents are valorized by the trainers as the accent to be imitated. In fact, from that session onwards, the trainees are encouraged to find faults of so-called Indianisms in their own and in their colleagues' accents and rectify them.

The accent training takes place through the regular practice of vowels, consonants and word chants before the training begins every day. It is often accompanied by a practice of tongue-twisters. They are also trained into specific aspects of accent acquisition depending on whether it is for the United States or the UK. For example, they are trained in specific accent acquisition rules for the USA, like the plosive rules, the TROLI, the mountain rule, the TH rule, and so on (for a review see Raina, 2004). In this way the training becomes the period when the employees gradually learn to conceal one set of identities, and get comfortable with and foreground another newly 'acquired' set of identities.

One needs to keep in mind, however, that though this training is rendered effective by its various rigorous sessions on accent and culture, its success also partly rests on a continuing desire for 'Westernization' in the postcolonial Indian subjects (Fanon, 1967). This desire is predicated on the elite status and continuing centrality of English as a language of power and upward mobility in postcolonial India in general (Viswanathan, 1989). In fact, this can be seen in the same light of the differential desire for the 'other' that determines the postcolonial variant of globalization as pointed out by Radhakrishnan (2001). The only observable change in the contemporary affinity for the English language would probably be the gradual prominence of American English along with, and in place of, the earlier dominance of British English (for a review see Kachru, 1983; Mishra, 2000; Trivedi, 1995).

AGENT REACTIONS

In the interviews conducted with the agents, they were asked about their experiences on this job, what they enjoyed and what they did not, how they thought this experience might have changed them, and their customer interactions. In general, the aim was to get access to the narratives of their work selves, the changes experienced, and their cross-cultural interactions. In these narratives of identity, the crucial aspect that emerged was the sense of disconnect or the bifurcated experience of leading two different lives that many of the agents shared. For example, according to Rajni, a female call center agent, the two identities she has are remarkably different – 'both of them belong to two different backgrounds. Lucy Matthews [the identity she enacts] works in Dish Network. She is based in Salt Lake City, Utah, whereas Rajni Basu-Chowdhury is a total house wife in Kolkata – doing a job in ABC – two different persons'. Similarly, according to Chiranjeet, a 20-year-old call center agent, 'Richard [his alias] is the kind of person who is comfortable being abused, in real life Chiranjeet is not that at all – they are very different people.' The interesting dynamic to note here is that there is no 'real' Lucy Matthews or Richard that exists, except when they are enacted by the respective agents, and therefore this role identity is dependent on the imagination of the agent-actor and the scripts of the organization. This also provides us with the sense of how identities are being de-stabilized – since Lucy Matthew's and Richard's roles are dependent on Rajni and Chiranjeet concealing their other, salient social identities.

It is also interesting to note how imagination plays a crucial role in this enactment. According to Arjun Appadurai (1996), our contemporary world of global cultural processes is characterized by a new role for imagination in social life – it has become a 'social practice,' a 'form of work', which now combines the functions of everything from fantasy and escape to contemplation and aspiration (1996: 31). The salient identities of the agent's 'real' life of being from Kolkata, India, of being a wife, working in their specific call centers and so on are thus being masked to be able to imagine and enact the identity of a Lucy or a Richard. The agents also had mixed reactions to living such double lives – for some like Tapan, another call center agent, it was a source of fun: 'Hardy is a very naughty guy, who would do anything, but Tapan Chatterjee is a very serious, typical Bengali guy, Hardy is a typical Aussie guy. Hardy lives in Melbourne with a room-mate, studying hotel management – see I have a good story for Hardy!' Some others like Jay said that he wanted to keep a different name even when he did not have to, 'because I don't want my identity to be associated with this work'. Such a sentiment stems from the fact that many of the campaigns that the agents have to work for are often 'scams' – and they don't want to be associated with this work.[3] For still others like Anirban: 'I did not want to take up a different name and be dishonest, I wanted to keep my name and when they did not agree, I called myself Anir – that's what anyways my friends call me.' In fact, the trainers often fall back on this fact of dual identity when they need to advocate a coping mechanism for the agents to deal with customer abuse: 'Krishna [one of the trainers] said that – if you get abused then don't worry, think who is this person abusing? – some poor guy called James who lives in Arizona – but its not me Shashi in Kolkata, so don't take it personally.' Such destabilization of identities is intimately tied to the experience of call center work that involves a transition from one self to another.

The agents also mentioned how their experiences at work gradually make them identify with the lives of their overseas customers. For example, according to Chandrima,

> In this industry, once you speak, you're not speaking to your own friends only, you're speaking to a person abroad. Their ideas are different . . . so we have to adapt to their ideas, their way of thinking . . . we're in the US right now, we're not in this place, we're not in India, we're in the US . . . so according to that we're thinking . . . even we get holidays based on them.

Similar sentiments are echoed by HR managers who believe that by talking all night with customers in the USA and the UK, the agents often get mentally transferred to those places. According to Sanchari, the HR manager in one of the call centers, 'The agents tend to follow a very different lifestyle. They think they live in the US when they are dialing. They tend to have multiple partners, go on drugs – you know just like it is in the US.' Such experience of the imagined 'other' and imagined identification with them, we argue, gives rise to an experience of 'unhomeliness'. Unlike the stories of the 'real' migrant's unhomely experience, here the 'virtual' migration (Aneesh, 2006) – enabled by the trained imagination – brings in another level of complication and creates a new form of self-consciousness that is produced 'in between' the discourses of globalization and national identities.

One can see the resonances of these emerging hybridities in the agents' narratives of how they think this job has changed them. According to Sumanto,

> I have a problem these days you know. For eight and a half hours in the office I speak with an artificial accent and when I come out and if I speak to my friends . . . I can't go back to my normal accent – I am getting stuck when I speak like that . . . When I hear the Americans I start speaking like them, and when I come out and I hear an Indian speak, I speak like that and my words get messed up. . . . it's become something in-between. That's a problem, a big problem.

Similarly, according to Mira,

> I think a big change in me is my accent – though I was fluent in English because I went to a good school, I have a different accent. And people, I mean Indians . . . now, I mean though I am not from UK or US, I speak like I am from UK/US.

Again, according to Sharif,

> Now I party a lot, I booze – I won't lie, sometimes . . . my family members don't know about that. They won't like it if they know. I come from a conservative Muslim family you see.

Again, for Chandrima,

> Yeah [I have changed] a lot in my way of dressing, in my way of behaving; I was totally like I used to wear *salwars* only . . . I'm wearing different clothes now, more fitting, Western clothes, I'm working on my figure as well.

They also talk of an experience of confusion in enacting the different selves at work and at home. For example according to Jatin,

> I mean there is nobody called Jason Foster – but everybody calls me Jason Foster. My friends call me at home and ask for Jason – and my family is like – 'who's Jason?' And sometimes when someone calls me Jatin – I feel who's calling Jatin – it's all about confusion.

We would like to argue that what all these excerpts from the interviews point towards is only a variant of the Anglicization process begun (in) famously by Macaulay's 'Minute on Education' (1835) in British India, and its long-term, dispersed effects. The similarity rests on the experience of an institutionalized process of inculcating a new breed of subjects: then, the creation of native civil servants through mimicry under colonial rule, now, a creation of teleservicing agents under conditions of contemporary globalization. The difference in this version is that the rhetoric of colonial governance is replaced by the logic of global capital.

The idea of Anglicization in postcolonial theory is closely tied to the colonial discourse of 'ambivalence' in the reactions of the British authorities to the newly English-educated Indian subjects. According to Bhabha (1994), there was a constant ambivalence that came into play in the behavior of the British officials who used strategies of mockery and derision towards these English-educated Indian 'mimic men'. This was necessary because the colonial authority rested on the notion of a civilizational superiority, and if mimicry could easily reproduce English subjects, the legitimacy of colonial rule would be lost. Hence, the subjects were Anglicized and not English – thereby maintaining a difference, and therefore 'a subject of a difference that is almost the same, but not quite' (1994: 86).

In the context of the call center, the experience of ambivalence emerges from the constant reminder of the subject's actual location and national affiliation by hostile customers. A large number of call center employees report the experience of being abused by customers, or being refused to be spoken to by them because they are Indians. For example, according to Rajni,

> when a customer asks 'are you an Indian' or 'are you calling from India', we say that yes, we are Indians – why should I lie to them? So I tell them that I am Indian – but I'm studying in the US and doing this job. And that's ok for them and ok for me. But then if the customer goes on about how they will not take anything from an Indian – then fine – I'm ok with it . . . [the customers say] I don't accept a call from an Indian – and all that. But from the beginning of our training we've been told that if the customer is abusing you, don't abuse back. And you can always tell them that this is a business call, and if they don't listen then just hang up. So we do the same thing. It's very bad – I mean they would also not like to hear that America is bad, but we can't do anything because this is our job. It feels very awkward – very bad – but then you have to do it.

Similarly Jamal says,

> If the person is a bit broad minded, if the person thinks globally, they won't mind. There are others who are really conservative and they say, 'if I'm getting something from my own country why should I buy something from someone sitting abroad?' This is how the mentality goes. But still sometimes people say 'you bloody Indians, you keep calling us, keep bothering us.' I really feel bad – I most – uhh – like – we can't say anything to them.

To project a direct parallel between the experience of ambivalence under colonial Anglicization and in contemporary global teleservice would be too simplistic. Yet all identities formed in-between, and all experience of hybridity is associated with a splitting of the image that is mimicked (Roy, 1998). While we are not suggesting that exactly similar processes are in operation here, the postcolonial lens of hybrid identity formations is useful for us to conceptualize the experiences of the Indian call center agents and the eventual formation of new hybridities. What is crucial here is to identify this dynamic – that while the agents' efforts are constantly aimed at concealing their Indian identities, their customers' efforts are often directed toward unmasking this concealment and challenging their authenticity. This can be thought to be similar to the audience's possession of 'destructive information' in a theater where the fore-knowledge of the audience retains the power to destabilize the performance by finding out what should have remained hidden from them (Goffman, 1959). Thus, the agents' salient identities are being erased and evoked at the same time through this constant experience of concealing and being exposed.

In addition to the experiences of such ambivalent identifications on the job, it is also interesting to note the perception of any new occupation by society at large in order to identify the legitimacy of the profession (Nelsen and Barley, 1997). The public perception of the call center employees, in this new booming industry with strange working hours and their make-believe 'Western' lives while living in India, remains ambiguous in the larger Indian society. Most agents complain that people tend to misunderstand call center jobs. For example, according Sumanto,

> People don't know exactly what happens inside a call center. They think it's a low end job that does not require any brains. . . Some people think that we are asked some questions and we have some scripts and we simply read them out, and forget about soft skills and communication skills.

However, these are also gendered narratives where the images of women working in call centers (especially in the night/US/UK shifts) are different from men. According to Indraneel, a manager in a call center, 'It is very difficult for girls working in call centers to get married. I mean arranged marriage, of course.' Many people seem to have confused the name call center with the word 'call girl' – which essentially is short-hand for a sex worker (generated from the ethnographic accounts). According to Srimanti, another call center agent, a common anecdote about the call center girls is:

> Just imagine a lady going out at night, a car comes and picks her up and in the friendly neighborhood, everyone peeks out of their windows and sees this lady

going out all dressed up. And when she is coming back after a night's work, the only discussions she has with her colleagues was last night this customer was saying this, and that customer was saying that. So you can imagine what people think.

DISCUSSION

What these interviews provide us with is a sense of the disturbing experiences of complex identifications and the varieties of ambivalence generated therein. These experiences of mimicry are associated with a double bind of ambivalence from both sets of people – the larger Indian society the employees need to go back to at the end of every shift, and the client countries they need to interact with. The identities are thus produced in-between, in the transition from 'Rajni' to 'Lucy' and back – in the pick-up and drop-back cars at strange times, in the liminality[4] of the office space, the unhomeliness of the international call center. The stress of such constant and different identity enactments is often borne out in various behavioral attributes that have now become the hallmark of call center life, such as increase in the consumption of drugs and alcohol, higher incidences of extra-marital relationships, and so on (Verma, 2006).

In this chapter, through the lens of postcolonial theories, we have made an exploratory attempt to build an understanding of the process of new and complex identifications that are a direct outcome of corporate globalization. We try to develop an emic perspective of 'how' this is done, and 'what' the experiences are, that go into and come out of it. Here, we hope to raise some of the critical issues that are central to the production of such new forms of hybrid subjectivities through a destabilization of identities.

By drawing on the notion of hybridity theorized by Bhabha and Fanon, we want to trace the new processes of indoctrinating the postcolonial 'desire' for the other, the systematic process of acquiring and performing new identities and concealing the others, and the slippages/ambivalence that are experienced in the process of such enactment/concealment. While Bhabha and Fanon develop the model of complex identifications with the 'other' in the colonial world, we try to delineate the similar experiences in identifications through mimicry and its consequent ambivalence in the postcolonial world. We try to understand this through an exploratory analysis of both the ethnographic accounts and the personal interviews conducted with the employees in the call centers. However, this chapter is a preliminary study at best that requires further refinement of the theoretical model and a more systematic analysis of the interviews. One limitation of this chapter remains that it is at present concentrated on only one location. While that is necessary to obtain in-depth information, there is a loss of breadth of data. In future we intend to extend our study to other parts of India. We also intend to build a comparative understanding of call center work in different countries like the Philippines, Ireland and parts of Eastern Europe. Moreover, while in this chapter we have mostly discussed the experiences of the agent body taken as a whole, we would like to eventually explore the heterogeneity within the experiences of the agents, such as the different nature of interactions depending on which country they work for, their religious affiliations, their gender and age profiles and so on. We would also like to extend this to other areas where globalization can affect work identities – for instance in the case of immigrant entrepreneurs.

NOTES

1. Thomas B. Macaulay – a senior British administrator, known for establishing the English education system in India – with the 'infamous' 'Minute on Indian Education' (1835), had made explicit how it was necessary to create 'a class of persons, Indian in blood and colour, but English in taste, in opinions, in morals, and in intellect'. This class was necessary for the British administration for governing the Indians effectively.
2. Anglicization has been defined as the process of 'making English' in language and characteristics. The process has been studied in detail by postcolonial theorists of South Asia and other British colonies. It marks the cultural and ideological influences of the colonial English rule that led to a form of creolization.
3. Many of the telemarketing campaigns conducted are not genuine, and the employees know that the customers they convince are going to be cheated. Agents also report a sense of dishonesty and discomfort in working for these campaigns.
4. Liminality (which literally means a threshold) is the stage of transition, where people are in between experiences, do not belong anywhere and are therefore in a flux. The concept was employed to understand the rites of passage in different societies in anthropology. It has also been used in performance studies to explain the transition of an actor from their everyday lives to the 'character' (Shechner, 2002). In organizational studies this has been explored in the context of role transitions, career transitions, job loss and so on (Ashforth, 2001; Ibarra, 2005). The experience of such liminality is the point where identity negotiations and reformulations take place (Ibarra, 2005). Postcolonial theorists (Bhabha, 1994) argue that it is in this liminality that hybrid identities get produced. However, this is not a physical or temporal state as much as it is a psychological state of rejecting one aspect of self and taking up another. It is a time that is characterized both by a sense of alienation, and also by a sense of adventure or riskiness – where one can indulge in imagination and in fantasy (Ibarra, 2005).

REFERENCES

Aihlon-Souday, G. and G. Kunda (2003), 'The local selves of global workers: the social construction of national identity in the face of organizational globalization', *Organization Studies*, **24**(7), 1073–96.

Albert, S., B.E. Ashforth and J. Dutton (2000), 'Organizational identity and identification: charting new waters and building new bridges', *Academy of Management Review*, **25** (1), 13–17.

Aneesh, A. (2006), *Virtual Migration: The Programming of Globalization*, Durham, NC: Duke University Press.

Appadurai, A. (1996), *Modernity at Large: Cultural Dimensions of Globalization*, Minneapolis: University of Minnesota Press.

Ashforth, B.E. (2001), *Role Transitions in Organizational Life: An Identity-based Perspective*, Mahwah: Lawrence Erlbaum Associates, Inc.

Batt, R. and L. Moynihan (2002), 'The viability of alternative call center production models', *Human Resource Management Journal*, **12**(4), 14–34.

Batt, R. and L. Moynihan (2004), 'Human resource management, service quality, and economic performance in call centers', Working paper No. 04-16, Center for Advanced Human Resource Studies, ILR School, Cornell University, under review, *Management Science*.

Batt, R., V. Doellgast and H. Kwon (2005), 'Service management and employment systems in U.S. and Indian call centers', in S. Collins and L. Brainard (eds), *Brookings Trade Forum 2005: Offshoring White-collar Work – The Issues and Implications*, Washington, DC: The Brookings Institution.

Bell, E. (1990), 'The bicultural life experiences of career oriented Black women', *Journal of Organizational Behavior*, **11**(6), 459–77.

Bhabha, H.K. (1994), *The Location of Culture*, London & New York: Routledge.

Chattopadhyay, P., M. Tluchowska and E. George (2004), 'Identifying the ingroup: a closer look at the influence of demographic dissimilarity on employee social identity', *Academy of Management Review*, **29**(2), 180–202.

Deery, S. and N. Kinnie (2004), 'Introduction: the nature of management of call center work', in S. Deery and N. Kinnie (eds), *Call Centers and Human Resource Management*, New York: Palgrave Macmillan.

Dossani, R. and M. Kenney (2003), 'Went for cost, stayed for quality? Moving back office to India', *Asia-Pacific Research Center*, http://APARC.standford.edu.

Ellemers, N., R. Spears and B. Doosje (2002), 'Self and social identity', *Annual Review of Psychology*, **53**, 161–86.

Fanon, F. (1967), *Black Skin, White Masks*, New York: Grove Press.

Fernie, S. and D. Metcalf (1998), '(Not) Hanging on the telephone: payment systems in the new sweatshops', Discussion Paper No. 390, Center for Economic Performance.

Frenkel, S., M. Korczynski, K. Shire and M. Tam (1998), 'Beyond bureaucracy: work organization in call centers', *International Journal of Human Resource Management*, **9**(6), 957–79.

Friedman, T.L. (2005), *The World Is Flat: A Brief History of the Twenty-first Century*, New York: Farrar, Strauss, Giroux.

Garson, B. (1988), *The Electronic Sweatshop: How Computers are Transforming the Office of the Future into the Factory of the Past*, New York: Simon & Schuster.

George, E. and P. Chattopadhyay (2005), 'One foot in each camp: the dual identification of contract workers', *Administrative Science Quarterly*, **50**, 68–99.

Gikandi, S. (2001), 'Globalization and the claims of postcoloniality', *South Atlantic Quarterly*, **100** (3), 627–58.

Goffman, E. (1959), *The Presentation of Self in Everyday Life*, New York: Anchor Doubleday.

Gopal, A., R. Willis and Y. Gopal (2003), 'From the colonial enterprise to the enterprise systems: parallels between colonization and globalization', in A.

Prasad (ed.), *Postcolonial Theory and Organizational Analysis: A Critical Engagement*, New York: Palgrave Macmillan.

Ibarra, H. (2005), 'Identity transitions: possible selves, liminality and voluntary career change', INSEAD working paper # 2005/51/OB.

Jack, G. and A. Lorbiecki (2003), 'Asserting possibilities of resistance in the cross-cultural teaching machine: re-viewing videos of others', in A. Prasad (ed.), *Postcolonial Theory and Organizational Analysis: A Critical Engagement*, New York: Palgrave Macmillan.

Kachru, B.B. (1983), *The Indianization of English: The English Language in India*, New York: Oxford University Press.

Macaulay, T.B. (1835) 'Minute on Indian education', in *Norton Anthology of English Literature*, available at http://www.wwnorton.com/college/english/nael/victorian/topic_4/Macaulay.htm.

Mirchandani, K. (2004), 'Practices of global capital: gaps, cracks and ironies in transnational call centers in India', *Global Networks*, **4**(4), 355–73.

Mishra, P.K. (2000), 'English language, postcolonial subjectivity, and globalization in India', *ARIEL: A Review of International English Literature*, **31**(1 & 2), 383–410.

Nelsen, B.J. and S.R. Barley (1997), 'For love or money: commodification and the construction of an occupational mandate', *Administrative Science Quarterly*, **42**, 619–53.

Prasad, A. (ed.) (2003), *Postcolonial Theory and Organizational Analysis: A Critical Engagement*, New York: Palgrave Macmillan.

Radhakrishnan, R. (2001), 'Globalization, desire and the politics of representation', *Comparative Literature*, **53** (4), 315–33.

Raina, A. (2004), *Speak Right for a Call Center Job*, India: Penguin Books.

Roberts, L.M. (2005), 'Changing faces: professional image construction in diverse organizational settings', *Academy of Management Review*, **30**(4), 685–711.

Roy, P. (1998), *Indian Traffic: Identities in Question in Colonial and Postcolonial India*, Berkeley: University of California Press.

Rushdie, S. (1988), *The Satanic Verses*, New York: Viking.

Schechner, R. (2002), *Performance Studies: An Introduction*, London: Routledge.

Sitt, G. (1997), *Diverted to Delhi*, New York: Filmmakers Library.

Taylor, P. and P. Bain (2005), 'India calling to faraway towns: the call center labor process and globalization', *Work, Employment and Society*, **19**, 261–82.

Trivedi, H. (1995), *Colonial Transactions: English Literature and India*, Manchester: Manchester University Press.

Verma, V. (2006), 'More sex please, we are BPO – It's common to find couples cuddling in the cafeteria', *The Telegraph*, 16 May, www.telegraphindia.com/1060514/asp/opinion/story_6215232.asp.

Viswanathan, G. (1989), *Masks of Conquest: Literary Study and British Rule in India*, New York: Columbia University Press.

Whetten, A. and G. Godfrey (eds) (1998), *Identity in Organizations: Building Theory Through Conversations*, Thousand Oaks, CA: Sage.

9. Globalization and social change: the Polish experience

Martyna Sliwa

INTRODUCTION

The first democratic parliamentary elections in Poland in June 1989 marked the end of the communist era in Polish post-World War II history and brought about an exposure of the country to the processes of globalization to an extent previously not known in Poland. Since then, the political transformation has resulted in the accession of the country to the North Atlantic Treaty Organization (NATO) and to the European Union (EU), and in an economic opening marked by the proliferation of companies from abroad, most notably multinational enterprises (MNEs), competing within the Polish market. The present membership of Poland in the EU is often quoted as evidence that the country has succeeded in reaching the goal first articulated by the former Polish minister of finance, Leszek Balcerowicz, that is to move away from undemocratic and economically inefficient modes of governing and organizing, and to become a politically stable and economically sound 'Western-style market economy' (Balcerowicz, 1989: 5).

Within extant literature, data referring to the economic conditions in Poland post-1989 are widely available. However, little is known about the socio-cultural effects on individuals participating in and affected by the political and market reforms, and affected for the first time by the processes of globalization (Kelemen, 2002; Kelemen and Kostera, 2002). Using the example of one of the major cities in Poland, this chapter aims to contribute to filling this gap in our present knowledge. In this research, a qualitative perspective was taken in order to build an understanding of the subjective perceptions of individuals of certain aspects of the transition from a centrally controlled to a market economy, and from a relatively closed country to one strongly involved in the processes of globalization. As such, the main contribution of this chapter to extant literature stems from its preoccupation with the experience of the processes of globalization considered at the level of the individuals involved.

The empirical data analysed here consist of material gained through participant observation and individual interviews. The picture emerging from the collected narratives is a complex one, combining accounts of positive and negative changes, and perceptions of successes as well as failures. Insights are gained into the new social inclusions and exclusions, marked by the distinction between 'winners' and 'losers' which, as noted and discussed by Kelemen (2002), has emerged throughout the transition period in post-socialist countries of Central and Eastern Europe. However, the externally attributed labels of 'winning' and 'losing' are also problematized in a reflection on the interpretative frames and criteria used by individuals in making sense (Weick, 1995) of their experience. To shed light on the changes that have affected different aspects of Polish society since 1989, this chapter draws on Brown and Lauder's (2001) argument about the emergence of new rules of eligibility, engagement and wealth creation accompanying globalization. This particular framework is chosen to develop an understanding of the current situation in Poland as resulting from those impacts of the globalization processes, as a result of which contemporary societies are 'characterized by difference rather than uniformity and widening rather than narrowing inequality' (Perrons, 2004: 1).

The remaining parts of this chapter are organized as follows. First, an overview of the literature pertaining to globalization and social change, with a particular consideration of the emergence of new rules of eligibility, engagement and wealth creation, is offered. Then, an account of the methods adopted in the empirical part of this research is given. Further, the globalization processes in Poland, as experienced by the individuals affected by them, are analysed. Finally, this chapter draws conclusions regarding the contribution of this research to extant literature on globalization and social change within the Polish context, as well as providing directions for future studies.

GLOBALIZATION AND SOCIAL CHANGE

The effects on society of the various processes, commonly referred to under the umbrella term of globalization, have been discussed by a number of authors (see Beck, 1992; Perrons, 2004; Schmidt and Hersh, 2000; Stiglitz, 2002). Of particular interest here is the extent to which globalization is related to the progressing prevalence of capitalism as an economic and social system, with its logic of production efficiency and profit maximization, and the prominent role of commercial organizations within it – facilitated by technological advances in transportation and communication technologies, and by the 'shift in policy orientation as governments everywhere have reduced barriers that had curbed the development of domestic markets and their links to the international economy' (World Bank, 2000: 1). Perrons (2004) argues that the motives of profit and competitiveness, which underlie the production of social output and its distribution within a capitalist society, also underlie the processes of globalization, the organization of work and industrial relations. As such, they have an impact on changes within society, especially evident in the case of a country such as Poland, that is, one that has been moving towards a capitalist economy while being intensively exposed to globalization.

Globalization and the Rules of Eligibility

The processes of economic globalization have not necessarily brought positive outcomes for societies in general (e.g. Banerjee and Linstead, 2001; Easterly, 2006; Giddens, 2000; Held and McGrew, 2002; Milanovic, 2002; Perrons, 2004; Rapley, 2004; Stiglitz, 2006; Wade, 2004). For example, Perrons (2004) argues that as a result of these processes, despite the increased economic integration, the social and spatial divisions in the world are becoming ever wider. Reich (2001) points out that because of the present unequal distribution of profits from production to capitalists and workers, resulting in a polarization of incomes, many of those participating in the processes of production cannot afford to purchase the goods and services they deliver. Brown and Lauder (2001), in their discussion of the simultaneity of increasing wealth and poverty, point to the emergence of the new rules of eligibility, engagement and wealth creation, which presently determine the ways in which, within the global economy, individuals, organizations and nations function, and in particular earn their living and make profits. The first of the three, the rule of eligibility, is related to the opening up of domestic economies, whereby the role of national governments in protecting workers and companies in their countries from competition from abroad decreases as a result of the reduction and removal of barriers to trade, foreign exchange and financial services. In the case of Poland, the rules of eligibility started to change at a quick pace from the beginning of the economic and political transition in 1989, as exemplified by the move from a centrally planned, 'walled' economy, to one governed by market principles and characterized by a strong presence of companies from abroad.

Globalization and the Rules of Engagement

While neo-classical economists have been enthusiastic about the changing rules of eligibility, the related potential for greater wealth creation by companies, and for increased consumer power stemming from wider choice and cheaper prices, others have seen this shift as contributing to growing economic insecurity and inequality (Brown and Lauder, 2001). The insights into these mechanisms of deepening inequalities, which result from the changing rules of eligibility, can be obtained through consideration of the changing rules of engagement. As Brown and Lauder (2001) argue, until the early 1970s the rules of engagement were based on the principles of economic nationalism, whereby government, employers and trade unions agreed on the view that all parties involved should share the fruits of prosperity. This approach was underpinned by the assumption that workers needed regular pay increases in order to maintain their families and ensure a high level of domestic consumer demand; and that employers were interested in high domestic demand as this enabled them to generate healthy profits. However, since the time of the decline of profits in 1970s, the rules of engagement based on economic nationalism were replaced by those underpinned by global market competition, with companies gaining and exercising their power to 'go abroad' and 'go global' (Hymer, 1976). This, in turn, has enabled multinational companies to develop strategies for avoiding the negative effects of economic downturn by shifting the risks involved in operating within a volatile market environment onto the employees who, as a consequence, have lost their previous long-term job prospects. Moreover, as a result of the globalization of enterprises, the power of the trade unions, which lack the kind of cross-border organization that would improve their chances for success in negotiating with multinationals on behalf of the workers, has also weakened (Acker et al., 1996). This aspect of the changing rules of engagement has had particularly severe impacts on low paid workers, who have become subject to weak labour regulations, and contingent and flexible working conditions (Perrons, 2004).

Relevant to the discussion of the social consequences of new rules of engagement is Beck's (1992, 2000) idea of 'individualization', related to his concept of risk society. Commenting on the social impacts of globalization, specifically on the processes underpinned by the changing rules of engagement, Beck (2000: 53) concludes that 'instead of the promised classless society the fine old distinctions are suddenly changing into intense social polarization. Instead of an elevator effect for all layers in society, a revolving door effect admits a few winners and casts many losers'. Beck (2000) sees the increase in flexible and temporary employment, brought about by globalization, as being part of one of the two major risks for society – affecting it as a whole and through the impacts on the everyday life of individuals within it – which he refers to as individualization. According to Beck (2000: 128), in general, individualization comprises three dimensions: the 'liberating dimension', which relates to the 'removal from historically prescribed social forms and commitments in the sense of traditional contexts of dominance and support; the 'disenchantment dimension', associated with 'the loss of traditional security with respect to practical knowledge, faith and guiding norms'; and the 'control (or "reintegration") dimension', involving the construction of 'a new type of social commitment'. As a result of these three dimensions of individualization, from the perspective of an individual, traditional commitments and support relationships disappear and are replaced with

> the constraints of existence in the labor market and as a consumer, with the standardizations and controls they contain. The place of traditional ties and social forms is taken by secondary agencies and institutions, which stamp the biography of the individual and make that person dependent upon fashions, social policy, economic cycles and markets, contrary to the image of individual control which establishes itself in consciousness. (Beck, 2000: 131)

Insights into the different social phenomena stemming from the new rules of engagement as pertaining to contemporary Polish society, are offered in the discussion of the empirical research conducted for the purposes of this chapter.

Globalization and the Rules of Wealth Creation

In relation to the third mechanism described by Brown and Lauder (2001), namely the changing rules of wealth creation, the authors argue that the situation has shifted from one where the main emphasis was on improvements in efficiency, as first introduced through the systems of mass production invented in the era of scientific management, to one where the generation of economic development is contingent on the ability of nations to create large numbers of high-skilled jobs, characterized by a level of complexity that precludes the possibility of delivering them according to Fordist principles. Rather than emphasizing the need for efficiency, the necessity to produce goods and services capable of satisfying the precise needs of customers and clients is given priority. However, as Brown and Lauder (2001) point out, the emphasis on the role of high skills does not automatically translate into an evolution from a low- to high-skill economy, as companies are still able to benefit from the labour of low-skilled, low-wage employees. Instead, the changing rules of wealth creation have given rise to the expansion of professional and managerial jobs, providing high earnings for those occupying these positions. These types of workers have high disposable incomes, but they are short of time outside work, and hence have demands for a range of personal services, which in turn are delivered by low-wage workers. As Perrons (2004) observes, the working lives of both high and low earners in a globalized economy present challenges for reconciling work with family lives, because of the expectations of long working hours. While the affluent ones can afford child minders and cleaners, lower paid employees struggle to afford families or are forced to give up on having children.

Another social consequence of the changing rules of wealth creation, and of the resulting divide between high and low earners is the spatial segregation of different income or ethnic groups, whereby the rich have the freedom to choose which locations they live in, as they 'join communities as consumers not as participants' (Reich, 2001), whilst the poor, who for financial reasons are not able to move to the same areas as those inhabited by the rich, are often spatially excluded from the consumerist lifestyles. Exploring this phenomenon in the American context, Marcuse (2002) distinguishes between three forms of spatial segregation, which he terms citadels (gated communities), enclaves (which are voluntarily inhabited by members of certain ethnic and national groups), and ghettos (in which the poor live not out of choice, but out of the lack of other options). The different consequences for individuals functioning within an economy governed by the new rules of wealth creation, in the Polish context, are explored later in this chapter.

Implications for this Research

The empirical research presented here and discussed in the context of the social changes considered at the level of individual experiences resulting from the new rules of eligibility, engagement and wealth creation in Poland post-1989, is organized according to the following themes:

- the decreased role of the government in protecting Polish workers and enterprises;
- the emergence of new employment conditions, resulting in lower job security and flexible working hours;
- the deepening of social and economic inequalities;
- the spatial segregation of different sections of society.

While the impacts of the processes of globalization can be addressed in reference to different geographical foci, in the research carried out here attention was paid to one particular location in Poland, namely the city of Krakow, as an example of a microcosm representative of the situation in the whole country. In that city, extremes of wealth and poverty, as well as contradictions of global capitalism, can be found. Being certainly a much more provincial location than places such as London, New York, Tokyo, Paris or Frankfurt, which tend to be classified as 'global cities' (see Perrons,

2004), Krakow has a number of features that Sassen (2000, 2001) associates with global cities. Specifically, it constitutes a geographical base for companies in sectors requiring high-skilled professional workers, but also is the place of living and working for a considerable proportion of low-income earners. Hence, similarly to the situation in other global cities, the population of Krakow is characterized by high income disparities, even though, as a result of Poland's recent economic and political history, the comparative extent of earning differentials and income inequalities within the country may not be as drastic as in the case of some other regions in the world. However, relative to other locations in Poland, Krakow represents a city where a wide variety of economic activities take place, and thus a broad range of workers, with correspondingly varied levels of remuneration, reflecting the overall national levels of wealth and poverty, are employed there. For these reasons, it is taken as the geographical focus of the discussion of the impact of some of the processes associated with globalization on Polish society, as presented here.

RESEARCH METHODS ADOPTED

The empirical research conducted here focused on collecting narratives addressing the changes that have affected members of the Polish society as part and consequence of the transition and globalization processes since 1989, with an emphasis on phenomena associated with the changing rules of eligibility, engagement and wealth creation. To avoid constructing a reductionist meta-narrative that either romanticizes the past or glorifies the present, and to gain an understanding of and to be able to problematize the new social inclusions and exclusions – marked by the distinction between 'winners' and 'losers' that has emerged throughout the transition period – in the empirical research, views from a wide range of individuals in terms of age, gender and occupation were included from a sample of 30 participants divided into the following age groups:

- Under 25 years of age – those who have little experience of living in communist Poland.
- Between 25 and 39 – those who were brought up pre-1989, but who have lived most of their adult life in the country in transition.
- Between 40 and 54 – those who by 1989 had already made the most significant life and career choices.
- 55 years of age and above – those who experienced many years of life under the communist regime, and for whom the 1989 transition came relatively late in life.

Within each group, the sample of participants comprised female and male individuals, with different types and levels of education, different places of residence (e.g. upmarket estates versus blocks of flats), and varying with regard to their financial and broader social status. Participants were asked to comment on different aspects of their private and professional lives in the past and currently; and to recount and evaluate the changes they have experienced since 1989, with a focus on impacts of the new rules of eligibility, engagement and wealth creation. The interviews were carried out in Polish. In the analysis of the empirical data gathered, emphasis was placed on the complexity of the narratives, and the types, extent and normative evaluations of changes experienced by the participants. Moreover, the analysis paid attention to whether, within the collected narratives, patterns can be identified with regard to factors such as age, gender, education, place of living, and financial and broader social status of the participants.

In the discussion, the qualitative data were complemented by reference to quantitative research, in particular to the publications of CBOS (2000, 2003), and Paczynska (2005).

INTRODUCTION TO TRANSITION IN POLAND

The liberalization and opening up of the Polish economy commenced soon after the official fall of communism in the country. The original plan of economic reforms, commonly referred to as the 'Balcerowicz plan', which was presented to Sejm, the lower chamber of the Parliament, in October 1989, put addressing inflation, budget deficit and foreign debts as the economic priorities of the first democratic government in post-communist Poland. An overall 'shock therapy' was applied to the Polish economy – as an immediate result of which the GDP decreased by 11.9 per cent in 1990 and by 7.6 per cent in 1991; industrial output by 24.4 per cent in 1990 and 11.9 in 1991; whereas the inflation level reached 585.5 per cent in 1990 before falling to 70.3 per cent in 1991. At the same time, the Poles were faced with the previously unknown phenomenon of unemployment – the figure grew from 0.3 per cent at the beginning of 1990 to 11.8 per cent by December 1991, and reached 15.7 per cent by the end of 1993 (Institute for World Economics, 1994).

The initial fall in GDP was overcome and between 1995 and 1999 the Polish economy grew on average between 4.5 per cent and 6.5 per cent per year. This trend, while slower, has continued from 2000 onwards. The unemployment rate, however, has not been reduced; by 2004, it reached 20 per cent – the highest level among all EU members. Moreover, the high percentage of unemployment has been accompanied by spread of poverty, which has had negative impacts on a large proportion of society. It is estimated that during the first 2 years of transition, as a result of unemployment, a fall in real wage levels and the decreased value of savings, the number of people affected by poverty increased significantly, to double from 20 per cent in 1989 to approximately 40 per cent in 1999 (Zagorski and Strzeszewski, 2000). As of 2009, the scale of poverty in Poland remains at a similar level.

While there is an abundance of aggregate quantitative data addressing the present condition of the Polish economy and society, individual-level analyses of the effects of transition and globalization processes have attracted much less research attention to date. The discussion below presents the results of qualitative research conducted in order to elucidate the aspects of individuals' lives related to the decreased role of the Polish government in protecting domestic workers and enterprises, the changes in the employment conditions, the rise in social and economic inequalities, and the spatial segregation of different sections of Polish society.

Decreased Role of Government

One of the aspects of the changing rules of eligibility in Poland has been the proliferation of companies from abroad within the Polish market. It has been accompanied by a decreased role of the government in setting up the rules of competition and employment. While the presence of foreign investors is considered an important contributor to the country's economic development post-1989, the removal of barriers to commercial activity, in particular the privatization of previously state owned enterprises and the associated unemployment, have also resulted in the growth of economic insecurity and inequality for the citizens. For Polish workers, the opening up of the economy has necessitated an adjustment to the new situation of an increased power of the employers to dictate the working conditions for the employees.

This withdrawal of the state from the role of helping its citizens to secure a workplace was quickly recognized by the Poles. Paczynska (2005) states that although at the outset of the transition the majority of Poles (57 per cent) believed that they could rely on the state's support in the case of unemployment, by the end of the 1990s this proportion was only slightly above one quarter of society (27 per cent). Furthermore the citizens in general have increasingly developed a belief that the country's authorities do not care about them. In 2000, 61 per cent of Poles expressed the opinion that the government was not concerned about them and their needs, and did nothing for them (CBOS, 2000), whereas in 2003, 92 per cent stated that, rather than looking after the interests of the electorate, the country's leaders only focused on their own careers (CBOS, 2003).

Polish authorities have also withdrawn from their protection of domestic enterprises from competition from abroad, which has had an impact on how Polish firms relate to their own employees. Piotr (34), a co-owner of a family firm in the construction industry, is confident that the protection of workers' interests is, in the present circumstances, an unreasonable luxury: 'I would never allow trade unions in my firm. It is hard enough to survive in the kind of market conditions we have in Poland right now; having to deal with employees' demands would make it impossible.' It might appear surprising that in the country of Solidarnosc and with a strong unionist tradition, less than 20 years after the beginning of the political and economic reforms the approach represented by the comment above seems to have been adopted and taken for granted by many in Poland. Both employers and workers accept that the lack of governmental protection from companies abroad requires that they need to look after their interests themselves. As a consequence of this, as Paczynska (2005) points out, the efforts of the majority of Polish society are directed towards ensuring that their social position and security, as well as their living standards, do not deteriorate further – that is, towards issues of economic survival, pursued in conditions of public apathy, scepticism and alienation. At the same time, it is not generally contested that the freedom from state control that came with capitalism often denotes the freedom of companies to hire and fire workers, rather than the freedom of the latter to choose their place and influence their conditions of employment.

New Employment Conditions

The new employment conditions, associated with the decline – or in many workplaces, the absence – of trade unions, have had important implications for the ability of workers to manage their family lives. The observations made in the literature on globalization regarding its impact on the issues of reconciling work and family life (Beck, 1992, 2000; Perrons, 2004) can be seen as relevant in the context of contemporary Poland. One of the participants, Joanna (35) has a well paid and highly time-demanding job in Krakow. She has two children; 9 and 4 years old; but returned to work within 18 weeks after each birth in order to keep her position in the organization she works for. She comments on how her ability to cope with the simultaneous demands of work and family depends on the support of her and her husband's parents:

> I feel very lucky because both mine and my husband's parents live in Krakow and they take care of most of the childcare and a lot of the family logistics. In the morning, my mother or my mother-in-law comes to our house and takes both children to school and to the kindergarten. She also brings them back

> home and looks after them for a few hours every evening until I and my husband return home after work. Without the help of our parents, one of us – probably me – would have had to give up working, but then I don't know how we could support a family of four.

Joanna, of course, is in the fortunate situation of enjoying well paid employment coupled with family support. Those on lower incomes and whose parents cannot afford to help them either through giving up their time or financially, to enable them to settle in the city, struggle to keep work and to maintain themselves in Krakow because of the high costs of living in the city.

Not only the time demands of and the wages paid by the employers, but also other aspects of the working conditions require that the workers are prepared to compromise their family lives in order to maintain employment. Barbara (29) has first-hand experience of flexible working hours in a supermarket belonging to a multinational chain. In her case, this means that she works on some Sundays but not on all, and the manager calls her at home when there is a need to open more cash tills. She explains: 'On a Sunday one can earn more, but Sunday work is not always guaranteed. They may call me up any time when there are many customers and they want to open more cash tills.'

The constraints of existence in the labour market, as discussed by Beck (2000), to a large extent show through the above narratives – although within the Polish context, it appears that Beck's thesis about the removal of individuals from traditional commitments and support relationships, such as family structures, cannot be confirmed. This is not a surprising finding, considering the traditionally important role of family in the Polish society. However, other phenomena – such as the organization of family logistics around the demands of work; the subordination of private life decisions to issues of job prospects and income; and the preparedness to allow the professional sphere occupy what was previously considered as private time – provide evidence for the relevance of Beck's 'individualization' thesis in the Polish context.

Rise in Inequalities

In addition to the withdrawal of the government from its role of protecting domestic workers and companies, and changes in the working conditions within the Polish labour market, the emergence of the new rules of wealth creation has also had a direct impact on Polish society. For some, the new conditions have brought the opportunity to earn high incomes and to move up the economic ladder, whereas for others they have resulted in the lack of a chance to take up any other than low-skilled, low-wage, and low-security employment. The differences in economic effects of transition on the various social strata are reflected in the extant perceptions of the outcomes of transition, whereby as Paczynska (2005: 597) points out 'the more educated and urbanized ones tend to view the post-1989 period in a positive light. Those with less education and living in small towns and the countryside tend to be more critical about the changes and more nostalgic about socialism'.

The introduction of the new rules of wealth creation has brought for Polish society a shift in both absolute and relative earnings levels. Up to 1989, salaries of different types of workers did not vary considerably. Among those remunerated particularly highly were workers in sectors such as coal mining and the steel industry. The liberalization of the labor market post-1989 has meant that the skills of some have become valued more than those of others. The contrasting views of two participants, made in relation to this process of re-valuing skills and qualifications according to market demand, illustrate how the emergence of the new rules of wealth creation, and the associated increase in income inequalities, has been experienced at the level of individuals. Rafal (60), an established researcher specializing in a sought-after area of expertise, is an example of someone whose financial status has improved considerably in the new circumstances. He comments on how his new situation is a source of great satisfaction for him:

> Before the transition, I used to earn half of the salary of a steelworker. Nowadays, these kinds of workers still earn about twice the country's average – provided there is work for them – but I make three to four times as much as they do. I am very happy about the way things have changed in Poland as I have managed to improve my standard of living, and to advance my social status . . . The only problem is the pace of all the changes and of life in general. It is so hard to catch up with things and to find the time for contacts with others. The thing is that in the past, on many days I could go out and meet other people after work but nowadays, at the end of a long working day, I don't even feel like talking to anyone at all.

Feelings of contentment are also expressed by Jerzy (62), presently a successful entrepreneur:

> The change in my life situation has been beyond expectations. From an engineer in a state-owned company – even though I have never complained because I was always able to earn extra money by working on construction sites in Iraq, Libya, and Germany – after the transformation I have reached a financial status I have not even dreamt about. I opened my own company which soon monopolized the national market and I then started exporting to other countries in Eastern Europe. Today I employ 300 people and sell in over 20 countries. Poland is a country of great opportunities – one just has to work hard and not be lazy.

On the other hand, Ryszard (56), who used to work as a welder in a large state owned company, lost his employment when the firm was privatized. At present he works for a medium-sized private enterprise. Ryszard speaks about how his situation has deteriorated since 1989:

> I used to be the only bread winner in my family, because my wife was looking after the children when they were young. We were able to buy everything we needed, and in summer we always went on holidays. Now I work here, my wife is currently in Italy cleaning people's houses, but everything in Poland is so expensive that we hardly make enough money to survive from one month to next. And there is no way we could afford going on holidays these days. I am very suspicious of those who have made money after 1989 – surely, this couldn't have been done based on honesty and hard work.

While this kind of a sense of satisfaction among the 'winners' and frustration on the part of the 'losers' would have been expected as a logical reaction to the improvement or worsening of the situation for particular individuals (Kelemen, 2002), a closer engagement with how these changes are perceived allows for problematization of the concepts of 'winning' and 'losing' in this context. In the case of Poland, as with other countries of Central and Eastern Europe, the exposure to the changing rules of wealth creation has come in a sudden rather than gradual manner, and has affected society within a relatively short period of time. Those who previously would have shared similar lifestyles and were each other's neighbours or friends suddenly found themselves in separate social strata. This has been a difficult process to deal with not only for those who have lost in terms of their financial status, but also for the supposed winners. Jerzy (62) comments on how, at present, he finds it difficult to maintain his old friendships because of the new income divides:

> Some of my old friends are jealous about the fact that my standard of life has improved, whereas they have not been successful in the capitalist Poland. Also, we often do not share the same views on the current situation in the country. I support the changes and the transition, as well as the EU enlargement. I see it all as a great chance not only for myself but also for others. Those who are jealous and are 'losers' do not trust the transition and the changes that are happening. They do not move on and are frustrated. When I speak to some friends who have not succeeded, they are bitter and frustrated, and therefore we cannot find a common language any more. I have lost contact with a lot of old friends because of that.

The above examples might be taken as indicative of the shift in interpretative frames used by individuals as a consequence of changes in their economic situation. Those who have 'made it' attribute their success to their hard work and to what they perceive as positive changes in the situation in the country; those who have not, question the ethics of the actions of the successful ones. However, there exists also a realization that the emergence of new economic divides has had a varied impact on the social lives of individuals. The narratives show that for those involved, the evaluation of whether they see themselves as 'winners' or 'losers' takes place according to more complex criteria than merely that of their current economic standing, and involves a more holistic assessment of factors such as one's relationship with the broader social environment. Ricoeur (1978) explains that the meaning of present experiences is never separated from the experiences of the past – and as the content of the narratives suggests, the current life situation is viewed by individuals in a complex manner, in reference to a variety of aspects of their existence in the past, rather than according to any set criteria of personal wealth. Comments about the lack of time for cultivating acquaintanceships and about the disintegration of old circles of friends point to broader phenomena of individualization (Beck, 1992, 2000) and the feelings of isolation experienced by the members of Polish society under the new conditions. These aspects of experiences are even more evident when considered from the point of view of spatial segregation of different social strata that has been taking place in Poland since 1989.

Spatial Segregation as Manifestation of Social Stratification

Bauman (2000) argues that, because of the processes of globalization, the external appearance of contemporary cities is determined by the consumption patterns of the rich – as exemplified by upmarket restaurants, hotels and shops dominating the cityscape. The presence of the poor, on the other hand, is not granted the same visibility. In Krakow, low-wage workers, although needed as a labour force in the city, are not able to pay the property or rent prices that would allow them to live close to their workplace. Barbara, while being appreciative of having a job in a supermarket in Krakow, cannot afford to live in the city. The daily commute of over 2 hours takes about 12 per cent of her salary, and she tries to save money whenever possible:

> I live in the countryside in my parents' house. With my and my husband's income, we could not afford living in the city, so although getting to work every day costs a lot, it is cheaper than living in Krakow. I normally don't buy products from the supermarket I work for – they are expensive, and we grow the basic foods at home.

In contrast, Jan (57), a successful entrepreneur, is not only able to cover the costs of living in Krakow, but since the mid-1990s has been living in an upmarket new residential development. His satisfaction with the current situation in his life shows in the pride with which he speaks about the fact that he does not live on the same estate of blocks of flats any more. He sees his move to a big house in the suburbs of the city as an important symbol of his social position:

> I am happy that I do not have to live on a big estate with blocks of flats any more. Looking at who still lives in those blocks, one can easily see who has made it in new conditions . . . I am so glad I now do not have to put up with all that was going on in the neighborhood: the smells coming from other people's flats, the noises of their quarrels and the music they listened to.

Under the new rules of wealth creation (Brown and Lauder, 2001) brought about by the globalization processes in Poland post-1989, the life paths of low and high earners are not likely to cross very often. On the present map of Krakow, it would be possible to draw lines showing the potential living and working areas of the economic 'winners' and 'losers'. Of course, the phenomenon of spatial segregation of different social strata stemming from the differences in incomes is not unfamiliar in Western societies. In the case of Poland, however, this aspect of the processes of individualization (Beck, 1992, 2000) is still a novelty and is affecting the lives of individuals in ways that, again, challenge the assumption that personal financial success in a capitalist country unambiguously denotes 'winning'. For example, Jan recognizes that the move away from what he saw as the disadvantages of living in a block, has exposed his family to threats from potential burglars – altogether leading to a feeling of isolation and fear he had not known previously:

> It is great where I live now although I miss the chance to chat with my old neighbors, as I used to do. Also, one cannot trust people that much any more. You never know when someone can break into the house or try to steal your car. Mind you, we are connected to a security company, so if someone were to break in, the guys will be here within three minutes . . . I do not know many people where I live now. Even my wife who normally finds it easy to get on with people, over the last 10 years has not managed to develop genuine bonds with other women in this neighborhood.

The ability to move away from the block estate to a newly built 'gated community' (Marcuse, 2002) is a symbol of economic success. However, it also denotes the breaking down of previously existing social bonds. Living in a community with which one is familiar, trust and a feeling of personal safety are replaced by loneliness, isolation and living in houses equipped with alarms and monitored by security companies. Considering this phenomenon using Beck's (2000) argumentation, the spatial segregation of different social groups in Poland constitutes yet another aspect of the processes of individualization, whereby 'the place of traditional ties and social forms is taken by secondary agencies and institutions' (2000: 131), and hence people have to 'rely on themselves and their own individual fate with all its attendant risks, opportunities, and contradictions' (2000: 92).

FINAL REMARKS

This chapter presented insights gained from qualitative research conducted in the city of Krakow in the south-east of Poland and focusing on some of the social and economic impacts of the accelerated globalization processes in Poland post-1989. The empirical data obtained throughout the research process have been related to literature on globalization and social change, in particular in the context of Brown and Lauder's (2001) argument about the emergence of new rules of eligibility, engagement and wealth creation accompanying the globalization processes. The particular phenomena addressed in the discussion have included the decreased role of the Polish government in protecting domestic workers and enterprises from the employment practices and competition from companies from abroad; the changes in the employment conditions within the labour market in Poland; the rise in social and economic inequalities; and the spatial segregation of different sections of the Polish society.

In terms of this chapter's contribution to the current knowledge about globalization, three major points need to be made in conclusion. First, through being founded on primary qualitative data, the research presented here complements macro-level studies, addressing the globalization-induced changes within the whole economy of a country or a region. It builds on extant writings on globalization and social change by providing additional empirical evidence, gathered in the Polish context, of phenomena discussed by authors such as Bauman (2000), Beck (1992, 2000), Brown and Lauder (2001), Kelemen and Kostera (2002), Paczynska (2005) and Perrons (2004). In particular, this chapter offers insights into the individual-level experience of the various processes related to globalization, and hence helps us develop an understanding of the sense-making (Weick, 1995) that happens at the micro-level of an individual. Through addressing the processes of globalization and social change from this perspective, it becomes possible to engage with the questions of how individuals relate to the various changes, how they find themselves in the new circumstances, and how they evaluate the outcomes of the changes for themselves.

Second, the findings of this research constitute a commentary on the categorizations found in the extant literature discussing the problems of new social and economic divides (e.g. Bauman, 2000; Brown and Lauder,

2001; Kelemen and Kostera, 2002; Perrons, 2004) by drawing attention to the problematic nature of attaching labels such as 'winners' and 'losers' to individuals based on the external manifestations of their situation as exemplified by their social and economic status. The narratives collected here show that whether individuals perceive themselves as 'winners' or 'losers' is determined by more complex criteria than merely that of personal economic standing, and involves also an assessment of factors such as, for example, one's relationship with the broader social environment in which one functions.

Moreover, from the stories of the participants in this research, it emerges that while a number of social phenomena commonly associated with globalization can be identified within the Polish context, there exist also important differences. Therefore, caution needs to be applied when generalizations are made about the nature of the globalization processes in different countries. For example, in relation to Beck's (1992, 2000) concept of individualization, the narratives show that the constraints imposed on Polish society by the present labour market have not led to the disappearance of traditional family support structures. Rather, contrary to Beck's (1992, 2000) analysis, there are signs of an increased importance of extended family support in a situation where help with childcare and pro-family employment policies are not any more guaranteed by the Polish state for its citizens. Hence, in discussing the impact of globalization on Polish society it is important to take into account the specificity of the Polish context, and the way in which history and culture underpin the responses of individuals to globalization and economic transition.

As far as the directions for future research are concerned, there is scope for further empirical investigation, including extended data collection in Poland, as well as in other countries of Central and Eastern Europe. This, in turn, would create a basis for developing theories of social impacts of the processes of globalization and transition in that region. Perhaps such theories would offer non-reductionist insights into these processes, and would be a useful resource for building an understanding of what has been happening within the post-communist European societies since 1989.

REFERENCES

Acker, P., C. Smith and P. Smith (1996), *The New Workplace and the New Unionism*, London: Routledge.

Balcerowicz, L. (1989), *Biuletyn nr. 41/X Kadencja*, Warszawa: Komisja Polityki Gospodarczej, Budzetu i Finansow, Kancelaria Sejmu, 5–6.

Banerjee, S.B. and S. Linstead (2001), 'Globalization, multiculturalism and other fictions: colonialism for the new millennium?', *Organization*, **8**(4), 683–722.

Bauman, Z. (2000), *Globalization. The Human Consequences*, New York: Columbia University Press.

Beck, U. (1992), *Risk Society: Towards a New Modernity*, London: Sage.

Beck, U. (2000), *The Brave New World of Work*, Cambridge: Polity Press.

Brown, P. and H. Lauder (2001), *Capitalism and Social Progress*, Basingstoke: Palgrave.

CBOS (2000), *Public Opinion Survey (January)*, Warsaw: Centre for Public Opinion Research.

CBOS (2003), *Public Opinion Survey (September)*, Warsaw: Centre for Public Opinion Research.

Easterly, W. (2006), 'The rich have markets, the poor have bureaucrats', in M.W. Weinstein (ed.), *Globalization: What's New?*, New York: Columbia University Press, pp. 170–95.

Giddens, A. (2000), *Runaway World: How Globalization is Reshaping Our Lives*, New York: Routledge.

Held, D. and A. McGrew (2002), *Globalization/Anti-globalization*, Cambridge: Polity Press.

Hymer, S.H. (1976), *The International Operation of National Firms: A Study of Direct Foreign Investment*, Cambridge, MA: MIT Press.

Institute for World Economics (1994), *Transformation in Progress: Proceedings of the First Roundtable Conference, Budapest, March 2–3, 1994*, Budapest: Institute for World Economics, p. 20.

Kelemen, M. (2002), 'Reinventing the past: stories about Communism and the transition to a market economy in Romania', in M. Kelemen and M. Kostera (eds), *Critical Management Research in Eastern Europe: Managing the Transition*, Basingstoke: Palgrave, pp. 143–63.

Kelemen, M. and M. Kostera (2002), *Critical Management Research in Eastern Europe: Managing the Transition*, Basingstoke: Palgrave.

Marcuse, P. (2002), 'Urban form and globalization after September 11th: the view from New York', *International Journal of Urban and Regional Research*, **26**(3), 596–606.

Milanovic, B. (2002), 'True world income distribution, 1988 and 1993: first calculations based on household surveys alone', *Economic Journal*, **112**, 51–92.

Paczynska, A. (2005), 'Inequality, political participation, and democratic deepening in Poland', *East European Politics and Societies*, **19**(4), 573–613.

Perrons, D. (2004), *Globalization and Social Change. People and Places in a Divided World*, London: Routledge.

Rapley, J. (2004), *Globalization and Inequality. Neoliberalism's Downward Spiral*, London: Lynne Rienner Publishers.

Reich, R. (2001), *The Future of Success: Work and Life in the New Economy*, London: Heinemann.

Ricoeur, P. (1978), 'Can there be a scientific concept of ideology?', in J. Bier (ed.), *Phenomenology and the Social Sciences*, The Hague: Martinus Nijhof.

Sassen, S. (1991 and 2001), *The Global City: New York, London, Tokyo*, 1st and 2nd edns, Princeton, NJ: Princeton University Press.

Sassen, S. (2000), *Cities in a World Economy*, London: Pine Forge Press.

Schmidt, J. and J. Hersh (2000), *Globalization and Social Change*, London: Routledge.

Stiglitz, J. (2002), *Globalization and its Discontents*, New York: Michigan State University Press.

Stiglitz, J. (2006), 'The overselling of globalization', in M.W. Weinstein (ed.), *Globalization: What's New?*, New York: Columbia University Press, pp. 228–61.

Wade, R. (2004), 'Is globalization reducing poverty and inequality?', *World Development*, **32**(4), 567–89.

Weick, K. (1995), *Sensemaking in Organizations*, Thousand Oaks, CA: Sage.

World Bank (2000), 'Poverty in an age of globalization', www.worldbank.org/html/extdr/pb/globalizatoin/povertyglobalization.pdf (Accessed 15 June 2006).

Zagorski, K. and M. Strzeszewski (2000), *Nowa rzeczywistosc: Oceny i opinie*, Warszawa: Wydawnictwo Akademickie Dialog.

PART V

Conclusion

10. Towards an anthropology of globalization

Vanessa C.M. Chio and
Subhabrata Bobby Banerjee

We started this book with Paul Rabinow's (1986) call to anthropologize the West. In this conclusion we return to his call, and locate the contributions and theoretical framing of the book in terms of the insights offered by such endeavors in relation to globalization. By attending to the 'domains of truth and economy' that make globalization real, the intent is to show its historicized character and socially constructed nature.

At the center of this anthropology is a bid to simultaneously problematize and resituate what globalization is by focusing attention on what it is constituted by and constitutive of. Following on from insights offered by Dorothy Smith (1987) about the 'problematic of the everyday', the entry point for this possibility is the active recasting of globalization into an object and subject for investigation. Rather than accepting prima facie the 'fact' of globalization as an economic and social form of organization (e.g. trade, outsourcing, economic growth, FDI), the intent is to defamiliarize what has become taken for granted. To enable such defamiliarization we need to pose some questions: What makes globalization possible? What sustains it and what does it sustain? Who are the actors and players involved? How does it organize and transform social reality and the actions and intentions of those organized by it? What are the social, political, economic and academic or organizational factors organizing these actors' engagement with the phenomenon? The contributions in this volume have explored different aspects of these questions.

Our aim is to offer an alternate way of understanding and investigating globalization that can actively counter mainstream and dominant knowledge by 'situating' the phenomenon in trajectories of knowledge, power, political economy and history that anchor and make possible its 'facticity' as a form of organization and organizing (Haraway, 1988). This is especially critical as most mainstream research on globalization in the management and organization sciences is silent about history. Most of our management and organization theories are functional, focused on a present that is attenuated from any past, intent on documenting the managerial and organizational factors at play, using primarily self-referential categories and forms of knowledge to do so. Where 'history' is attended to, functional categories representing other nations' contexts are offered, treated often as a substitute for history but devoid of any analysis of historical relationality (Chio, 2005). As we noted in our introduction, this silence and absence are particularly egregious in the context of the Third World as their histories have been singularly forged in relation to histories of the West (Chakrabarty, 1992; Prakash, 1990; Radhakrishnan, 1994). Within the colonial and imperial trajectory organizing relations between the West and the Rest, this ahistoricism is part and parcel of what makes and perpetuates the colonial and imperial contours of the global and globalizing terrain. Globalization is a result of a web of institutional and institutionalized practices of knowledge and relations between capital, development agencies, academia, and states whose interactions produce the specific forms of organization, activities and subjects connected to and required for globalization (Chio, 2005; Harvey, 2003). Unmasking these institutions of rule and the myriad of ruling practices, relations and interconnections – part of its taken-for-granted character – is the task of an anthropological endeavor (Smith, 1987).

Each of the contributions in this volume has sought to resituate, re-historicize and deconstruct particular aspects of this global and globalizing order. Collectively, they make possible an understanding of the activities and actions – procedural, academic, institutional, economic, regulatory – that are required in order to *have* a 'global' order and *be* global. Each begins by questioning received understandings or practices connected to their respective topics in order to cultivate this alternate visibility and understanding. The chapters by Ali, Wong-MingJi, Fougère and Moulettes, and Fougère and Solitander, for example, problematize the configuration of received knowledge about theories of the firm, strategic conceptions of borders, international management texts, and constructions of the natural environment. By calling attention to what is missing and what is forwarded and what is problematic, these authors aim to recast knowledge about this global order that remains silent and invisible in most mainstream approaches to globalization.

If having globalization and being global is the story that needs to be told in this reconfiguration of knowledge we are calling for – rather than the de facto assumption and acceptance of a global order that is natural or naturally evolving – the existence and the possibility *for* this global order becomes the center-point for investigation and analysis. Put another way, if globalization and the global is neither natural nor neutral, then it must come from a somewhere and be the result of something. Bringing attention to this somewhere and something has been the key focus of this book and its contributions, and as we discuss below is precisely what allows for an alternate understanding and entry-point for investigating the phenomenon.

THE SOCIALLY ORGANIZED TERRAIN

The contributors in this volume call attention to the presence of an 'extra-local' (Smith, 1987) that is constantly involved in organizing and reorganizing societies and possibilities at the level of the social or economic, collective or individual. This socially organized terrain of globalization and its imperial formations are articulated in terms of the politics and the political economy governing interactions between a multinational corporation (MNC) headquarters and its subsidiary (Mir et al. in this volume), the focus on intellectual property and e-commerce (Wong-MingJi), the ruling interests of capital and organization theories/theorists (Ali), or the contextual and structural changes being put into place as a result of the transition to a neoliberal political economy (Sliwa) and movement of societies and nations (Dyer, and Das and Dharwadkar) into the new world order. At the center of this global unfamiliar is an institutionally mediated set of relations, interconnections and activities that configure actions and intentions at the local level (nation-state, economy, labor market, workplaces) whose effect is the production of what is taken to be and needed for globalization to take place.

Key to this extralocal is a particular development apparatus that mediates and orchestrates this global reality (Escobar, 1995). Rooted in neoliberal premises and an economic mode of production privileging the interests of capital (Colás, 2005; Harvey, 2003, 2005) this development-based entry point is discursively produced and supported by a series of institutional mechanisms and procedures of rule. Organized around a focus on markets and underpinned by an assumption governing the implied superiority of markets to effect the transition of nations from underdeveloped to developed end-states, it is enabled by a construction of 'underdevelopment' (as a representational category rather than as a condition of Third World impoverishment connected to colonialism and imperialism; see Frank, 1967) as a fundamental problem of inefficient resource allocation because of target nations' reliance on non-market means of allocation (World Bank, 1991). Framed by this discursive production of the problem and a 'problem other', this knowledge and belief is procedurally reconstituted into a mode of regulation under the auspices of structural adjustment policies of the World Bank and institutionally inscribed into the conditions required for the renegotiation of debt and aid by the IMF (Banerjee and Linstead, 2001; Harvey, 2003, 2005).

Procedurally, this conceptual mediation of development by the discourse of markets simultaneously incorporates and recasts international capital into an 'agent' of development and economic growth through its discursive relocation as source of innovation, investment, forms of know-how, rationality, management and the like. Capital becomes, in effect, the literal and metaphorical engine behind economic growth, and symbol of the efficiency and effectiveness of market mechanisms thus opening the way for a more active role by business, in particular MNCs. This reorganization of the local is in turn made possible by those with most immediate 'access' to this local – namely state and development agencies who become the agents of privatization and deregulation (Lieberman, 1990). As we have noted previously, received conceptions of globalization as an evolution towards a stateless end state is a false premise at best. At the very least, the jurisdiction of states over regulation and policy necessitate their participation in implementing and overseeing transformations to the legal, administrative and procedural changes embedded in and required by structural adjustment programs. What has been transformed by this discursive turn to neoliberal markets is not the required presence or efficacy of the state. Rather, what has been changed is the role that the state is now required to play *in* the interests of development and international capital: namely, as facilitators and organizers of this new world order (Banerjee, 2007; Chio, 2005; Harvey, 2003).

This entry point into the local relies on certain conditions of possibility created by the histories of colonialism and imperialism. Specifically, in constructing the problem of development as market inefficiency, the presence and effects of colonialisms and imperialisms past – underdevelopment, unequal distribution and control over resources, dependency, poverty, debt (Amin, 1976; Cardoso and Faletto, 1979; Frank, 1967) – are effectively transformed via the representational practices of development into distinctive conceptual categories that enter the planning and policy domains of local development and multilateral agencies as a fundamental series of 'lacks and absences' (Chio, 2005; Escobar, 1995; Mitchell, 1995, 2002). Discourses of capital, efficiency, infrastructure, investment, education and so forth – already organized around a focus on markets and propped up by modernist values and beliefs governing science, management, efficiency, progress and the like – are used to actively recast the debilitating effects of colonialism and imperialism into forms of knowledge that are subsequently amenable to the planning activities of development officials. Their reconstitution into 'facts' becomes a barometer to calibrate and locate the 'backwardness' of nations.

What is notable here is how basic premises regarding the efficacy of markets are institutionally inscribed and systematically interconnected to form a nexus that mediates between theory and action, development and capital, planning and implementation that render possible the reach of said institutions (development) and ruling interests (capital) into the terrain of the local. They function as conduits and institutions of rule – a veritable web of administration and policy making possible the institutional and organizational entry points needed to engage in the local terrain. As Mir et al., Das and Dharwadkar, and Sliwa note in their assessment of negotiations and interactions arising from introducing market reforms in India and Poland (knowledge transfer, outsourcing, class and community identity), structural changes in the political economy are made possible by a contextual and institutional reorganization of the local that originates from an institutionalized and development-based 'externality'.

MARKETS AND THE 'WORK' OF GLOBALIZATION

The reconfiguration of nations and societies under the norms of privatization and deregulation creates tensions between 'transition' (Rostow, 1960) and 'transformation'. Development discourses have generally focused on the former and have tended to remain silent on the societal transformation that accompanies transition to a neoliberal political economy. As contributors to this volume suggest, the active reconfiguration of reality, life, labor and possibilities is needed to support and sustain markets as a system and systematic form of organization. For markets to exist and capital to thrive, the ancillary 'spokes' needed to sustain them must be *put into place* to reflect the values and beliefs of a consumer society. As noted by Berthoud (1992: 79):

> To conceive of the market system as a man-made institution rather than as a self-creating, self-perpetuating order is a way of recognizing that the market is controlled by various traditional political, social and moral constraints, and reinforced by a number of political and cultural innovations. In other words, the existence and expansion of the market is dependent on institutions and cultural values.

Markets must thus be continuously fashioned and re-fashioned into being. To do so, however, requires transformations to the social and cultural – as well as the institutional and structural – edifice of nations and societies (e.g. values, work behavior, relations to self and reality) considered fundamental to the production and reproduction of capitalist modes of organization and accumulation.

As numerous contributors have sought to highlight, a requisite for sustaining and making *plausible* the existence of this global order is the active reconstitution of people into effective laboring subjects as required by the increasingly transnational character of markets and capital. Whether in reference to call centers (Das and Dharwadkar) or flexible workers (Dyer), subjects must be cultivated who are owners of skills and abilities needed for the efficient and effective functioning of markets and capital, including labor markets. Call centers produce workers who are adept at 'adopting-and-concealing' their selves to deliver 'seamless' transactions in the service of customers, thus sustaining the economic and organizational imaginary of the borderlessness of MNCs in an era of globalization. Creating flexible careers involves the production of workers who willingly 'consent' (Gramsci, 1971) to take responsibility for the 'management' of their careers and working lives and are thus effectively reconfigured as a flexible factor of production consistent with the flexible strategies of capital. It is not only the active reconstitution of skills and capabilities that are at stake, but also the reconstitution of people's location *in relation to* globalization and transnational capital that are critical, including their ability to locate themselves so.

This reconstitution of labor and laboring subjects applies equally well to managers and even communities. In the case of managers, conceptions of culture and the other embedded in textbooks are aimed to actively construct and disseminate to their audience (future managers at home and abroad) a very specific way of seeing and understanding themselves (as managers) so that the world can be made into a 'familiar place' and thus 'rationally managed' (Fougère and Moulettes). What is at stake here is the technocratic and functional capabilities required for the effective and efficient management of self, culture and firm. Or as Sliwa documents in her ethnography of changes occurring in Poland, locals not only find themselves confronting growing class inequalities (e.g. rural–urban, professional–nonprofessional) but are compelled to reassess themselves through market-mediated evaluations of labor, skills and identity that confer differential use and exchange values.

This active transformation or regulation of people into objects of capital and management by firms extends into the terrain of knowledge and nature. Whether articulated in terms of the territorialization of intellectual property and cybernetic space (Wong-MingJi), or the extraction of 'local knowledge' into the auspices of an MNC's storehouse of intellectual property (Mir et al.), knowledge is reconstituted as a matter of property, simultaneously the subject of contested ownership as well as an object for 'accumulation by dispossession' (Harvey, 2003). Or in the case of theories of the firm (Ali), the nature and configuration of these theories (knowledge about knowledge) construct the existence of firms in de-contextualized terms leading to the formulation of solutions (theories) that overlook the role of national policy and how firms may exist to serve the colonial or imperial interests of states. In the context of the natural environment, the progressive commodification, capitalization and appropriation of nature re-territorializes nature and subsumes it under the auspices of capital as an economic good whose existence can only be of value in relation to the economic, whether of development or corporate capital. Nature is not just an object for accumulation; it is part of accumulation as a matter of social and economic practice. The subtext to these accounts is the active rendering of previously non-commodified or non-corporate entities into a form that anchors them to capital rendering them manageable through commodification and the reconstitution of their relationship to markets and capital, and *our* relationship to them as objects of our gaze.

RULE OF EXPERTS AND THE SUBJECTS OF GLOBALIZATION

The production of the global requires the presence of a plethora of officials and professionals actively engaged in making the world. From development planners and policy regulators to human resource managers, academics, lawmakers and the like, the spectrum of activities spans an equally large terrain that ranges from policy formulation, development planning and implementation to training, management and administration, text-writing, theory generation and so forth.

The rise of a new class composed of financiers, CEOs and entrepreneurs associated with neoliberal globalization and imperialism observed by Harvey (2005) includes here the rise of a transnational cadre of technocratic experts who, along with the owners and managers of capital, have become the architects and planners of this new world order. This 'rule of experts' (Mitchell, 2002) is rendered possible through power/knowledge and organized by a political economy that valorizes knowledge as 'capital'. A central procedure of this 'ruling' resides in the power exercised by experts in constructing the type and forms of problems that need to be solved and resolved. This construction of problems and visibilities brings power into play as it delineates the manner by which they are to be apprehended, and stipulates the targets and problem subjects who become objects for subsequent action and intervention (Escobar, 1995; Foucault, 1979). Moreover, these constructions and constitutions of problems are often anchored by values that represent the modernist and disciplinary heritage belonging to these experts. In the case of flexible careers for example (Dyer), human resource managers and organizations' ability to recast careers as a matter of individual responsibility is brought about by a construction of the problem (lack of responsiveness, rigidity, inflexibility) that reflects specific values and beliefs (about individual initiative and independence, responsibility and responsiveness, effectiveness and efficiency) arising from a market rationality already embedded in organizational discourses. Not only are human resource managers able to actively link workers to firm success, they seek to ensure that workers are able to see themselves in such organization-centered terms. In doing so, the politics and political economy of labor and conditions of employment are actively neutralized and reconstituted as an issue of 'supply' rather than 'demand', the responsibility of labor rather than capital (firms), thus relieving corporations of their accountability or complicity for the growing inequalities and shifting this burden of accountability onto the shoulders of individual workers.

Such neutralization by knowledge is produced by the reliance on certain practices and procedures of knowledge construction and knowledge use. As Fougère and Solitander note, the reinvention of nature by discourses of sustainable development and natural capitalism is effected via its reconstitution into the concept of environment, and the subsequent 'erasure' of this 'border' between nature and organizations whose effect is a shift from domination to the appropriation of nature, a representational sleight of hand (Jay, 1988) that recasts business enterprises into agents of sustainability and corporate social responsibility, rendering possible the extended possibility for 'further appropriation of global space and local places'. Concurrently, the production of managers, objectification of culture and reduction of cultural sensitivity to a skill (Fougère and Moulettes) are enabled by a series of elisions – disclaiming while claiming the reliance on simplistic categories of cultural representation (power, distance, time use, efficiency) and practices of knowledge (binary oppositions, clustering) that subjugates culture and diversity under the managerial. Thus culture becomes a functional and universal category reconfigured as capability and skill that is understandable for the purposes of management and return on capital, in effect promoting a progressive economization of the social and cultural.

Often informed by modernist, Eurocentric or Orientalist premises of their claims to knowledge, the constructions of problems and procedures of knowledge often perpetuate the hierarchical stereotypes of others, and subject 'the other' of such knowledge (Third World, transition economies, workers, nature) to a variety of disciplinary and governance mechanisms, leading often to an extension of the decimation already produced by colonialism and imperialism. Most contributors to this volume have noted this endemic exercise and the effects of expertise knowledge and power. For example, in the case of call center workers (Das and Dharwadkar), individuals reported a variety of painful dislocations as they struggle with experiences of bifurcation and disconnection and negotiate the 'double lives' they find themselves inhabiting. The conditions of dislocation are reinforced in call centers where English is elevated and the local mocked (silencing of self and marginalization of local) by virtue of call center employees' market-mediated value as 'economic goods' and where customer service includes 'apologizing' for corporations' off-shoring/ outsourcing activities. As the authors note, it is a condition that exemplifies all too well how 'colonial governance' has been replaced by 'the logic of capital' – a state of being noted somewhat similarly by Dyer in her account of flexible workers and the actions aimed at 'manufacturing consent' that were set into play as a result of such flexible strategies. In the case of Poland (Sliwa), the transition to neoliberalism led to the creation of a center and periphery, development and underdevelopment within the country, not to mention the rise of a technocratic class and a vast reserve army of labor, both unskilled and skilled, awaiting further accumulation and investment by capital.

Whether articulated in terms of dislocations, underdevelopment, re-capitalization of nature (Fougère and Solitander), extraction of local knowledge (Mir et al.), or 'masking' of the political economy of MNC actions and strategies connected to international trade and intellectual capital (Wong-MingJi), expertise, knowledge and practices have been and continue, particularly in the case of relations between the West and the Rest, to be premised on a policy of 'colonial difference' (Chatterjee, 1993) that perpetuates the 'romance of globalization' (Radhakrishnan, 2003) enabled by and attached to the colonizing and imperializing power of knowledge and discourses of development and progress. In the process, what is produced is the progressive and systematic neutralization and re-objectification of these historical realities. This mediation of history by the 'techno-politics' (Mitchell, 2002) of modern disciplines and science simultaneously silences the historical complicity of the colonial and industrialized West while perpetuating and extending the inequalities and unevenness attached to the accumulations by dispossession that are now additionally possible via the progressive privatization and deregulation of sectors in the economy, and the economization of life and reality associated with this newly reconfigured connection between capital, colonialism and imperialism (Banerjee, 2003, 2008; Harvey, 2003).

PARTING COMMENTS

The theoretical and methodological aims organizing the framing and con-figuration of this book circulate around a deconstructive and reconstructive project targeted at unveiling the nexus of knowledge, practices and institutions that have been and are socially organizing the production and constitution of neoliberal globalization as a phenomenon. The objective for undertaking this resides in a bid to relocate globalization in terms of the historicized contours and procedures (e.g. epistemic, policy, culture) making it possible and real, be it capital, history, science or the modernist underpinnings of disciplinary knowledge. The resituating of the phenomenon in terms of these social particularities is critical because the phenomenon as we know it is already the result of these particularities and the claims to truth and domains of economy (Rabinow, 1986) indexed by them. Not doing so is to risk perpetuating the limitations of existing knowledge (e.g. ahistoricism), and so non-accountability for how this knowledge was configured to begin with and the effects resulting from this knowledge and configuration.

Within the rubric of these aims, contributors to the volume have sought to unpeel the layers and aspects of the 'what' and 'how' connected to globalization. In doing so, they highlight the specific features of how it rules, what produces it and what is produced by it, and the kinds of people, institutions, partnerships and knowledge that sustain it. What emerges is the location of knowledge as an institution of rule – the enabler and the glue that anchors the power of mediating institutions to the everyday practices of experts and technocrats who are centrally engaged in making possible and real the aims of certain ruling interests (capital, development, markets) that are connected to it (and development). In the process, contributors and this book begin delineating the analytical features to an otherwise abstract, generic, normalized and de-historicized concept that 'globalization' itself has been reduced to by mainstream investigations into the phenomenon, used often as a substitute and/or concept to represent and specify its own 'existence' (Cooper, 2005).

Significantly, the contributions in this volume have drawn attention to the intersections and interconnectivity between knowledge, institutions, people and practices and revealed, to quote Harvey (2003: 152), the 'contingency of it all'. This focus on intersections, interconnections and, indeed, social organization, provides a way to 'capture and mediate' between the various dichotomies – between social and economic, economic and political, knowledge and practice, macro and micro, local and global – that anchor modernist constitutions of reality and phenomena whose effect is the neutralization and making 'non-apparent' of the presence of power and the ruling that has been accomplished or is taking place (Chio, 2005; Smith, 1987). The reconstitution – or more appropriately, recasting and reinvention – of colonialism and imperialism under the guise of development and globalization has led to an increasingly sophisticated and 'masked' reality when it comes to how power and inequality have been perpetuated in recent time. Partially a result of the discursive and institutional 'fusion' between the development and organizational/management sciences that fostered a belief that nations and societies, like organizations, can be managed along with the reconstitution of international capital as an agent or intermediary of development (Chio, 2005), the construction and deployment of an institutional nexus under the neutralizing and objectifying auspices of science, management and development planning obfuscate the power and complicity involved in the production of this global reality, which is really about the geographical expansion of capitalism. Put another way, forwarded under the template of trade and development and fostered under the auspices of multilateral and state apparatuses, this 'capitalist form of imperialism' (Harvey, 2003: 143) is legitimized and normalized by the ostensibly objective and neutral lenses of science, economics and management.

Thus the political economy at play is not just one of capital, it is also one of knowledge, although it is definitively material and economic in its generation and effect. In the context of developing and transitioning economies, this reduction of all to singularly narrow parameters as defined by the language of trade (labor, capital, natural resources and the like) serves as a reminder that as objects of the 'scopic gaze' of modern disciplinary knowledge, the social particularities and histories of these nations and societies are constantly 'abstracted into a general' (Smith, 1987) and a global that not only silences them, but is simultaneously silent about the history of relations organizing them and their relations to the West. It is for this reason that we call for a greater focus on intersections and interconnections in researching and analyzing globalization – significant not just because doing so is part and parcel of being accountable to historical relationality; it is also about being accountable to the conditions of knowledge production (Radhakrishnan, 1994) that had given rise to this lack of historicism to begin with. This book and the contributions therein have attempted to relocate globalization back to the trajectories of knowledge, history, economy and organization within which it is embedded and around which it has been organized. In doing so, it seeks to provide an alternate understanding and possibility for investigating the phenomenon, one that is able and capable of moving beyond the economic chess game of globalization to consider the globalization and economics of this chess game.

REFERENCES

Amin, S. (1976). *Imperialism and Unequal Development*. New York: Monthly Review Press.

Banerjee, S.B. (2003). 'Who sustains whose development? Sustainable development and the reinvention of nature'. *Organization Studies*, **24** (1): 143–80.

Banerjee, S.B. (2007). *Corporate Social Responsibility: The Good, The Bad and The Ugly*. Cheltenham, UK and Northampton, MA, USA: Edward Elgar.

Banerjee, S.B. (2008). 'Necrocapitalism'. *Organization Studies*, **29** (12): 1541–63.

Banerjee, S.B. and S. Linstead (2001). 'Globalization, multiculturalism and other fictions: colonialism for the new millennium?'. *Organization*, **8**(4): 711–50.

Berthoud, G. (1992). 'Market', in W. Sachs (ed.), *The Development Dictionary. A Guide to Knowledge as Power*. London: Zed Books, pp. 70–87.

Cardoso, F.H. and E. Faletto (1979). *Dependency and Development in Latin America*. Berkeley: University of California Press.

Chakrabarty, D. (1992). 'Postcoloniality and the artifice of history: who speaks for "Indian" pasts?'. *Representations*, **37**: 1–26.

Chatterjee, P. (1993). *The Nation and Its Fragments*. Princeton, NJ: Princeton University Press.

Chio, V. (2005). *Malaysia and the Development Process: Globalization, Knowledge Transfers and Postcolonial Dilemmas*. New York: Routledge.

Colás, A. (2005). 'Neoliberalism, globalization and international relations', in A. Saad-Filho and D. Johnston (eds), *Neoliberalism: A Critical Reader*. London: Pluto Press, pp. 70–80.

Cooper, F. (2005). *Colonialism in Question: Theory, Knowledge, History*. Berkeley: University of California Press.

Escobar, A. (1995). *The Development Encounter: The Making and Un-making of the Third World, 1945–1992*. Princeton, NJ: Princeton University Press.

Foucault, M. (1979). *Discipline and Punish*. New York: Vintage Books.

Frank, A.G. (1967). 'The development of underdevelopment'. *Monthly Review Press*, **18** (4): 17–31.

Gramsci, A. (1971). *Selections from the Prison Notebooks*. London: Lawrence & Wishart.

Haraway, D. (1988). 'Situated knowledges: the science question in feminism and the privilege of partial perspective'. *Feminist Studies*, **14** (3): 575–99.

Harvey, D. (2003). *The New Imperialism*. Oxford: Oxford University Press.

Harvey, D. (2005). *A Brief History of Neoliberalism*. Oxford: Oxford University Press.

Jay, M. (1988). 'Scopic regimes of modernity', in H. Foster (ed.), *Vision and Visuality*. Seattle, WA: Bay Press, pp. 3–23.

Lieberman, I. (1990). *Industrial Restructuring: Policy and Practice*. Washington, DC: The World Bank.

Mitchell, T. (1995). 'The object of development. America's Egypt', in J. Crush (ed.), *Power of Development*. London: Routledge, pp. 129–57.

Mitchell, T. (2002). *Rule of Experts: Egypt, Techno-politics, Modernity*. Berkeley: University of California Press.

Prakash, G. (1990). 'Writing post-orientalist histories of the Third World: perspectives from Indian historiography'. Society for Comparative Study of Society and History. No. 0010-4175/90/2893.

Rabinow, P. (1986). 'Representations are social facts: modernity and post-modernity in anthropology', in J. Clifford and G. Marcus (eds), *Writing Culture: The Poetics and Politics of Ethnography*. Berkeley: University of California Press, pp. 234–61.

Radhakrishnan, R. (1994). 'Postmodernism and the rest of the world'. *Organization*, **1** (2): 305–40.

Radhakrishnan, R. (2003). *Theory in an Uneven World.* Malden, MA: Blackwell Publishing.
Rostow, W.W. (1960). *Stages of Economic Growth.* Cambridge: Cambridge University Press.
Smith, D.E. (1987). *The Everyday World as Problematic.* Boston, MA: Northeastern University Press.
World Bank (1991). *World Development Report.* Washington, DC: The World Bank.

Index